Sectarianism

Contemporary Issues Series

Sectarianism

Analyses of Religious and Non-Religious Sects

EDITED BY ROY WALLIS

PETER OWEN · LONDON

ISBN 0 7206 0403 6

BP
603
S4
1975

PETER OWEN LIMITED
20 Holland Park Avenue London W11 3QU

First British Commonwealth edition 1975
© Roy Wallis 1975

Printed in Great Britain by
Bristol Typesetting Co. Ltd
Barton Manor St Philips Bristol

Contents

Acknowledgments

All but one of the essays included in this volume are presented here for the first time. For permission to reprint 'The Aetherius Society : A Case Study in the Formation of a Mystagogic Congregation', which originally appeared in *The Sociological Review*, Vol. 22, No. 1, February 1974, I wish to thank the Editorial Board of *The Sociological Review*. For making possible the time and resources to devote to preparing this volume for publication I should like to record my thanks to Professor Duncan Timms, Chairman of the Department of Sociology, University of Stirling. For their patience and skill in typing the manuscript I owe a considerable debt of gratitude to Grace Smith, Marion Govan and Pam Drysdale.

R.W.

Roy Wallis

1 Introduction

Although there is no general agreement on the range of meaning of the term 'sect', a certain minimal consensus exists that the concept has to do with groups, organized around a common ideology, which in a variety of ways cut themselves off from, or erect barriers between themselves and the rest of society. The essays in this volume are a product of research into the theory and practice, the history and social organization, the membership and their motivations, of a wide variety of such collectivities.

Despite their many divergencies, all these groups have two central characteristics in common. Firstly, they are each organized around a belief-system held by their adherents to offer some unique and privileged means of access to the truth or salvation. Secondly, they are each concerned with producing or maintaining a thoroughgoing transformation in the identities of those recruited to them. Salvation is, of course, differently identified in each case. The recruit to Recovery, Inc. conceptualizes the world and its problems in a different language from the Jehovah's Witness or the De Leonist, but each has (or comes to acquire) a view of the past, the world, and himself couched in profoundly negative terms. The past is seen as unsatisfactory, unpleasant or evil to an extent which can only be remedied by means of transcendence, through a privileged revelation into the meaning of life, to some totally different and superior state.

Most of the groups discussed here embody a vision of their beliefs and practices which attributes to them not merely a *superior* status as means of transcending a devalued present, but rather a *unique* status. They are viewed not merely as one technique or path, but the *only* one. It is this claim to privileged and unique status as a means to the truth or salvation which Wallis (Chapter 3) takes to be the identifying characteristic of sectarianism. In his paper on

9

'The Cult and its Transformation', he argues that this dogmatic claim to salvational efficacy is closely related to a number of other features seen as central to prevailing conceptions of the sect.

On the basis of an analysis of the transformation which some ideological collectivities undergo from cult to sect, Wallis argues that sects are typically organized on the basis of a principle of 'epistemological' authoritarianism. While cults are individualistic in the sense that there is no recognized legitimate locus of attributions of heresy, no source of authoritative definitions of acceptable belief and practice, beyond the individual member himself, sects possess such a source of authority. The process of transforming a cult into a sect therefore entails the subversion of the principle of 'epistemological' individualism and the arrogation of authority.

This process is visible to a degree in the development of a flying saucer movement, the Aetherius Society (Chapter 2). In the process of providing a description of the movement's beliefs, practices and organization, Wallis touches on the manner in which the movement's founder progressively institutionalized the Society around his revelations, establishing himself as the sole channel for communication with the Space Masters, and effectively monopolizing the means of revelation. In these two papers Wallis elaborates some of the factors *internal* to the collectivity which lead to organizational and ideological change. In a later contribution (Chapter 6) he details the way in which such change may result from a complex interplay between the movement and the surrounding society.

The increasing severity with which social control was employed within Scientology during the 1960s, and the increasing hostility which it displayed to the outside world, was, he seeks to show, the result of a process of deviance-amplification wherein initial deviation motivated in part by internal dissension and in part by state intervention led to the development of a 'moral crusade' against Scientology, often on what now appear to have been rather spurious grounds. The 'strategic choices' made by the movement's leadership to increase both internal control and attacks on those members of 'outside' society who were seen as hostile, led to further conflict between sect and society.

Sugarman (Chapter 8) also touches on the issue of how involvement with the wider society can become a factor in organizational development. While organized initially as collectivities run for addicts by ex-addicts, the costs of running the therapeutic communities known as Concept Houses are so high that in order to secure government funding, a bureaucratic structure has had to be grafted on to the original communities. This has resulted in the emergence of new sources of strain within the movement.

Whitworth (Chapter 7) tackles a similar theme. In this paper on communitarian movements he shows the way in which the changing 'social climate' of American society reduced the probability of replacing personnel in the Shaker Church through evangelization. Since the movement early eschewed sexual relations and therefore the possibility of replacing them through natural increase, the Shakers became increasingly introverted and, after a lengthy and successful history, moved into decline. Whitworth similarly seeks to show how the contemporary 'social climate' of American society, and of the 'Underground' from which such movements emerge, are today unsupportive of communitarian developments and render the probability of their survival very slight.

These cases illustrate the complex nexus of factors which may have to be considered in any concrete case of the development of a social movement. The ideology, the organizational structure, internal sources of strain, the motivation and goals of the movement leadership, the reception which the movement is accorded by press, legislators and other individuals and agencies concerned, may all play some part in determining the development of the movement.

The paper by Beckford (Chapter 5) analyses another aspect of the same general concern. All ideological collectivities face the problem of replacing personnel lost through death or defection. The ideologies around which some collectivities are organized, however, demand active evangelization and propagation of the faith. Beckford analyses the way in which two movements faced with the same imperative have implemented contrasting styles of recruitment. Both the Unified Family and the Jehovah's Witnesses have retained (the latter over several generations) an active, even aggressive, campaign of proselytization in the face of an indifferent and sometimes hostile world, and the disappointment of millennial expectations.

The political sects analysed by O'Toole (Chapter 9), however, have coped with the lack of objective success in world transformation by withdrawal into a passive elitist conception of themselves as a gathered remnant, ritualizing their proselytizing activities in what O'Toole describes as 'pseudo-evangelization', in which the members pursue recruitment practices of little objective efficacy in preference to potentially more cost-effective strategies which might be disruptive of their self-conception as a pure and embattled revolutionary enclave. This relative lack of success in recruitment is

itself interpreted as a sign of the essential correctness of their diagnosis of the state of capitalist society.

Two papers are addressed explicitly to the issue of the manner in
which the identities of recruits are transformed by sectarian
ideological collectivities. Daner, in her discussion of the Krishna
Consciousness movement (Chapter 4), isolates four phases in the
progression from new recruit to advanced devotee. For the typical
convert, experiences in the drug culture engender a set of expectations and lead to the acquisition of certain definitions and vocabu-
laries of motive which render him a potential convert to Krishna
Consciousness. The 'neophyte devotee' is provided with a set of
norms and practices which further structure his identity and the
meaning with which he endows himself and his environment. The
Krishna Consciousness temple is a 'total institution' in which the
recruit undergoes a drastic change in life-style and appearance as
he is progressively inducted into the esoteric doctrine, learns to
control his emotions, and experiences the transcendental rewards
of commitment. In the third phase, the recruit is endowed with a
new status marked by a new name and insignia which more firmly
link his identity with the community of which he has become a
member. New responsibilities are permitted him and the member
is mobilized for further recruitment and induction of converts. The
individual's goals in affiliating with the movement are progressively
transmuted to fit those of its 'dominant coalition'. Successful nego-
tiation of this phase of identity transformation issues in the phase of
the 'advanced devotee' available to fill leadership roles in the movement hierarchy, with further responsibilities but also a privileged
status and the right to deference from other members. The
individual has progressively redefined his identity until pursuing
the practices and tasks of the movement is seen as a unique source
of personal satisfaction and meaning.

In a rather different context, Sugarman discusses aspects of the
process of socialization in therapeutic communities for the drug-
dependent. The recruit to a Concept House undergoes a complete
break with his former life, is inducted into an ideology which re-
defines his past experience, and is provided with role-models as the
basis for a new identity. As in Krishna Consciousness, each member
acts as an agent of social control and socialization-reinforcement for
others. One of Daner's interview respondents comments on the way
in which his 'god brother' will persist in urging him to carry out
some required duty. This practice seems close to the technique of
'confrontation' in the Concept House, described by Sugarman. The

'encounter group' as a technique of socialization and social control is perhaps a more democratic functional equivalent of direct commands through the highly hierarchical Krishna Consciousness Society.

One important difference in the nature of socialization in the two types of community is the ultimate goal towards which it is directed. While the devotee of ISKCON seeks a fuller access to Krishna which requires increasing cognitive and affective withdrawal from the wider society, the Concept Houses seek to rehabilitate the drug-dependent and return him to the world. As Sugarman indicates, some communities in this field are increasingly moving towards utopian communities by further withdrawal from the world and retaining those whose identities they transform successfully. Others maintain a commitment to 'recycling' members back into society.

A similar dilemma of withdrawal into the collectivity or return to the wider society is faced by the members of two near-sectarian 'ex-patient' organizations described by Jones (Chapter 10). His account of Recovery, Inc. and Neurotics Nomine elaborates a number of features that such movements share with acknowledged religious sects. Both display separatist tendencies, although the extent to which they can move towards explicitly sectarian forms of organization is mitigated by their commitment to rehabilitation of the former mental patient, the limited scope of their ideology directed at enabling the individual to cope with his return to the world or with his neurotic symptomatology, and the fact that it is 'the world' itself which provides the criteria for salvation. Recovery, Inc. and Neurotics Nomine provide no model of the individual or the world claimed to be *superior* to that outside the confines of the collectivity. Like most of the Concept Houses, they offer the means of becoming more fully and competently a member of the world as it currently exists. Unlike the Concept Houses, however, they lack a recruitment base prepared to commit themselves to thoroughly heroic means to escape from a stigmatized and devalued status, and unlike Scientology they offer no techniques for becoming a vastly superior being in the current world.

Such groups display the continuity that exists between sectarian and non-sectarian organizations and movements. Moreover, the studies collected in this volume together demonstrate the utility of a conception of sectarianism as a form of belief and mode of social organization which cuts across a wide variety of belief-systems, exhibiting the continuities which exist in movements of a religious, political and therapeutic character, or those which fall at the boundaries of these categories. For this reason alone, the essays in this collection should be of interest to students of social movements and social organizations, as well as those whose central concern is with the field of sectarianism *per se*.

PART ONE

Cults and Their Development

Roy Wallis

2 *The Aetherius Society:*
A Case Study in the Formation of a Mystagogic Congregation[1]

A much underdeployed concept from Max Weber's typologies of religious virtuosi has been that of the *mystagogue*. His own examples, as befitted his broad historical and comparative scope, were drawn from ancient or oriental sources. I have been unable to locate any systematic application of this concept in the literature since Weber, however, and thus a descriptive and analytical account of a more recent example might prove profitable. A new magico-religious group, the Aetherius Society, provides the suitable raw material for the deployment of Weber's concept. The author engaged in participant observation with this group at a wide range of its lectures, services, pilgrimages and social gatherings in England over the course of some eighteen months and also systematically examined the literature of the society.[2]

This paper seeks to explore the emergence of the founder of the Aetherius Society, Dr George King, as a mystagogue. Of particular interest is the manner in which he was able to secure a monopoly of the means of revelation and to overcome the constraints on institutionalization which typically face movements founded on the systematic manifestation of charismatic gifts—for example, pentecostalism or, more appositely, spiritualism. These aspects are explored in the context of a description of the Aetherius Society, its leadership and membership, and an analysis of the factors which led to its emergence, modified its development, and limit its appeal.

The Leader, and the Emergence of the Aetherius Society

The history of the Aetherius Society is largely the history of its leader, George King. Of his own biography, only limited information is available. Born in 1919 in Wellington, Shropshire, King came

17

from a family imbued with occult inclinations. His mother was known as being 'psychic' and a clairvoyant, and practised as a spiritual healer. These attributes were also recognized in King as a child and encouraged by his mother. At twelve or thirteen years of age he experienced a vision and performed a healing of his sick mother by prayer. In later life, King was a London taxi driver and a Fire Warden during the Second World War, in which he was a conscientious objector. He appears to have been keenly interested in metaphysical thought and yoga for a number of years before founding the Aetherius Society, and to have been actively working, at least part-time, as a spiritual healer before his first public lectures.

During the period prior to the emergence of his own distinctive vocation, he passed through most of the available metaphysical and fringe religious groups in London. His own writings include elements typical of theosophy and other gnostic groups based on eastern religions. The Great White Brotherhood invoked originally by Madame Blavatsky as a source of much of her own 'wisdom' figures prominently in King's writings. New Thought ideas of the physical world lying within and surrounded by a 'Sea of Mind', and that 'Thoughts are things', make a not infrequent appearance. Even locutions typical of early Dianetics, with its conceptualization of the mind as a computer with references to 'memory banks', etc., have been used by Dr King. The healing practices he advocates might have been a synthesis of theosophical conceptions of the *chakras* and *pranic* energy, and of the manipulation technique of Harry Edwards—whom he claims to have known.[3]

Yoga, Tantric Buddhism, homeopathy and radionics all figure prominently. King was clearly deeply immersed in the 'cultic milieu'[4] and synthesized its ideas in a very eclectic fashion. Atlantis and Lemuria are occasionally invoked, together with elements typical of spiritualism, but the most distinctive components of the belief system of the Aetherius Society are to be located elsewhere. Dr King first emerged as a public speaker in 1954, and that emergence coincided with two prominent concerns in public thought of the time—reported sightings of space-craft and contact with their personnel, and apprehension regarding the testing of nuclear weapons.[5]

King was obviously something of a solitary. Thirty-five years old when his first major revelation came to him and unmarried, we are told that :

For ten years previous to this, he had been a keen student of spiritual philosophies of East and West. He had practised the ancient mystic science of Yoga for as long as nine hours per day. Many times through this ten-year period, sleep, spare time and vacations were given up to the practice of the greatest forms of spiritual development and Yoga known to mankind. Urged on by some great inner power, he drove himself relentlessly to practise, for hours each day, Mantra, Kriya, Raja, Gnani and the secret Kundalini Yoga, until he developed the ability to throw off the veils of basic materialistic thought and by the *conscious control* of the great *Power of Kundalini* within himself, he was able to enter the deeper, more lasting states of true Meditation.[6]

In contrasting the divergent implications of the imperatives of ascetic versus mystic religion, Weber argued :

For the ascetic, . . . the divine imperative may require an unconditional subjection of the world to the norms of religious virtue, and indeed a revolutionary transformation of the world for this purpose. In that event the ascetic will emerge from his remote and cloistered cell to take his place in the world as a prophet in opposition to the world. But he will always demand of the world an ethically rational order and discipline. Now a mystic may arrive at a similar position in relation to the world. His sense of divine inwardness, the chronic and quiet euphoria of his solitary contemplative possession of substantively divine salvation, may become transformed into an acute feeling of sacred possession by or possession of the god who is speaking in and through him. He will then wish to bring eternal salvation to men as soon as they have prepared, as the mystic himself has done, a place for god upon earth, i.e. in their souls. But in this case the result will be the emergence of the mystic as a magician who causes his power to be felt among gods and demons; and this may have the practical consequence of the mystic's becoming a mystagogue, something which has actually happened very often.[7]

In May 1954, Dr King received a disembodied command to 'Prepare yourself, you are to become the voice of Interplanetary Parliament.' A few days later, whilst in a meditative trance, he received a visit through his locked door from an Indian Yoga Master who gave further instructions and secret yogic practices and announced to him that he had been selected by the Cosmic Intelligences who man the space-craft, to act as their 'Primary Terrestrial

Channel' for the important messages they were shortly to transmit to Earth.

He set himself during the ensuing months to the task of practising the yogic techniques passed on to him, and before the end of 1954 was able to enter into telepathic rapport with a Cosmic Master living on Venus, named Aetherius. In January 1955, at one of the centres of the cultic milieu in London, the Caxton Hall, King gave the first public performance of his thaumaturgy, going into a yogic trance on the platform to relay a message from the Master Aetherius to the audience.

His immediate following was small. We are told that: 'In the early days he had to face much prejudice and opposition from all sides. He stood alone, save for one or two people who recognized that the contact was in every way genuine.'[8] He continued with his lectures nevertheless. The messages grew longer and more regular, and their urgency increased. Apparently, during this time, King continued to work at his job often twelve hours a day, going into trance only on his return from work.

King's 'command' and the mission with which he was entrusted initiated his transformation from mystic and magical healer to mystagogue. As Weber indicated, the mystagogue is only distinguished from the magician as a matter of degree, 'the extent of which is determined by the formation of a special congregation around him.'[9] The magician, unlike the mystagogue, practises on the basis of a professional-client relationship, either independently or as a member of a guild-organized craft.

A small following began to accumulate for his lectures and the first step toward institutionalizing them into a collectivity was the circulation of a single-page, duplicated news-sheet. In the course of time, King made contact with other space notables—Saint Goo-Ling, a member of the Great White Brotherhood living on Earth, a Martian scientist, Mars Sector 6, Mars Sector 8, and Jupiter Sector 92. King began to receive invitations to lecture to other groups, his following increased and in August 1956 he founded the Aetherius Society. It was at this stage that he began to devote himself full-time to his mission.

The messages of the Cosmic Masters during this early period related mainly to health and healing practices, the friendliness of the Space People (to still the doubts of those who thought them most probably hostile), the dangers of atomic experimentation, the nature of the other inhabitants of the solar system, and the metaphysical activities of the Cosmic Masters, who through the manipulation of spiritual energies unknown to human beings were seeking to save man from destroying himself by his indifference, selfishness and greed.

With the founding of the Society a regular magazine was established to provide news and a means of distributing the important messages being transmitted to those who could not attend all the meetings. Early editions contain frequent accounts of flying saucer sightings, and King reported a voyage on a Martian satellite in March 1956.

It was not until some time after King had begun to receive messages from the Cosmic Masters that he was 'over-shadowed' or contacted by the Master Jesus. Jesus, like Aetherius, was apparently a Venusian, and had contacted King to relay assurances of his existence. Some two years later he began relaying a set of new prayers and teachings suitable for the 'Aquarian Age'. Jesus's reassurances appeared in print alongside a terrifying story of King's role in repelling the fiendish invaders from outer space who threatened to take over 'Terra', which as he himself admits, 'reads like science-fiction'.[10] During the ensuing years a number of similar situations occurred which threatened to bring the whole of mankind to complete destruction, prevented only by the brave and timely intervention of King and the Cosmic Masters. The threat of imminent or hardly averted catastrophe is a prominent one in King's writings. Man by his evil thoughts and actions is close to bringing disaster upon his own head through the operation of the basic Law of Karma : action and reaction are opposite and equal. Curiously, this does not mean that good will be returned for evil, but that man's evil will shortly return to him and only a few spiritually worthy souls such as Dr King stand between man and cataclysm.

Apart from Dr King's healing activities, in these early days ritual centred primarily on those occasions when a satellite from Mars was believed to come close to the Earth in order to increase the potency of the spiritual energy activated at that time by prayer directed to the benefit of mankind.

The transmissions from the Space Masters were recorded and circulated in the increasing literary output of King and his society. *The Twelve Blessings*, Jesus's 'Aquarian Age Bible to this Earth'[11] was transmitted in July 1958, after King had met the Master Jesus in person on top of Holdstone Down in Devon. This meeting produced a considerable change in the Society's activities, for King was commissioned to 'act as an essential link between Earth and the Higher Forces'[12] in the 'charging' of a number of Holy Mountains throughout the world with Cosmic Energy which could be released through prayer for the good of mankind. This was known as Operation Starlight. Nine such mountains were charged in Britain. Meanwhile, King was receiving increasing publicity through radio and television appearances, and invitations to lecture, some from the United States.

In June 1959 he left for the United States accompanied by one disciple to begin a lecture tour and extend Operation Starlight to America. This tour was eventually to lead on to Canada, Australia and New Zealand. It appears to have been organized by accepting and soliciting invitations to speak to flying saucer, metaphysical, and theosophical groups,[13] and promotions through radio and television appearances, and to have been financed at least in part through their sale of King's books. The limited resources of The Aetherius Society at this stage are evident from several reports by King and his disciple of the privations and discomforts they suffered during this tour.

Support for King gradually emerged, however, together with funds to enable him to continue, and small groups of adherents formed across the States. In Los Angeles the following was sufficiently large to establish an American headquarters and to incorporate the Society as a religious organization under American law. King's long absence in the United States was not without repercussions at home, since in later lectures by leaders of the Society reference has been made to secessions of membership and a decline in recruitment. America proved sufficiently spiritually rewarding, however, for King to take up residence in California shortly after his initial tour.

From an essentially passive, mediumistic role in the early years, King progressively emerged as an active agent in cosmic affairs. From being a channel activated as required to receive messages and charge Holy Mountains, he moved on to initiating contacts with the Space Intelligences and autonomous metaphysical manipulations to save man from disaster. From being an 'unworthy and ignorant servant', he progressed to colleague, confidante and even advisor of his erstwhile superiors. From harbinger of the coming of a new Master, the equal of Jesus, Buddha, and Krishna, it was clear from around 1958 that Dr King was himself destined for a greater role. In April 1959, during a transmission from the Space Masters, the Master Jesus said to King : 'My Son, you are now one of Us, and We now declare this to all men.'[14] And while much of the earlier literature of the Society stressed the *coming* of a new

Master, it is now customary to refer to King himself as a Master.[15]

In recent years King has ceased to give public transmissions of the messages of the Cosmic Masters, devoting his energies to the performance of a variety of esoteric ritual operations: Operation World Healing; The Ejection of the Alien; Operation Karmalight; Operation Bluewater; Operation Sunbeam; etc., and has restricted his personal contact to the permanent members of his staff and a few core members who have assisted in these operations. During the six-year period when most of these operations were taking place, King made only two visits to his followers in Britain. Recruitment slackened considerably during this period, to such an extent that in 1971 Operation Expansion was proclaimed. A permanent headquarters organizer was appointed in London, the formation of branches outside the metropolis encouraged, and in 1972 Dr King visited England for a one-month lecture tour. It is as yet too early to say what permanent effect this will have on recruitment.

Beliefs and Practices

The belief-system of the movement, as indicated earlier, constitutes a complex synthesis. It hinges fundamentally on a paradox: the Cosmos is governed by a Law of Karma: as ye sow, so shall ye reap. The karma of individuals and races is then constantly in the process of being 'balanced' as they progress through reincarnation towards higher spiritual development, or regress to a lower plane. Mankind, one of the least evolved entities of the solar system, at some very early stage elected to have free will, unlike most other beings in the Cosmos who elected for 'Freedom under Karmic Law'. The consequence of this is that man is liable to gross acts of selfishness and greed, which not only retard his own spiritual development but threaten that of other Beings in the Cosmos—such as the Being on which we live, Terra.

Explosion of nuclear bombs and despoliation of the Earth causes her damage and a nuclear war or the launching of interplanetary and lunar missiles threaten to endanger the status of a vast array of Beings inhabiting the solar system on various dimensions of aetheriality/materiality. While we may be foolhardy enough to upset our own karmic balance we cannot be allowed to threaten that of other Beings. So, since the more advanced among them have been sympathetic to our plight, they have intervened periodically by sending their representatives: Jesus, Krishna, Buddha, etc., to warn us of the consequences of our actions, as well as sending space-craft to monitor our activities.

In brief, however, we have almost used up the goodwill available to us. If we do not take radical action now and improve our ways, we shall be brushed off the face of this planet into cosmic obscurity. These are the last days. Through Dr King one final attempt is being made to avert disaster. We must 'manipulate karma' for mankind by employing spiritual energy—particularly under the auspicious circumstances made available to us by the Space Masters which enable us greatly to increase its potency—to the benefit of mankind.

Hence, in Operation Starlight, the Space Masters made further energy available through the charging of the Holy Mountains, turning them into storehouses of spiritual energy to be tapped whenever required, by means of prayer. Correct utilization of this energy can help to avert war, such as in the Lebanon and at the Cuba confrontation, or natural disaster such as the earthquake which it has been predicted will engulf Los Angeles, turn tornadoes aside, or quell forest fires. These natural disasters as well as the more obviously social ones are caused by man's evil thought and action, in exploding nuclear devices for example. With the emergence of a concern for ecology during the 1960s, pollution has tended to replace the testing of atomic bombs as a central cause of concern in the Society.

Man has taken so much from the Earth that it has seriously upset the karmic balance of mankind. This debt must be repaid eventually, and operations such as Bluewater and Sunbeam are devoted to this end. Some of the energy stored in the Holy Mountains, instead of being used directly for the benefit of mankind is redirected to the Psychic Centres of Earth as a token repayment of this karmic debt.

Since mankind is so evil, it attracts other evil forces to it from other parts of the Cosmos, forces which seek to enslave man and employ his potential for evil to further their own ends. Operation Karmalight thus involved a cosmic battle of gigantic proportions, with Dr King playing an active role alongside the Space Masters, to save mankind and repel these evil forces.

The undertaking of these operations has forced Dr King to develop a range of technological aids to expedite them, including batteries which store spiritual energy generated by prayer, and a spiritual energy radiator which will facilitate the transmission of such energy unerringly over transatlantic distances.

The time of the active member is fully committed. Services are held on Sunday and Monday evenings, classes, lectures and dynamic prayer circles throughout the week, as well as less frequent metaphysical seminars and pilgrimages. Extra prayer meetings are arranged when Satellite 3 enters Earth orbit, and the core members pledge whatever other spare time they may have to assisting in the upkeep of the headquarters, the production and distribution of literature, and other chores required in running an active voluntary association.

Analysis

Weber devoted far more attention to the prophet than to the mystagogue, seeing the prophet's influence on social organization as considerably more profound. The primary criterion that Weber had in mind in distinguishing the *prophet* from the *mystagogue* was that the latter offers a largely magical means of salvation rather than proclaiming a radical religious ethic or an example to be followed. Unlike the guru who 'implements an established order' the mystagogue may, in common with the prophet, proclaim a new dispensation and call for a break with the established order. Dr King's message is not entirely non-prophetic. Indeed he not infrequently produces prophecies, among others, that Los Angeles would not be engulfed by a tidal wave in 1972 as predicted by a prominent astrologer; that there is a further moon to Jupiter and a further planet in the solar system to be discovered; vague warnings that man will soon be abandoned to his fate unless he changes his ways; and even vaguer auguries of the coming of a New Age—on which subject he has offered little specific information. This usual lack of specificity in Dr King's prophecies has the obvious advantage that they are unlikely to experience a clear refutation, while receiving daily corroboration. The attention of members to reports of world events in the media to follow the realization of King's prophecies is often as close as that of many adventists.[17] The Cuban confrontation, Arab-Israeli War, etc., are seen as but paler reflections of cosmic battles, and as an indication of the karmic balance and the nearness of the New Age. Members are quite convinced that events such as the China-US rapprochement were the consequence of Dr King's role in Operation Karmalight.

Talcott Parsons suggests that 'The essential difference from the prophet is that the mystagogue defines his source of legitimation primarily in *magical* terms not those of a *religious ethic*. He is not an agent of rationalization, but of escape from the problems of meaning which exert pressure to rationalize, i.e. to establish new levels of normative order.'[18] While this is clearly true of King, his message is not entirely non-ethical.

Continued evil thought and action will result in extinction in our current form and regression to a very much less advanced spiritual plane. But while the world is enjoined to behave more morally, it is not altogether clear what this morality entails. We must cease despoiling the planet, exploding atomic bombs and thinking evil thoughts, and must pay greater attention to spiritual matters, particularly as elaborated by Dr King, but what other ethical steps we may take are left rather vague. Smoking is denounced as a pollutant, although Dr King smokes in order to 'lower his vibrations' and most of his staff are heavy smokers. There is no ban on alcohol, and only sex is strongly discouraged as tending to weaken one's vital energies. King recently contracted a 'celibate union' with a prominent disciple. Apart from these specific injunctions and a vague ethic of 'Do as you would be done by since you will be done by as you did', there are few explicit moral constraints for members. Salvation lies less in following a radical morality and rather more in trusting to and assisting in the Doctor's ritual manipulations of cosmic energy for karmic ends. It is a complaint I have heard from members more than once that they are not always certain of the practical application of Aetherius Society teaching in their everyday lives.

Dr King first began to proclaim his message at the height of the Cold War. In the aftermath of the Second World War and the development of nuclear weapons, the situation of mankind looked precarious. The 'free world' seemed to be threatened by an enormous force of evil whose potential was unthinkable. For the little man without any apparent influence on world affairs and in the grip of forces he could not understand, both at home (the struggle between organized labour and the managerial bureaucracies of vast corporations) and abroad (the struggle between 'democracy' and 'communism'), the Weberian problem of meaning was posed acutely. For some, meaning was supplied through the Campaign for Nuclear Disarmament, for others more alienated from political institutions in America, meaning emerged through McCarthy's cry of communist conspiracy,[19] for others yet further politically alienated into a sense of powerlessness, mundane political categories of explanation appeared to offer no salvation. They looked instead for signs and clues of some higher order of explanation. It was into this situation of anxious expectancy that the first flying saucer 'sightings' emerged in America in 1947. As H. Taylor Buckner suggests, 'Insofar as its social impact is concerned the flying saucer might as well have been a flying Rorschach blot.'[20] While books began to appear on the subject in the USA, exchange control regulations may have limited their diffusion to Europe. It was not until the early 1950s that the European press publicized flying saucers widely. Moreover, as Buckner indicates, it was around this time that flying saucer interest shifted from uncrystallized popular excitement to an interpretation in occult terms with the appearance of personal contact stories.

Some enthusiasts interpreted the flying saucers as hostile forces, thus projecting their terrestrial anxieties on a broader screen. Others, like George King, interpreted them as a sign of salvation. Minor modification to traditional occult thought easily assimilated the flying saucer pilots to the role of mystical beings with supernatural powers, previously located in Tibet or India. Indeed in some ways this was a happy coincidence. As the West grew relatively more familiar with the East through the media, the plausibility of the claim that amongst the dirt, squalor and poverty of the East lived mankind's most highly developed members or his spiritual protectors was beginning to be undermined. The locus of occult knowledge could conveniently be shifted to a point outside the visible empirical world.

Since man, through forces that seemed beyond his control, appeared about to precipitate his own extinction, the space people could credibly be cast as friendly spiritual guides and superiors hopeful of saving man from his own folly if he was prepared to change his ways. Such an interpretation afforded hope and reassurance, resolving the problem of meaning through the elaboration of a Cosmic Plan. Terrestrial irrationality made sense when located within a super-terrestrial framework. King provided such a framework without the objectionable limitations of earlier versions. Despite the anti-materialism of the occult reaction, no supernaturalist scheme can afford to ignore contemporary science totally. Thus on the one hand science and scientists are denigrated: 'Even though medical science can cure things now they could not a few years ago, nevertheless our hospitals are still overflowing and people are still dying of "old age".'[21] On the other hand King produced a cosmic picture replete with scientism and technology. These appear in a number of forms, for example scientific asides between the Space Masters during transmissions:

B

'Nehone in infinitely variable pattern. Beam six, six, zero. Transmission state—good, but full protective measures must be given because of the value of the information factor.[22]
'Neem six. Divorce. Nehone. Divorce isolation beam collective neem, neem, two zero.'
'Executed.'
'Acceptable. Temperature?'
'Ninety-nine.'
'Neem six. Relate. Divorce. Temperature?'
'Normal.'
'Acceptable. Your opinion?'
'Heart, deviation nil, nil par six.'
'Neem two seven. Relate M.C.I. Divorce. Your opinion?'
'Heart normal.'
'Acceptable. Gamma radiation?'
Etc.[23]

and in descriptions of King's radionic equipment:

The whole apparatus was specially designed so that a collector could be placed on a Charged Mountain in England which would collect energies radiated to it and transmit them through a crystal linkage to a carefully designed receiver 6,000 miles away. The energies would be carried through a capacitor chamber in the main body of the apparatus, where they would be compressed and directed through special booster coils into a physical battery which was engineered for the purpose of reception and retention of this type of ultra-high frequency energy. At a later date, the position of the battery could be reversed on the machines and energies stored there could be taken out of the battery by a demand imposed by the main machine itself. These energies could then be radiated in powerful pulses through underwater transducers into a Psychic Centre of the vibrant Mother Earth.[24]

Both anti-science and scientism are apparent in the following words of George King: 'Einstein didn't know what he was talking about when he said light was the ultimate velocity. I have spoken to him since and he's beginning to change his mind.'[25] King, one of the 'uneducated and undegreed people',[26] could challenge the words of Einstein on his own ground.

Alienation from science is matched by alienation from politics. King has claimed that thirteen men have manipulated the world for 2,000 years.[27] (It is apparently not difficult to live 2,000 years if you are powerful enough.) Behind most contemporary political events lie the machinations of these thirteen Black Magicians. An English leader inquired rhetorically at a recent lecture: 'How long are people on Earth going to be hoodwinked by politicians?'[28]

At least part of the motivation for membership of the Aetherius Society then would seem to lie in cognitive insecurity resulting from an awareness of forces at play in the world beyond man's control, political alienation and apathy, a rejection of contemporary materialism and particularly materialistic and deterministic science, and a desire to take some active part in alleviating the world situation.[29] An essential prerequisite is sufficient education to cope with the extensive occult literature and its abstruse terminology, but insufficient to penetrate its tortured logic and thin veneer of 'science'. It also seems plausible that a sense of personal insignificance and inadequacy is a prerequisite for the acceptance of ritual rather than empirical means of self-improvement. This rather suggests one of the limitations of the Society's appeal. Scientology has been vastly more successful in terms of numbers of adherents than the Aetherius Society not perhaps because it has eschewed flying saucers, since it contains its own equivalent component of science fiction, but rather because it offers practical individual techniques for manipulating one's own destiny. The return on Aetherius Society ritual to the individual is too indirect. Scientology will save mankind by saving individuals, the Aetherius Society promises only that through assisting mankind one will assist one's own karma. What Dr King has gained in altruism, he has possibly lost in membership.[30]

Having joined, however, a member of the Aetherius Society can justifiably feel a part of profound events. He is numbered among those who address their petitions and warnings to prominent scientists and heads of state. His leader, supported by his members' ritual activity, visits the inner realms of the earth and the outer reaches of space, participating in cosmic events of unimaginable proportions. Through practice of the ritual, the member can have a hand in averting fire, earthquake, pestilence and war, and in saving the world from enslavement by Satan and Black Magicians.

As Weber indicated, the congregations of mystagogues 'generally remained associations that were open to the outer world and fluid in form'.[31] The boundaries of the Aetherius Society are not rigidly drawn. Entry is simply a matter of paying a regular subscription and signature of an affirmation that one supports the aims of the society and is not a member of a communist organization or an associate of known communists.[32] Active members have only recently been distinguished from mere sympathizers, and an internal hierarchy has begun to emerge. A minimal condition of membership was recently established in terms of the adherent's willingness to participate fully in one particularly important day of ritual.[33] While there has been differentiation between the staff members of the Society and ordinary members, the former being recognized as closer to Dr King and more spiritually advanced, a 'hierarchy of sanctification which the unilluminated [are] excluded from attaining'[34] is beginning to emerge, based on the award of certificates of merit for commitment to Aetherius Society activities, and through 'Temple Degree examinations' as a test of level of understanding of King's message and the practices of the Society. King intends to perform 'Initiations' when this merit structure is firmly established, and to institutionalize a range of degrees of Initiation.

The Aetherius Society can be located in a religious tradition which stems most directly from the nineteenth-century spiritualist movement. The Theosophical Society was founded as a reaction to the inability of spiritualism to develop beyond its limited ideological rationale, seeking to investigate the common mystical foundations of the world religions and to realize a wider framework of meaning and a metaphysics which would provide an explanation of spiritualist and other occult phenomena.

The Theosophical Society is the clearest source of King's revelation. Theosophical thought is one of the predominant elements of King's teaching and there is a pronounced cultural overlap between these two movements. Similarly, an adherent of spiritualism would not feel altogether out of place at Aetherius Society meetings. The voices of the Space Masters and their messages do not sound so different from those of the dead produced by spiritualist mediums.[35]

Spiritualism, however, failed to transcend the level of thaumaturgy. Its limited personal-service oriented rationale, and the access of all who have the sensitivity to the role of mediumship, have restricted the degree to which it can generate cohesive organizations.

King however has been successful in institutionalizing his mystagoguery around a stable collectivity. This success has been achieved through his ability to monopolize access to his own charismatic legitimation. He early established his link to the Cosmic Masters as the 'Primary Terrestrial channel' through whom they would communicate with the world, and defended the legitimacy of his own contact with the flying saucers against other published claims, refuting their validity on the basis of his own superior knowledge. As editor of the Society's publications he published reports of flying saucer sightings by others, but the only report ever published of an actual contact, other than his own, was one by his mother which further supported his own primacy. Finally, he subordinated the Society's spiritual healing role, with its tendency to fragmentation on the basis of its professional-client relationship, by establishing it as a secondary object of the Society, and devalued it as a source of authority by placing it within everybody's competence.[36] The Society's primary object was established as that of spreading 'the teachings of the Masters Aetherius, Jesus or other Cosmic Masters', and performing the collective rituals this entailed.

King also developed the putative theodicy of the Theosophical Society through his stress on the role of Karma in the explanation of the current situation of the individual and the social order. Offering a wider framework of meaning than spiritualism, King could demand higher levels of involvement from the Society's membership. By these means King avoided the difficulties, which have generally faced spiritualistic mediumship, of aggregating loosely and segmentally committed participants of a professional-client relationship into a stable collectivity.[37]

Summary and Conclusions

Employing Max Weber's concept of the mystagogue, this paper seeks to interpret the appearance of a contemporary metaphysical group and its leader. Dr George King commenced his occult career as a mystic and (magical) healer. Deep yoga trances produced in Dr King an awareness of spiritual beings who wished to employ him as a medium for the transmission of guidance in a period of acute cognitive ambiguity. His public thaumaturgy progressively institutionalized into stable mystagoguery and with a congregation able to provide economic security for his mission of magical manipulation on their behalf, his passive, dependent thaumaturgy atrophied in favour of an active role as co-participant in cosmic events. Cognitive insecurity of politically alienated members of the cultic milieu is invoked as a limited rationale of the membership of his congregation, and the failure of his belief-system to provide the means of direct magical manipulation of one's own situation in this life is invoked as a partial explanation of its limited appeal. It is argued that the institutionalization of his mystagogic congregation was successful due to his success in monopolizing access to charismatic legitimation, elaborating a theodicy, and subordinating spiritual healing to evangelistic and ritual goals.

NOTES AND REFERENCES

1 Among those who have kindly commented on this paper I have particularly benefited from the thoughts of Dr Bryan Wilson.

2 For earlier commentary on the Aetherius Society, see John A. Jackson, 'Two contemporary cults', *The Advancement of Science*, 23, 108, June 1966, pp. 60–64; and John Jackson & Ray Jobling, 'Towards an analysis of contemporary cults', in David Martin (ed.), *A Sociological Yearbook of Religion in Britain*, No. 1, S.C.M. Press, London, 1968, pp. 94–105. Unfortunately, the *Advancement of Science* paper, while a sympathetic analysis, is factually inaccurate concerning both the Aetherius Society and Scientology at a number of points.

3 See Louis Rose, *Faith Healing*, Penguin Books, Harmondsworth, 1971.

4 On the notion of the 'cultic milieu' see Colin Campbell, 'The cult, the cultic milieu and secularisation', in Michael Hill (ed.), *A Sociological Yearbook of Religion in Britain*, No. 5, S.C.M. Press, London, 1971.

5 See Martin Gardner, *Fads and Fallacies in the Name of Science*, Dover, New York, 1957, particularly Chapter 5 'Flying Saucers' and pp. 329–31.

6 Anonymous, *The Story of the Aetherius Society*, The Aetherius Society, London, n.d., p. 1, emphasis in the original. As studies of sensory deprivation suggest, these are not unlikely conditions for the appearance of hallucinations and 'voices'.

7 Max Weber, *The Sociology of Religion*, Methuen, London, 1965, p. 175.

8 *The Story of the Aetherius Society*, p. 3.

9 Weber, op. cit., p. 54.

10 *Cosmic Voice* (edited by George King), Vol. 1, p. 54.

11 *The Story of the Aetherius Society*, p. 4.

12 Ibid., p. 4.

13 E.g. Keith Robertson, the accompanying disciple says of their intention to go to California: 'Letters were immediately sent out to numerous Flying Saucer and Metaphysical groups through the States telling them that George King was on his way.' *Cosmic Voice*, issue 21, December 1959–January 1960, p. 3.

14 Ibid., p. 6.

15 E.g. a circular advertising metaphysical classes September–November 1972: 'Those of us who were fortunate and privileged enough to attend any of the lectures given by Doctor King during his recent highly successful tour of England, will have been struck most forcibly by the awe-inspiring range of this Master's abilities. His vision and practical accomplishment,

as demonstrated during this visit, stretch from the healing requirements of an individual to those of a World, as exemplified in the mighty Cosmic Energy manipulation of Operation Sunbeam. From being a Spiritual Healer of men Doctor King has become The Great Healer of a Planetary race.'

16 Weber, op. cit., p. 54.

17 See e.g. John Lofland, *Doomsday Cult*, Prentice-Hall, New Jersey, 1966; or Bryan R. Wilson on the Christadelphians in *Sects and Society*, Heinemann, London, 1960.

18 Talcott Parsons, Introduction to Weber, op. cit., p. xxxv.

19 See e.g. Frank Parkin, *Middle Class Radicalism*, Manchester University Press, 1968; A. Rebecca Cardoza, 'A modern American witch-craze', in Max Marwick (ed.), *Witchcraft and Sorcery*, Penguin Books, Harmondsworth, 1970, pp. 369–77.

20 H. Taylor Buckner, 'The flying saucerians: a lingering cult', *New Society*, 9 September, 1965, and 'The flying saucerians: an open door cult', in M. Truzzi (ed.), *Sociology and Everyday Life*, Prentice-Hall, New Jersey, 1968, pp. 223–30. Possibly, however, the cults observed by Mr Buckner were rather different from the Aetherius Society since he characterizes the membership of flying saucer cults as predominantly female, aged, widowed or single, upper-working-class to lower-middle-class, with low formal education, bad physical health ('Many members are deaf, many have very poor vision, many walk with aid of sticks and many more display obvious physical handicaps of other types.'); and with a high prevalence of mental illness ('If one were to attend a meeting and watch the action without knowing in advance whether the audience was in a mental hospital or not, it would be very difficult to tell, because many symptoms of serious illness are displayed.'). Mr Buckner has 'never seen a male member who could make a successful presentation of normalcy', while I have never met a member of the Aetherius Society who had any such difficulty, nor have I seen more than one would expect with sticks, obvious physical impairment or symptoms of mental illness. Most of the members I met seemed altogether 'normal' but for some rather curious beliefs concerning flying saucers. Buckner also draws attention to the prevalence of a 'Do as you would be done by' ethic.

21 George King, lecture at Caxton Hall, London, 2 August, 1972.

22 *Cosmic Voice*, issue 25, November–December 1961, p. 29.

23 Ibid., p. 31.

24 *Aetherius Society Newsletter*, 10, issues 5 & 6, March 1971, p. 1.

25 George King, taped lecture played at a Metaphysical seminar, 15 April, 1972.

26 The doctorate was awarded by a Californian evangelistic college for his book *The Nine Freedoms*. Dr King also sometimes employs the style M.R.P.S. after his name. These initials stand for Member of the Royal Photographic Society.

27 George King, lecture at Kensington Library, 17 August, 1972.

28 For similarities in this and many other respects, see H. T. Dohrman, *California Cult: The Story of 'Mankind United'*, Beacon Press, Boston, 1958.

29 Donald Warren has employed Gallup Poll data in an attempt to show that social marginality, alienation and cognitive dissonance resulting from

status inconsistency are responsible for UFO sightings. Donald J. Warren, 'Status inconsistency theory and flying saucer sightings', *Science*, Vol. 170, 6 November, 1970, pp. 599–603.

30 On the contemporary occult revival of which the Aetherius Society forms a part, see Daniel Bell, 'Religion in the sixties', *Social Research*, Vol. 38, No. 3, Autumn 1971, pp. 447–97; Marcello Truzzi, 'The occult revival as popular culture: some random observations on the old and the nouveau witch', *Sociological Quarterly*, Vol. 13, No. 1, Winter 1971, pp. 16–36; Andrew Greeley, 'Superstition, ecstasy and tribal consciousness', *Social Research*, Vol. 37, No. 2, 1970, pp. 203–211; John R. Staude, 'Alienated youth and the cult of the occult', in Morris Medley and James Conyers (eds), *Sociology for the Seventies*, New York, Wiley, 1972, pp. 86–94.

31 Weber, op. cit., p. 61.

32 This because King's appeal for unilateral nuclear disarmament by Britain was attacked as 'communist' by the right-wing *Empire News*.

33 This day is July 8th, the anniversary of the Primary Initiation of Earth:

> '. . . *we do not want any Members unless they are willing*
> *to observe this one day of thankfulness in the right*
> *spiritual manner—no matter who they are.*'

> 'Sympathisers, yes—but Members no.' *Aetherius Society Newsletter*, 10, issues 17 & 18, September 1971, p. 1. (emphasis in the original.)

34 Weber, op. cit., p. 124.

35 Interestingly the voices of these Cosmic Masters as relayed by Dr King have much of the quality of those produced by spiritualist mediums. Despite their excellent command of the English language they tended often to employ rather vulgar stylistic locutions, e.g.: 'It has caused me great suffering to keep plugging away at you all'; 'they will know that you speaketh the Truth' (this from the Master Jesus!); 'now is the hour when the Karmic bell tolls', (*Cosmic Voice*, No. 26, July–August 1962, p. 23); 'two wrongs will not make a right'; 'watch the world go by'; 'there's no great mystery about it' (tape-recorded lectures heard at meetings of the Aetherius Society). The sing-song, highly aspirated and distinctively inflected quality of their speech has since become the normative ritual mode in Aetherius Society services and prayers.

36 Although a regular healing practice is carried on at the Society's headquarters, conducted by the Staff Members, the literature and lectures of the Society stress that 'every man, woman and child can give healing. It is not an art confined to the few'. George King, lecture, Caxton Hall, 2 August, 1972.

37 Geoffrey K. Nelson, *Spiritualism and Society*, Routledge & Kegan Paul, London, 1971. See also the anonymous review of this book in the *Times Literary Supplement*, 26.6.69, pp. 706–707.

Roy Wallis

3 The Cult and Its Transformation

Current Concepts of Cult[1]

Sociological concepts have a fluidity and an open-textured nature which engenders perennial debate over their application. The best-known case, of course, is *class*, a term whose range of meaning is so wide and yet whose sense is so intuitively clear as to permit the suspicion that our opponents in debate are quite wilfully trying to mislead and misunderstand us. The concepts of *role* and *status* are sources of similar difficulties. Closer to home, in the sociology of religion, the concepts which identify and define religious collectivities are a prominent source of anxiety and their reconceptualization a source of persistent occupational mobility. How many dozens of articles must now lie unread in university libraries on the concept of *sect*, for instance? It is, therefore, at first glance, a matter for relief that a new orthodoxy has emerged concerning one item in the battery of concepts of religious collectivities, the *cult*.

Out of the struggles of Troeltsch with the notion of *mysticism*, Becker and early Yinger, this elusive and slippery concept has at last been thoroughly pinned down by Geoffrey Nelson. He assures us:

> The crucial criteria [sic] of cults, that which distinguishes them from all other types of religious bodies, is that which is represented by Stark's assertion that cults 'draw their inspiration from other than the primary religion of the culture, and therefore represent a break with the religious tradition of the society in which they exist.[2]

And here, it can be seen, he speaks with the consensus: Glock and Stark define cults as:

> religious movements which draw their inspiration from other than the primary religion of the culture, and which are not schismatic movements in the same sense as sects whose concern is with preserving a purer form of the traditional faith.[3]

35

Lofland's already classic study of a 'Doomsday Cult' adopts a similar position. Cults, he maintains, are 'little groups' which break off from the 'conventional consensus and espouse very different views of the real, the possible and the moral.'[4] Dohrman too rests on such a view :

> Here the concept 'cult' will refer to that group, secular, religious, or both, that has deviated from what our American Society considers normative forms of religion, economics, or politics, and has substituted a new and often unique view of the individual, his world, and how this world may be attained.[5]

A Critique

Since this conception of the cult has achieved such widespread acceptance, it behooves anyone who wishes to disturb the consensus to offer some sound justification for his action. What, after all, is wrong with this conceptualization? Why not let sleeping dogs lie?

Concepts are tools which enable us to grasp aspects of reality in a manner relevant to our particular problems. The problems which concern Nelson, Lofland, Dohrman, Glock and Stark, and myself are, I take it, *sociological*. We are severally interested in such questions as : Who joins cults and why?; Why are cults typically short-lived, loosely structured and individualistic?; How do cults develop as forms of social and religious organization?; How are deviant views of reality generated and maintained?

There are undoubtedly other areas of interest, but these are among the more central. Thus an important question that we need to ask is : Does the view of the cult presented above provide the basis for any explanatory advance? Has it been associated with theories or hypotheses which explain features of cult collectivities or their membership which we deem significant? The radical claim presented here is that, sadly, it has not, and indeed it cannot in the nature of the case, since such conceptualizations bear no relationship to the *sociological* problems at hand. They are either too vague and woolly to capture the phenomena in any theoretically useful way, or their basis is *theological* rather than *sociological*.

As an aside, let me say here, that my dissatisfaction is based on no mere disciplinary imperialism. It is conceivable that the solution to certain kinds of problem *is* theological rather than sociological—

or indeed psychological, ecological or whatever. In such a case, of course, a theological definition might be most useful. But the authors mentioned above do not conceive their enterprise in this way. They locate their work within a sociological tradition and identify their problems in sociological terms. Why, for example, did spiritualism prove a difficult ideological basis around which collectivities could institutionalize? What are the socially structured motivations which lead to affiliation with cults rather than sects, churches, etc?

In case studies such as those of Lofland and Dohrman the problem does not arise with any urgency since the definition of cult which they employ is not mobilized in a theoretically central way. However they may *define* cult, the definition has only marginal significance for the descriptions they proceed to offer. The problem does become significant, however, when any attempt is made to develop a set of generalizations concerning phenomena which the definition is used to identify.

This problem is characteristic of the work of the major advocates of this conceptual form : Glock and Stark, and Nelson. In a curiously oft-cited paper, Glock and Stark seek to illuminate the origin and evolution of new religious groups. The secret of origin and evolution they discover to lie in relative deprivation : 'Deprivation, as we conceive it, refers to any and all of the ways that an individual or group may be, or feel disadvantaged in comparison either to other individuals or groups or to an internalized set of standards.'[6] They outline five kinds of deprivation to which individuals or groups may be subject :

1 *Economic deprivation* : 'differential distribution of income in societies and in the limited access of some individuals to the necessities and luxuries of life' lies at the root of economic deprivation.

2 *Social deprivation* : rests on the differential distribution of socially valued attributes and rewards—prestige, power, status, etc.

3 *Organismic deprivation* : refers to the differential distribution of 'physical or mental deformities, ill health, or other such stigmatizing or disabling traits'.

4 *Ethical deprivation* : 'refers to value conflicts between the ideals of society and those of individuals or groups. . . . They can occur because some persons perceive incompatibilities in the values of society, or detect negative latent functions of rules and standards, or even because they are struck by discrepancies between ideals and realities.'[7]

5 *Psychic deprivation* : refers to the situation of persons who 'find themselves without a meaningful system of values by which to interpret and organize their lives.'[8]

These five types of deprivation, Glock and Stark suggest, are systematically related to five 'forms of religious group', respectively : economic deprivation—sect; social deprivation—church; organismic deprivation—healing movement; ethical deprivation—reform movement; and psychic deprivation—cult. Here, however, we face a problem since the only one of these 'forms' for which they specify identifying criteria is the cult (as above) and hence their 'theory' turns out to be no theory at all, offering no means of refutation.

Is it, then, a useful heuristic scheme? Their own examples would seem to suggest not. Cults are religious groups which make a fundamental break with the religious tradition of their society and will contingently be found to have their origins in psychic deprivation. The Black Muslims are therefore a clear case of a cult. But that turns out not to be the case, since Glock and Stark tell us : 'The Black Muslim movement . . . in its strong tone of social protest and its doctrine of Negro superiority . . . exemplifies the kind of religious movement which grows out of economic deprivation (with, of course, its accompanying social deprivation).' and 'the religious movement which grows out of economic deprivation need not have its theological base in the traditional religion of the society.'[9] What should we conclude? That the Black Muslims are a cult but cults do not uniformly have their origins in psychic deprivation? That the Black Muslims are a cult but that not all cults make a fundamental break with the traditional religion of their society? That the Black Muslims are a sect, having their origins in economic deprivation, but some sects, as well as cults, make a fundamental break with the traditional religion of their society? That we have a legitimate right to feel confused? The types seem not only to be impure, as Glock and Stark confess, but elegantly arbitrary.

Nelson develops a number of features of the Glock and Stark view of the cult, specifically their suggestion that successful cults may develop into new religions.[10] To summarize Nelson's argument : Cult and sect do not fall on the same typological continuum. Sects reject the social order and find their theological basis within the prevailing religious tradition. Cults are (a) groups based upon mystical, psychic or ecstatic experiences; (b) represent a fundamental break with religious traditions and (c) are concerned mainly with the problems of individuals.[11]

They emerge as *local* cults, spontaneously or around a charismatic leader, and may disappear on the death of the leader or through internal dissensions. Successful cults may be established as *permanent local cults, unitary centralized cults,* or *federal centralized cults.* In situations of breakdown of the traditional religious system, new cults flourish and one may secure a dominant position as a new religion.

Well and good. One may marvel at the leap from centralized cult to new religion, but no matter, let us look at some of Nelson's cases to assess the utility of his conceptualization in the light of the examples he offers us and others that seem appropriate.

New Thought does not, in most of its branches, 'emphasize the importance of all . . . members having a deeply personal religious experience of a type which would be defined as psychic, mystical or ecstatic.'[12] Moral Rearmament does, however, but it does not appear to 'represent a fundamental break with the religious tradition' of western society.[13] The Aetherius Society does appear to make such a break, but then it does not appear to be 'concerned primarily with the problems of individual(s) rather than those of social groups.'[14]

But perhaps to offer countervailing examples is unjust. Nelson may claim to be offering an ideal-type which we cannot expect to fit every case. The problem with this argument however is that what the examples seem to demonstrate is that what Nelson offers us is not a cohesive syndrome at all, but a set of characteristics which appear to vary independently of each other.

The problem stems, I believe, from a weakness in 'the crucial criter(ion)' of the cult which is employed.

1 The definition identifies the cult in terms of the *content* of belief. If *deviance* is the crucial feature of content, as with Lofland and Dohrman, then we have no good ground for not classifying a range of Christian schismatic and 'heretical' forms of belief as the ideology of cults[15]—Jehovah's Witnesses, the Mormons, the Salvation Army. That is, we lack any distinction between cult and sect.

2 Definition in terms of a 'fundamental break with the religious tradition' seems to provide such a distinction. Appearances can be deceptive, however. How *fundamental*, after all, is 'fundamental'? What makes Jesus's break with the Jewish tradition of messianism any more fundamental than Charles Taze Russell's with Christianity? Yet Nelson would have us classify one as cult, the other as sect.

3 The classification groups together cases which not only seem different (that after all, is partly the purpose of the exercise) but which do not have anything in common other than the definitional

criterion. What features do Scientology and the Freemasons share, other than their break with the religious tradition, that makes it useful to classify them together at all?

4 Finally, these definitions rule out any appreciation of a developmental pattern, which although by no means universal, has coherently been attributed to some cults, namely the transition from cult to sect. Within the scheme offered, such a transition is *a priori* impossible, sects are schismatic from traditional religions, cults are theologically alien. Hence we have an enormous hiatus between cult and new religion in which centralization may occur, according to Nelson, but nothing much else of interest seems to be going on. How then do we account for the similarities in patterns of development of such movements as Christian Science, Scientology, the Jehovah's Witnesses, etc?

It is here that the crux of the matter lies. Groups which have similar patterns of social organization and development have diverse belief-systems, some Christian, some non-Christian. A theological criterion of classification thoroughly blurs this sociologically relevant feature of new religious movements. The conceptualizations of cult and sect employed by Glock and Stark, and Nelson fail to capture the organizational features which distinguish these forms of religious organization.

Reformulation

The criterion provided fails to differentiate cult and sect unambiguously. Both cult *and* sect are deviant in relation to the dominant agnostic/denominational Christian orthodoxy. That is, sect and cult are deviant in comparison to prevailing indifference and to churchly or denominational orthodoxy. Church and denomination embody normatively approved forms of religious belief and organization. Cult and sect are deviant in contrast to churchly or denominational respectability.

Having distinguished cult and sect from church and denomination, we now need to distinguish *between* cult and sect. A feature which usefully distinguishes these two forms of religious organization is that, like the church, the sect is conceived by its members to be *uniquely legitimate* as a means of access to truth or salvation. The cult, like the denomination, is conceived by its members to be *pluralistically legitimate*, one of a variety of paths to the truth or salvation.

A TYPOLOGY OF IDEOLOGICAL COLLECTIVITIES

	Respectable	Deviant
Uniquely legitimate	Church	Sect
Pluralistically legitimate	Denomination	Cult

The remainder of this paper will be concerned largely with *cult* and *sect*.

Having distinguished cult and sect typologically, it remains to be shown that the typology has any utility.

A Theory of Cult Development

As Glock and Stark argue, new religious movements may emerge in a variety of organizational forms. Martin has argued that many Protestant denominations were born in that form rather than as sects[17] and Steinberg suggests that Reform Judaism emerged as a church.[18] Although not as frequently as Niebuhr would have us believe, some religious movements do emerge as sects and develop into denominations. It is an argument central to this paper that some new religious movements emerge as cults and, of these, some develop into sects.

Cults develop as eclectic syntheses of ideas and practices available in the prevailing cultic milieu.[19] Typically, the cult is conceived as loosely organized, with no clear distinction between members and non-members, tolerant of other groups and beliefs, and often transitory. It is precisely these characteristics of the cult which require explanation.

These features of the cult relate to the characteristic which underlies cult organization—individualism.[20] In the cult, there is no locus of authority beyond the individual members. Unlike the sect, the ideal-typical cult has no source of legitimate attributions of heresy. It operates on the basis of a principle of 'epistemological' individualism which leaves the determination of what constitutes acceptable doctrine in the hands of the member.

This individualism is evident in many accounts of cults. Discussing spiritualism, Nelson writes of the 'suspicion of formal organization, many local societies failed to survive as a result of the individualistic nature of spiritualists. . . .'[21] Braden refers, albeit less directly, to the same phenomenon in his discussion of New Thought : 'Since knowledge of God—aided, to be sure, by scriptures and the revealed insights of others—is ultimately a highly personal, intuitive, experiential matter, how can it submit to any limitation upon its freedom of expression?'[22] In Dianetics, the same sense of individual autonomy was a prominent feature of the movement: 'In a healthy and growing science, there are many men who are recognized as being about equally competent in the field, and no one man dominates the work,'[23] or 'there are many, many roads to a higher state of existence . . . no man can say "This is the road for all to follow". . . .'[24]

The individualistic nature of the cult provides the explanation for those characteristics most typically identified as features of cult organization. Lacking any authoritative source of attributions of heresy there can be no clear boundaries between cult ideology and the surrounding cultic milieu, nor between cult members and others. Hence there are few barriers to doctrinal fluctuation and change. Since the determination of doctrine lies with the members, cults cannot command the loyalty of their membership, which remains only partially committed. Commitment being slight, resources for the control of members are lacking. Members typically move between groups and belief-systems, adopting components to fit into the body of truth already gleaned—loyalties of members are thus often shared between ideological collectivities, leading to tolerance. Membership will change rapidly as members move from one group to another, and the collectivities themselves will tend to be transient as charismatic leaders emerge and attempt to control the activities of the following, thus leading to alienation, or as dissension arises due to the relatively limited basis of shared belief. Since the particular cult is only one among many possible paths to the truth or salvation, membership may decline through sheer indifference. A paradigm case here would be the flying saucer cult described by H. Taylor Buckner.[25]

Sects emerge in various ways. They may emerge as schismatic movements from existing denominations, as Niebuhr, and Glock and Stark suggest. As others have shown, sects may also emerge as a result of interdenominational crusades. They may also emerge through a process of development from cults.

The dimensions of the sect have been much debated. Among those that have been advanced a number, such as Troeltsch's stress on the sect's eschatological nature, but also asceticism, the achieved basis of membership, an ethical orientation, and egalitarianism all seem in retrospect to have been features of the sect in particular socio-historical situations rather than universal characteristics. The concept of the sect therefore seems to centre on a self-conception as an 'elect' or elite, the right to exclusion, totalitarianism, and hostility towards, or separation from the state or society.

These dimensions of sectarianism are related to the characteristic which underlies sect organization—'epistemological' authoritarianism.

David Martin has observed : 'the sect recognizes no valid alternatives or independent orders of truth outside the inclusiveness of its vision,'[26] and Alan Rogerson, in his discussion of Jehovah's Witnesses, suggests : 'the Witnesses persist in being certain of everything they believe . . . (the Society is always right). When the Society changes its mind the Witnesses then stay just as certain, but now of the opposite thing.'[27] Possession of the truth implies a superiority over those too blind to see, too deaf to hear. The purity of the truth must be maintained against those who might pollute it and its protection therefore requires extensive control over those to whom access is permitted. Hostility to state and the wider society is generated by actual or threatened conflict over alternative versions of the truth.[28] In those areas in which it claims legitimacy the state may buttress its own version of right conduct or civil obligation by coercive means, sometimes forcing the sect to defend its vision by withdrawal and isolation.

The need to define the boundaries of true doctrine and true believers carries the further implication of an *authoritative locus* of attributions of heresy. In sects in general this authority may be variously located—in a body of literature, a bureaucracy, a group of elders, or an oral tradition. It is here that the central theoretical argument of the paper lies. In order for a cohesive sectarian group to emerge from the diffuse, individualistic origins of a cult, a prior process of expropriation of authority must transpire. This centralization of authority will be legitimized by a claim to a unique revelation which locates some source or sources of authority concerning doctrinal innovation and interpretation beyond the individual member or practitioner, typically the revelator himself.

Such a transition is evident in the cases of Harris's Brotherhood of the New Life, and Katherine Tingley's Point Loma Community.

THE REVELATION OF HARRIS

Spiritualism has proved a precarious ideological basis upon which to organize cohesive sectarian collectivities. Upon the revelation of its practice by the Fox sisters it rapidly diffused throughout the United States and beyond, organized on a largely amateur basis, or

around competing mediums and their clienteles. Mediumship proved
to be a highly contagious form of charisma and the movement
rapidly developed a predominantly democratic ideology and multiple leadership, and was synthesized with many existing forms of
religious belief, Christian and non-Christian, and socialism and free
love. Spiritualism was thus seen as an 'added blessing', a further
route to the truth or transcendental knowledge, rather than a unique
salvational system.

Thomas Lake Harris was a Universalist preacher who came into
contact with Andrew Jackson Davis and discovered mediumistic
abilities. He later became estranged from Davis, but received a
revelation from an angel which led him and James L. Scott to form
a spiritualistic community in which they acted as the mediums
through whom the colony was divinely directed. The Mountain
Cove colony proved an economic failure.[29] During a period as a
minister of the Church of The New Jerusalem (Swedenborgian) he
began receiving further revelations which led to the alienation of
his congregation but to a growing following of New Churchmen and
spiritualists, and to the founding of the Brotherhood of the New
Life. Communities were established in New York state and later
in California. These communities were founded on the basis of
Harris's revelations from the Lily Queen and later directly from
God himself. Harris was considered as 'God's Shadow', a second
incarnation of Christ. He proscribed general mediumship among
his followers as 'profitless, dangerous and even profane'[30] and arro-
gated sole authority in the direction of the colonies to himself.

The Brotherhood of the New Life imposed a rigorous regime
upon its followers. New converts were expected to turn over their
property to the common fund in Harris's name. Members promised
unconditional obedience to Harris. Sanctions were imposed for
failure to live up to the standard set by him, culminating in
exclusion from the colony. Any challenge to Harris's authority was
regarded as heresy : 'Harris and his friends regarded Oliphant's
claim to mediumship, his receiving and transmitting messages as
the beginning of his treason.'[31] Laurence Oliphant persisted, however, and caused a schism in the Brotherhood on the basis of his
own revelations.

KATHERINE TINGLEY'S REVELATION

The Theosophical Society was never democratic. It incorporated
from its inception a hierarchical structure related to degree of

proximity to the Masters or Mahatmas. However, *chelaship* and hence access to the Masters was in principle open to all. Moreover, the ideological basis of the movement was founded on a search for the common truth in all religions and the rejection of a single creed or dogma. Since all religions contained the truth, theosophy was not conceived as the sole available path.

Madame Blavatsky's charisma was founded on her thaumaturgic performance and her superior access to the Mahatmas. Leadership within the theosophical movement was distributed, however, between Madame Blavatsky and Colonel H. S. Olcott, the co-founder who had secured rational-legal authority as President-for-Life and administrative head of the movement.

On Madame Blavatsky's death, the leader of the American Section of the Theosophical Society, W. Q. Judge, seceded from the parent body which progressively moved toward an 'open-door' cult,[32] introducing a range of further items into the belief system, leading to ideological diffuseness and lessened relevance for salvation. Ellwood observes of the present day Theosophical Society in America, i.e., the body which remained 'loyal' after Judge seceded : 'To a great extent, Theosophical Lodges seem to be coming to play the role of forums where speculative spiritual ideas can be freely presented by all sorts of speakers.'[33] The cultic tendencies within theosophy have been fully asserted.

However, on the death of William Q. Judge, Katherine Tingley, hitherto almost unknown in the Theosophical Society, secured the leadership of the (schismatic) American Society on the basis of messages transmitted through her mediumship from Judge.

Since mediumship had been denigrated by Madame Blavatsky, along with all other features of spiritualism, after her own break with it, Mrs Tingley later legitimized her authority by claiming to have been contacted by a Mahatma while she was in India. Challenges to her authority from other officers of the society led her to secure autocratic powers to appoint or remove officers and veto amendments to the by-laws. On the basis of her new revelation of the nature of theosophy she established a community at Point Loma in California in which she exercised sole authority, ejecting those whom she considered insubordinate.[34]

DISCUSSION

In both of these cases we see the emergence of a cohesive, rigorously controlled, authoritarian sect from a fissiparous, loosely controlled, individualistic cult. In each case the transformation was effected on the basis of a new gnosis which located the revelator as the authoritative source of doctrinal innovation and interpretation.

It is the argument of this paper that the common pattern exhibited in the two examples briefly discussed is a general feature of all cults which negotiate the transition to sectarianism. Cults become sects as the leadership differentiate the movement's ideology from competing belief-systems, endowing it with a unique status as a mode of access to truth or salvation. Hence the arrogation of authority through the revelation of a new gnosis is a necessary condition for sectarianization. This new revelation incorporates an authoritarian epistemology which locates a source (or more precariously for sect persistence, sources) of doctrinal innovation and interpretation beyond the individual member or practitioner, typically in the person of the revelator himself. It thereby establishes a locus for attributions of heresy and provides a legitimation for the exercise of more rigorous control over access to the doctrine and the behaviour of members.

A further necessary condition for the emergence of a sect from a cult, is the appearance of a following for the new revelation. The motivations of the initial following will have as their central feature anxiety and insecurity or uncertainty in a situation of cognitive ambiguity. This may arise in at least two ways. Firstly, the anxiety may derive from the conflicting and competing views of doctrine and ritual which have emerged during the lifetime of the cult. The new revelation, offering an authoritative resolution of the problem of which path to follow, will appeal to those suffering doubt and uncertainty in the face of emerging ideological pluralism. Secondly, it may derive from a crisis of leadership, on the death of the incumbent leader and in the absence of any clear alternative. The new revelation authoritatively locates a new leader, resolving uncertainty.

The revelation of a new gnosis incorporating an authoritarian epistemology, and its acceptance by one or more members suffering uncertainty in the face of cognitive ambiguity, are conceived as contingently sufficient conditions for the development of a sect from a cult.

Conclusion

The argument of this paper has been that a definition of cult and sect on the basis of differences in the content of doctrine is irrelevant to the sociological problems posed by these types of ideological collectivity. A distinction is proposed in terms of the conception of access to the truth or salvation incorporated in the belief-system, i.e. whether it is seen as uniquely or pluralistically legitimate.

While empirically new religious movements may emerge at any point on the cult-sect continuum, those which negotiate the transition from cult to sect will do so as the result of the arrogation of authority from individual members and practitioners. This process is legitimized by appeal to a new revelation which typically locates the revelator as the source of future doctrinal innovation and interpretation. Prior cognitive insecurity provides the basis for the acceptance of the revelation on the part of a section of the cult's following.

NOTES AND REFERENCES

1 My thanks are due to Dr Bryan Wilson for his comments on a version of this paper. The author's research into marginal religious movements has been supported by a grant from the Social Science Research Council.

2 Geoffrey K. Nelson, 'The spiritualist movement and the need for a redefinition of cult', *Journal for the Scientific Study of Religion*, Vol. 8, 1969, p. 158.

3 Charles Y. Glock and Rodney Stark, 'On the origin and evolution of religious groups', in *Religion and Society in Tension*, Rand McNally, Chicago, 1965, p. 245.

4 John Lofland, *Doomsday Cult*, Prentice-Hall, New Jersey, 1966, p. 1.

5 H. T. Dohrman, *California Cult: The Story of Mankind United*, Beacon Press, Boston, 1958, p. xi.

6 Glock and Stark, op. cit., p. 246, emphasis omitted.

7 Ibid., pp. 246–247.

8 Ibid., p. 248.

9 Ibid., p. 250.

10 Ibid., p. 258.

11 Geoffrey K. Nelson, 'The concept of cult', *Sociological Review*. Vol. 16, No. 3, 1968, p. 345.

12 Geoffrey K. Nelson, 'The analysis of a cult: Spiritualism', *Social Compass*, Vol. 15, No. 6, 1968, p. 470. On New Thought, see Charles Braden, *Spirits in Rebellion*, Southern Methodist University Press, Dallas, Texas, 1963.

13 Nelson, 1968, op. cit. On Moral Rearmament, see Allan W. Eister, *Drawing-Room Conversion*, Duke University Press, Durham, North Carolina, 1950.

14 Nelson, 1968, op. cit. On the Aetherius Society, see Roy Wallis, 'The Aetherius Society: a case study in the formation of a mystagogic congregation', *Sociological Review*, Vol. 22, No. 1, 1974, pp. 27–44; or Chapter 2.

15 As theologians do, e.g. A. H. Hoekema, *The Four Major Cults*, Eerdmans, Grand Rapids, 1963.

16 This dimension is employed by Roland Robertson in *The Sociological Interpretation of Religion*, Basil Blackwell, Oxford, 1970, p. 123, but there it refers to 'the bases of religious legitimacy as perceived by the effective leaders of the organization . . .' and is employed to slightly different effect.

17 David Martin, 'The denomination', in his *Pacifism*, Routledge & Kegan Paul, London, 1965.

18 Stephen Steinberg, 'Reform Judaism: the origin and evolution of a church movement', *Journal for the Scientific Study of Religion*, Vol. 4, 1965, pp. 117–129.

19 On the notion of 'cultic milieu' see Colin Campbell, 'The cult, the cultic milieu and secularisation' in Michael Hill (ed.), *A Sociological Yearbook of Religion in Britain*, No. 5, S.C.M. Press, London, 1972, pp. 119–136. See also Roy Wallis, 'Ideology, authority and the development of cultic movements', *Social Research*, Vol. 41, No. 2, 1974, pp. 299–327.

20 David Martin, 'Sect, order and cult', Chapter 9 of his *Pacifism*, op. cit.

21 Nelson, 'The analysis of a cult: Spiritualism', op. cit., p. 475.

22 Charles Braden, *Spirits in Rebellion: The Rise and Development of New Thought*, Southern Methodist University Press, Dallas, Texas, 1963, p. 24.

23 Correspondent to a dianetics newsletter, 1952.

24 Anonymous, 'Introduction' to *Jack Horner Speaks*, (transcript of a lecture given to the New York Dianetics Society), Eidetic Foundation, Fairhope, Alabama, 1952.

25 H. Taylor Buckner, 'The flying saucerians: a lingering cult', *New Society*, 9 September, 1965.

26 David Martin, 'Sect, order and cult', op. cit., p. 184.

27 Alan Rogerson, *Millions Now Living Will Never Die*, Constable, London, 1969, p. 121, emphasis omitted.

28 Hostility to the researcher may be similarly generated. See Thomas Robbins, Dick Anthony and Thomas E. Curtis, 'The limits of symbolic realism: problems of empathic field observation in a sectarian context', *Journal for the Scientific Study of Religion*, Vol. 12, No. 3, 1973, pp. 259-272; also Roy Wallis, 'Religious sects and the fear of publicity', *New Society*, 7 June, 1973, pp. 545-7.

29 Geoffrey K. Nelson, *Spiritualism and Society*, Routledge & Kegan Paul, London, 1969, pp. 18–19.

30 Herbert H. Schneider and George Lawton, *A Prophet and a Pilgrim*, Columbia University Press, New York, 1942, p. 201. My brief account of Harris is heavily indebted to this work.

31 Ibid., p. 336.

32 H. Taylor Buckner, 'The flying saucerians: an open door cult' in Marcello Truzzi (ed.), *Sociology and Everyday Life*, Prentice-Hall, New Jersey, 1968, pp. 223–30.

33 Robert S. Ellwood Jr., *Religious and Spiritual Groups in Modern America*, Prentice-Hall, New Jersey, 1973, p. 95.

34 Emmett A. Greenwalt, *The Point Loma Community in California 1897–1942*, University of California Press, Berkeley, 1955. My brief account of Katherine Tingley is heavily indebted to this work.

PART TWO

Structure and Process in Sectarian Movements

Francine J. Daner

4 Conversion to Krishna Consciousness:
The Transformation from Hippie to Religious Ascetic

An unknown, seventy-year-old Hindu swami, A. C. Bhaktivedanta, arrived in the United States in 1965. By 1966 he had attracted enough disciples to found the International Society for Krishna* Consciousness (ISKCON). The society is popularly known as the Hare Krishna movement, it is small but widespread, and has attracted much attention from the press and from youth.[1] Bhaktivedanta is accepted by his membership to be an *ācārya*, a spiritual master. *Ācārya* means to teach by example. The *ācārya*'s word is taken by his disciples to be law and a disciple must surrender completely to him. The swami claims to be thirty-second in the direct line of succession stemming from Lord Krishna himself. By this claim, the movement links itself to the Hindu Vedic tradition. Bhaktivedanta states that 'The International Society for Krishna Consciousness is a bona fide religious society strictly following the principles described in the Vedic scriptures and practised in India for thousands of years.'[2] Krishna is believed to be the 'Supreme Personality of Godhead' and his form and personality are to be worshipped along with the disciplic succession, who are the *ācāryas* credited with providing their devotees with the absolute truth. The basic beliefs of ISKCON are outlined by Bhaktivedanta as follows :

1 The Absolute Truth is contained in all the great scriptures of the world, the Bible, Koran, Torah, etc. However, the oldest known revealed scriptures in existence are the Vedic literatures, most notably *Bhagavad-gītā*, which is the literal record of God's actual words.

2 God, or Krishna, is eternal, all-knowing, omnipresent, all-powerful and all-attractive, the seed-giving father of man and all living entities. He is the sustaining energy of all life, nature and the cosmic situation.

* For typographical convenience the English spelling 'Krishna' is used in preference to the Sanskrit 'Krsna' (Editor).

3 Man is actually not his body, but is eternal spirit, soul, part and parcel of God, and therefore eternal.

4 That all men are brothers can be practised only when we realize God as our common father.

5 All our actions should be performed as a sacrifice to the Supreme Lord. . . .

6 The food that sustains us should always be offered to the Lord before eating. In this way He becomes the offering, and such eating purifies us.

7 We can, by sincere cultivation of bona fide spiritual science, attain to the state of pure, unending blissful consciousness, free from anxiety, in this very lifetime.

8 The recommended means to attain the mature stage of love of God in the present age of Kali, or quarrel, is to chant the holy name of the Lord. The easiest method for most people is to chant the Hare Krishna *mantra* : Hare Krishna, Hare Krishna, Krishna Krishna, Hare Hare. Hare Rama, Hare Rama, Rama Rama, Hare Hare.

Our basic mission is to propagate the *sankirtana* movement (chanting of the holy names of God) all around the world. . . . It is not recommended that a Krishna conscious devotee go into seclusion to chant by himself and thereby gain salvation for himself alone. Our duty and religious obligation is to go out into the streets where people in general can hear the chanting and see the dancing. We have already seen practically how by this process many, many boys and girls of America and Europe have been saved from the immoral practices of this age and have now dedicated their lives to the service of Krishna.

As devotees of Lord Krishna, it is our duty to teach the people how to love God and worship him in their daily life. This is the aim and destination of human life.[3]

This portrait of the devotees of Lord Krishna is based on a two-year study of the members and their temples in Boston, New York, Amsterdam and London. As an anthropologist seeking to learn of their life-ways, their values, their rituals and commitment to the movement I began to learn why young people join this society. Elsewhere[4] I have presented the devotees' life histories, in order to demonstrate who is drawn into the movement. In this paper I shall limit myself to the analysis of why individuals join the movement, the stages from recruit to devotee, the sex roles within a temple, and the lines of authority within temple life.

A member characterized his fellow devotees as former 'young, psychedelic, middle-class renegades searching for alternatives to their legacy of lies and materialism.'[5] Young people turn to ISKCON seeking an ideology and life-style which they believe modern society does not offer them. Entrance into a Krishna Consciousness temple involves a crucial self-degradation ritual whereby many disoriented individuals find new identities as devotees. The temple itself is a 'total institution', as Goffman[6] defines it, '. . . a place of residence and work where a number of like situated individuals, cut off from the wider society for an appreciable period of time, together lead an enclosed formally administered round of life.'[7] Four phases are discernible in the progression from new recruit to advanced devotee. With some individuals these changes are gradual, with others they can be abrupt transitions. Of course, individual differences and varied backgrounds influence each person's development. The first phase, predevotee life, sets the stage for eventual involvement in ISKCON and is characterized by a rejection of middle-class values and experimentation with the different life-styles available to modern youth. Secondly, we have the neophyte devotee, whose life is marked by entrance into an ISKCON temple and socialization into new roles as a devotee. Next, the devotee becomes an initiated member of the society. He receives a new name, a new status and has superficially internalized his new identity as a devotee. Finally, the devotee successfully integrates his new identity and role in ISKCON.

Predevotee Life

The life-style of most devotees prior to entrance into ISKCON can best be described as permissive with regard to work, drugs and sexual mores. Most described their predevotee lives to me as a psychedelic drop-out process. Their preoccupation with drugs and sex led the prospective members to a disenchantment and boredom with these pastimes even before their involvement in ISKCON. Consciousness-expanding drugs produced a kind of 'inner revolution' and were fundamental in producing new orientations and perspectives for them. In a subjective article on psychedelic drug experience, Russ Rueger explains that these drugs bombard the individual with sensory stimuli.[8] This excess of external information is augmented by unusual images from the unconscious. Simple objects become filled with profound meanings. This overload of subjective and objective data may create a 'synesthesia' effect which is produced by crossing 'sensory wires', so that sound may be seen as flashes of colour and sights heard as loud noises. The mind is awakened to thoughts, impressions, and objects in the environment.

With heavier dosages stronger psychic reactions occur and Rueger observes that the user may detach himself from the world of ordinary meanings and view life as a composite of artificial roles, games or habits. Many users become overwhelmed by the beauty and power of their experience. For the potential devotee these experiences tend to be mystical. A female devotee describes her experience with mescaline :

> Everything seemed so messy, dirty, and horrible to me, but I did get a strange feeling of power. I even knew that I could walk through the walls of a nearby building if I wanted to. I guess I knew, for a moment, that I was not this body.

A young man tells us :

> In graduate school I began studying eastern philosophy and experimenting with drugs. Drugs made me very conscious that there was something to achieve, that there was a realm beyond the level of the senses. With drugs one may believe he is on that spiritual platform, or even think he has become God. . . .

> At that time I thought I had reached the goal, but looking back, all I gained was the awareness. This awareness led me to abandon my studies and go to India because I was disgusted, frustrated with the whole material world. Everything seemed meaningless.

Preconversion drug experiences are viewed by most devotees as temporary, but life-altering events. For them these events are unsatisfactory and incomplete and the potential devotee finds it impossible to recapture the transcendental insights that fade away so rapidly. A male devotee presents this point of view clearly :

> I was actually looking for a spiritual master. In my LSD experiences and my other life experiences I had come to a point where I didn't know what the truth was. I was looking for someone to tell me. I was generally involved with Tim Leary and the LSD thing through his books. When I read Śrīla Prabhupāda's[9] books I could see that he was a person who knew every place where I was at and had been on these LSD trips and something far beyond which I couldn't fathom. Śrīla Prabhupāda is perfectly situated in knowledge. He led me to a consciousness that I could never experience with Timothy Leary's psychedelic experiences, much less by

reading other philosophers, such as Alan Watts. Watts really didn't know—he was speculating from a few LSD experiences. I could tell that from my own LSD experiences.

LSD opened up an awareness that's impossible to describe on the material level of consciousness. I saw a completely different level and displays of energy things going on.

The life experiences of the predevotee are crucial because they represent what Mandelbaum calls a 'principal turning'.[10] These psychedelic experiences are major transitions because they pave the way for a new set of roles, new relationships with people, and a new self-concept. The potential devotee's other experiments with such things as a vegetarian diet, sexual permissiveness, travel, and various philosophies and religions seem to be contributing factors, but less important than the awareness leading from psychedelic drug experiences. In order to purify himself enough to reach the joyful spiritual platform he seeks, the prospective devotee joins an ISKCON temple.

Entrance into an ISKCON Temple

A desire to escape his former 'hippie' life and the belief that he can change his personal consciousness without the use of drugs cause a new devotee to submit himself voluntarily to the austerities of temple living. Commitment and unquestioning loyalty to the authority of Bhaktivedanta are rooted in personal commitment and free choice, not force or coercion. It is a personal decision based on a vision of stability and harmony which is to replace the former 'hippie' state of instability with its helter-skelter value orientation. The transformed consciousness of each person will automatically bring about this state of stability and happiness, according to the swami.

Following the regulative principles required of all devotees is requisite to the personal transformation desired by the neophyte devotee. In addition to chanting the Hare Krishna *mantra* all devotees are required to follow four rules:

1 *No gambling.* This rule also excludes frivolous sports and games. In addition devotees are advised not to engage in any conversation that is not connected with the teachings of Krishna Consciousness or with the execution of duties. All other speech or

reading is called mental speculation and is a luxury in which the devotees do not engage.

2 *No intoxicants.* This rule includes all narcotics, alcoholic beverages, tobacco, coffee and tea. ISKCON's efficiency in getting its members to abandon the use of drugs such as marijuana, LSD, etc., has drawn commendations from the mayors of New York and San Francisco.

3 *No illicit sex.* Sexual relations are permitted only between individuals married by a qualified devotee in Krishna Consciousness. There is no dating or courtship allowed. Marriage is an arrangement for two devotees of Krishna to serve and worship in this way. A swami stated it succinctly : 'If a devotee believes he can serve Krishna better by being married, then he gets married. Marriage is primarily for the purpose of raising children in Krishna Consciousness.'

4 *No eating of meat, fish, or eggs.* The only food that can be eaten by devotees is food prepared under strict dietary regulations and offered by prescribed ceremony to Krishna. When travelling or under unusual circumstances, devotees may eat foods such as fruit or milk which can easily be offered and which do not necessarily require preparation; under no circumstances may unoffered food be eaten. In ISKCON, eating is an act of worship and must be conducted accordingly.

A new devotee is taught to follow temple rules and regulations, how to behave in the temple during ceremonies, how to prostrate himself before the deities, how to say various prayers and hymns in Sanskrit, how to eat with his fingers Indian-style, how to maintain temple standards of cleanliness and hygiene, how to do a job (if he does not already have a skill), how to chant, how to follow temple routine, and how to use a vocabulary of Sanskrit words that will replace English words. Entrance into a temple also means a shift to communal living. Although some married couples live outside the temple, most devotees live within temple walls. The devotees eat together, chant and dance together, work together and sleep together. There is no furniture in a temple other than the spiritual master's *vyasasana*, a few desks and a small table or two to hold religious articles. There are no chairs except those used for elderly guests, so all desks and tables used for work are sawed down to floor-sitting size. At night the devotees unroll sleeping bags and sleep on the floor, men in one section of the temple and women in another.

A male devotee entering a temple must be prepared to shave his head except for a remaining lock of hair called the *sikha*. The *sikha* and Indian-style garments are worn by the men to identify them to the public as devotees. Women devotees wear traditional Indian-style *saris*. All devotees always carry a string of 108 prayer beads worn in a cloth bead-bag around the neck, convenient for chanting the Hare Krishna *mantra* in any spare moments. Devotees also wear small beads made of *tulasi*, the sacred plant, around their necks to signify a lifetime commitment to Krishna. Clay markings (*tilaka*) are also worn on the body to mark it as a temple. The most prominent mark is worn on the forehead and bears a resemblance to an exclamation mark, going from the hairline and ending in a point on the nose. The strange clothing and hair-styles gain attention and fulfil the function of changing a person's social identity from 'hippie', office worker, construction worker, or whatever the person was in his former life.

In addition to the drastic changes of life-style and appearance, the neophyte devotee must learn to follow the orders of the spiritual master and his representatives, the temple presidents and task leaders. A neophyte devotee is allowed to ease himself slowly into this strictly regulated life. The only demand at first is that the four temple rules are strictly observed. A new devotee is considered to be a wild animal and is given kind and gentle treatment to help him adjust. Little by little he surrenders to the many austerities of temple life and learns to eat, dress and live according to Vedic prescription. The philosophy of the Vedic scriptures is taught in the daily classes given in all ISKCON temples.

Perhaps it is the belief that man should not identify with his body that gives the neophyte the most difficulty. The devotee learns that identifying with one's material body is one of the greatest pitfalls of the human form of life. The body is simply a vehicle for going back to Godhead. Therefore the devotees are advised to treat it as such. Material life is a disease, and having a material body is a symptom of one's diseased form of life. Controlling one's senses and bodily desires will help one to achieve release from rebirth. In order to change his social and self identity, a devotee voluntarily subjects himself to a series of abasements, degradations, and profanations of his self. The alienation from his society, from his family and friends begins before an individual becomes a devotee, but entrance into an ISKCON temple is a formal recognition of this alienation and tends to reinforce it.

Further, the identity of the new devotee is directly attacked by the deprivation of the paraphernalia of his prior status and self-concept as he seeks to redefine his identity. The most obvious

C

degradation a new devotee must endure is the appearance change
to which he finds himself committed. For many of the men, shaving
their beards and long hair is quite traumatic. New recruits usually
either give all of their property to the movement or distribute i
among friends. All property within the temple is not personally, bu
communally owned. With the exception of Bhaktivendanta's books
a pair of shoes, prayer beads, sleeping bag, and a few items o
jewellery, the devotee is stripped of his possessions. This stripping
of personal possessions together with the mandatory appearance
alterations divest a person of what Goffman calls his 'identity kit'.[1]
The sense of self is thus altered and his presentation of his former
image to others is curtailed. In addition, the individual become
totally dependent on the temple to provide the basic necessities o
existence, and is even reduced to begging on the street for
money.

A general mortification of the flesh is practised and the body i
viewed as an object of hatred. It is the body that entraps the devotee
and its needs are the obstacle to reaching God-realization. The body
is the cause of all suffering and misery and a source of great annoy-
ance in that it must be cared for at all. Under these circumstances
humility comes more easily.

The devotees readily admit that they are fallen and that they
are helpless unless they can seek a spiritual master.[12] All devotee
prostrate themselves before the deity images in the temple and
before their spiritual master or his photograph to show their
surrender to them. This act of putting one's body in such a
humiliating position is a further assault on the self. These
assaults on the self which constitute degradation rituals reinforce
the belief of a devotee that he is the most fallen, impure creature
in existence. This is another reason he deprives himself of all
possessions, renounces everything, and even claims to know nothing
It is only the swami who has wisdom; he knows all. Devotees are in
such a fallen state that their entire lives must become *tapasya*
(penance, austerity). A former devotee believes that the devotee
are rejecting the mind's ability to think. While she was in the movement and was attending *Gītā* classes, she would look around at the
devotees sitting in the temple chanting *japa* silently and listening to
the lecture, and all she could think of was Orwell's novel *1984*
When she was in the Philadelphia temple where Bhaktivedanta's
lectures are played over the loud-speaker system for twenty-four
hours a day, she was unable to sleep. She felt that in the ISKCON
movement 'there was a rejection of the individual ego and an

assumption of a community ego. The needs, desires, and knowledge of all individuals were subjected to service of Krishna, not even for the good of the community.'

The invasion of privacy in temple life is complete and all-pervasive. The devotees are instructed in detailed bathroom habits. They are not allowed the use of toilet paper, but are required to take a shower after passing stool. There is no personal privacy and all bathing and bathroom facilities are open, but segregated by sex. All sleeping rooms are shared, eating is communal, almost all activities are batch activities.

Devotees are supposed to find all joy in the performance of *bhakti* (devotion), and for this reason all devotees refrain from showing anger or any personal emotions. A good devotee should always feel happy, so devotees attempt to eradicate all moods completely. Anger is rarely expressed. When an Indian man yelled viciously at some devotees about their treatment of him, they expressed no feelings, but everyone present began chanting 'Hare Krishna, Hare Krishna . . .' aloud.

A male devotee speaks of his early participation in ISKCON :

I had turned into an atheist, but my LSD experiences convinced me of higher aspects of reality. My whole view of God was impersonal so that at first I accepted Bhaktivedanta's teachings only theoretically—it was hard for me to adjust to them.

From chanting Hare Krishna you can get to the higher level of consciousness. When I chant without offence I can reach the higher levels, usually, though, my chanting is almost always coloured by some offensiveness. From the point of view of my own development there are times when my chanting is more pure than at other times. When it is most pure I am associating with Krishna and feel happiness and joy in my heart that is different than speculating with my mind.

At different times Krishna would give you a taste of higher levels. Even at the very beginning he might give you a taste—you can feel the indescribable bliss of chanting Hare Krishna. Then you might not feel that again for a long time. You have to become totally purified before you come to a platform in a higher realm. The taste we get at the beginning we actually don't deserve. It only helps us in our devotional service. At different times you get different realizations which give you renewed energy to endeavour more and more until gradually you get to a platform of steadiness.

The neophyte devotee, consequently, is in a liminal stage of his development as a devotee. He is what Turner calls 'betwixt and between'[13] because he 'eludes the network of classifications that normally locate states and positions in cultural space'.[14] The neophyte has anonymity, no status or property, and his behaviour must be humble while his identity is refashioned to enable him to cope with his new existence. Persons in such transitional states are considered dangerous, inauspicious and polluting, according to Douglas,[15] until they are initiated and receive their spiritual name. Before this ceremony these devotees' activities are restricted, due to their polluting qualities, and they cannot perform certain activities, such as operating the stove and cooking.

The process of stripping, levelling and purifying the neophyte before his initiation prepares him by altering his identity in readiness to take on his new identity as a servant of the Lord.

Initiation: The Harynama[16] Ceremony and Sacred Thread Ceremony

The *harynama* ceremony takes place after an individual has been a devotee for six months or more. At this time he makes a lifetime commitment and receives a new spiritual name and insignia. The devotees are aware of and discuss the effects of this ceremony upon the person who undergoes it. One young woman said : 'A person really changes when he is initiated and gets his new name. I almost didn't recognize my own husband, he had changed so much.'

The devotee is now imbued with a revived sense of enthusiasm, a feeling of tremendous self-confidence. Other devotees may think the recent initiate is 'puffed up' because of his new confidence. The new initiate assumes roles of increasing leadership and may take on some responsible position such as temple commander or special task leader. Moreover, he is now a more experienced preacher and may even get to preach in public or to teach a class in *Bhagavad-gītā*. Due to his increased recognition and responsibility in the ISKCON organization the new initiate will experience a period of euphoria in which he feels extremely secure in his new identity as a devotee. This euphoric period may last a few months or as long as a year, before the initiate begins to feel less secure about his spiritual progress.

Six months after a devotee passes his *harynama* ceremony, he becomes eligible for his second initiation. Through this ceremony the initiate becomes a *brahmin* by receiving the sacred thread and a secret *mantra*, the *gayatri mantra*, which is never to be uttered aloud. The *brahmin* is now able to perform ISKCON ceremonies such as the *aratrikas* and fire ceremonies when necessary, and is considered to be a priest of ISKCON. The person becomes what Bhaktivedanta calls 'a brahmin by qualification' which is considered to be of higher merit than being born into this priestly caste.

Usually during his first year an initiate experiences at first a feeling of being what the devotees call 'fixed-up' in Krishna Consciousness, but later goes through a period of disenchantment. The devotee begins to feel unsure of his devotion to Krishna and ISKCON. In the words of a troubled devotee : 'Mornings were presenting a problem for me and I was having a terrible time each day coping with this life. I felt like I was in prison. . . . It reached the point where all the beauty and pleasure were gone for me and I was only suffering pain and misery. I could not believe that God wanted us to live like that. One really had to work to get fixed up for the day, whereas before I joined, it was no problem at all.'

The devotee sees himself as falling and again feels the need to purify himself. Some devotees leave the movement when these feelings become too overwhelming. Most of the 'bloopers' (the ISKCON name for defectors) leave with a feeling of regret that they were not able to purify themselves enough to remain in the service of Krishna. Many feel that they may someday return to the movement when they can get themselves straightened out. A blooper knows from reading the *Bhagavad-gītā* that the man who practises devotional service (*bhakti yoga*) and cannot quite succeed will immediately be reborn in his next life into a very pious family. A person begins each new life spiritually where he left off in his former life.

The individuals who remain in ISKCON face a constant struggle to maintain their position as servants of Krishna. Great stress is placed on the fallen, impure condition of the devotee which causes his suffering in this life. Assaults on the self, in the form of degradation and mortification of the body, are invited because of these beliefs. The self is relegated to an inferior, unclean status. To surrender to Krishna is to give one's entire being to him. One surrenders desires, thoughts, and actions and it is no longer *myself*, at least for those moments. These are the exceptional moments, the experience of grace; for, on the whole, failure is the rule. The effort is to love God through Bhaktivedanta from the point of failure, because the love of God is extraordinarily difficult. This path of love of God is brutal revelation to the devotee that he may never achieve his goals. Following one's desires is the path of least resistance : the path of illusion. The purification of the soul requires a constant vigil over thoughts, actions and speech. When a devotee has thoughts of anger, lust or greed and can refrain from expressing them, it is a very great achievement. A devotee must be prepared to give his entire self to lead a life of day-to-day obedience and service.

A young man told me about his struggles :

I still have falls. I'll feel steady and I'll remain steady for quite a long time, but then I fall down again. When I fall down it is usually due to material desire. The worst desire is female attraction—it's always there and you must learn to be free from it. There is no correct mechanical process of becoming free—it is a question of changing your whole consciousness. You must surrender your soul to the Lord—to change your attraction from mundane things to an attraction to the Lord.

Eating is another problem—over-eating. When you eat too much you become attracted to mundane things and your consciousness drops. When mine drops I want to go off by myself to the mountains and chant Hare Krishna alone in the woods. When I was in the New York temple I had to struggle with myself every day not to leave and go to the mountains. Once when I was in another temple near the woods I did go out intending to chant all day, but all I did was to sleep all day in the woods. That helped me understand that the best thing is just to stay in the temple and associate with other devotees. This is part of the feeling of agitation that a devotee sometimes feels.

Women are the worst stumbling block on the path to God realization in almost every instance. For a person who is advanced marriage is a dangerous proposition because you are living right with *maya* (illusion). Woman attracts the soul away from God. The form of a woman is attractive—no one can deny this—and she talks nicely. If you fall a little bit you have someone to shelter you. If you take shelter with your wife you sit around and talk to her and forget your spiritual life. Of course, that can lead to sex and sex is just like committing suicide—a really dangerous proposition! The only way to free yourself from this temptation is to become attracted to Krishna's form.

So one can artificially stop being attracted to the material world by being austere and keeping aloof from old associations. But this does not stop the desire in the heart. You have ups and downs and you seek your freedom in material ways when you fall down.

A lot of your advancement comes from finding another devotee who you really like. With him you can read Bhaktivedanta's books and discuss the philosophy. Together we find new meanings in the philosophy. Instead of just sitting alone, reading and maybe falling asleep we help each other. So if I eat too much he will say 'Hey, come on what are you doing?' Or if one of us is sleeping too late in the morning we wake each other up.

Among my godbrothers events just happen. Maybe a god-brother tells me to do something and I don't want to do it. I say that I have something else to do and instead of letting it be he keeps hassling you. 'No, you have to do it!' It ends up that you get angry because he is bothering you and it can get to be a very passionate thing. An event like this can wreck your consciousness for a couple of days. But it is through these different trials that we learn. This also helps to purify the soul because this shows you your own insincerities. It shows you that you are not humble, but very puffed up.

To become a devotee an individual undertakes a task of immense difficulty and often cannot succeed in transforming his consciousness to the point of stability. The individual has redefined his goals to dovetail with those of ISKCON and has made a public commitment to a new deviant identity.

The Advanced Devotee

The ideal of all ISKCON devotees is spontaneous love of God, a selfless dedication to Krishna from which the individual experiences pleasure. Bhaktivedanta states it thus in his *Bhagavad-gītā*:

A person acting in Krishna Consciousness is naturally free from the resultant action of work. His activities are well performed for Krishna and therefore he does not enjoy or suffer any of the effects of the work. . . . Because everything is done for Krishna, he enjoys only transcendental happiness in the discharge of this service. Those who are engaged in this process are without desire for personal sense gratification.[17]

The paths of work, ritual and knowledge are all sanctified by the dedication of the action to Krishna. Belief in this ideology is the binding factor for the devotees, who voluntarily submit themselves to the communal temple life and discipline for the purpose of furthering their common goal—the performance of devotional service. In this sense all members of ISKCON are equal, but in practice there is a hierarchical political structure to administer the bureaucratic organization of the movement.

Social control through the use of authority is the primary basis around which the formal political structure of ISKCON is built. All authority technically rests with the guru, Bhaktivedanta. He, as God's representative on Earth, is the last resort and the ultimate authority in all conflict solution and in questions of doctrine and practice. His devotees say, 'The order of our spiritual master is to be taken as one's life and soul.' Because the society grew too large for Bhaktivedanta to preside over all the temples he established a governing body commission (GBC), creating a formal structure for ISKCON. Twelve male devotees, who were considered by Bhakti-vedanta to have outstanding managerial talents and to be very advanced spiritually, were appointed to relieve him of managerial tasks. Their main responsibilities are to decide where new centres will be established, and who will be sent to open them, to ensure that the temples are following Bhaktivedanta's orders and cere-monies, and to maintain high standards in all temples.

The line of authority extends from the regional GBC member to the president of each temple, who is responsible for carrying out the orders of the guru and the GBC in his temple. He is also res-ponsible for his devotees much as a father is responsible for his children, and like the head of a household, he must be able to settle disputes, offer spiritual guidance, delegate authority, assign work, and advise devotees on practical, everyday problems that arise. It is he who decides who may stay in the temple and who may not and this authority may be exercised without recourse. The president must be informed of all business matters; he plays the role of father confessor; he is responsible for the health of his devotees; he is the congregation leader; he is the authority on scripture and ceremonies. Even the personal decisions of the devotees come under his jurisdiction. Some of the members have remarked that a temple is run like a military regime, commenting on the rigid schedule which is observed and the necessity to be able to take orders.

If a temple president needs managerial assistance, he may appoint a temple commander, who presides in his absence and helps to carry out his orders. In addition, various tasks are allocated to several task leaders such as the woman in charge of deity care, who directs the work of the women assigned to sewing, garland making and deity work, and the cook, who is in charge of the kitchen.

Not subject to the jurisdiction of any particular temple are the *sannyāsas*, the very spiritually advanced renounced order, who have special austerities and responsibilities. These *sannyāsas* are com-pletely independent of everyone in the movement except the spiritual master. The special duties of the *sannyāsas* are to study scripture and preach; therefore they are not attached to a temple but travel around, especially to new territories, accepting as students those who are seriously inclined towards Krishna Consciousness. When one of the ISKCON's *sannyāsas* visits a temple, he is expected to enliven the devotees in the temple. The temple presidents work with the *sannyāsas* as well as with the GBC and accord all respect to *sannyāsas* as a higher authority. All devotees give special service to a *sannyāsa*, offering their obeisances each morning when he appears and giving him a special room in which to stay while visiting the temple. If a *sannyāsa* will allow it, one or more devotees will attach themselves to him as his personal servants.

The structure of ISKCON allows the spiritually mature devotee and those with special talents to advance within the society. They are accorded special status, privileges, responsibility and deference as they mature as devotees. The advanced devotee has reintegrated his identity and has successfully fitted himself into the structure of the ISKCON community. A temple president has summed up his role as follows:

It is my business to engage people in service by discovering their best qualifications and what they like to do and suit this to time and circumstance. It is also my duty to collect money for the temple—this is part of managing. I also am father, advisor, confessor. I am father to the children because I represent the real father, Prabhupāda.

And a *sannyāsa* says of his spiritual development:

I now feel that I have fulfilled the Bible. Jesus Christ said he had one commandment, and if you fulfil that one commandment, you have fulfilled them all. This is that 'thou shall love the Lord thy God with all thy heart, with all thy soul, with all thy might, and thy neighbour as thyself'. If we carry out the orders of our spiritual master we fulfil all of that.

In conclusion, we see that an advanced devotee is able to derive personal satisfaction in executing devotional service to his beloved Krishna and through the status he earns in the society. If he must do mundane tasks such as typing or cooking he gains the satisfaction of a job well-done and sanctifies this activity by dedicating all of his activities to Krishna. He is steady in his role as a member of ISKCON because he has successfully redefined his identity and, moreover, he is able to achieve personal satisfaction as well as recognition for his achievements within ISKCON. This stage of maturity is the goal of new recruits coming into the society. The personal history of an individual before entering ISKCON will influence success or failure as a devotee.

It will be interesting to learn from future studies what percentage of neophytes are able to achieve a stable, coherent identity within ISKCON and what percentage of those who attain advanced devotee status will remain in ISKCON or drop out. It will also be useful to learn if the movement will continue to grow at its present rapid rate or if the number of devotees will level off or fall and why. These are, however, long-term trends which cannot yet be determined only nine years after ISKCON was founded.

NOTES AND REFERENCES

1 No membership records are kept, but some ISKCON leaders estimate the number of devotees to be between two or three thousand. The movement has established 63 ISKCON centres around the world and can justifiably be called international.

2 *Back to Godhead*, No. 40, p. 5. *Back to Godhead* is the magazine of the Hare Krishna movement, published by its own press, ISKCON Press.

3 Ibid., p. 5–6.

4 See Francine J. Daner, *The American Children of Krsna: A Study of the Hare Krsna Movement*, unpublished doctoral dissertation, University of Illinois, 1973.

5 Hayagrīva dasa Adhikārī 'Chant (Part 1)' in *Back to Godhead* No. 36, p. 24.

6 Erving Goffman, *Asylums*, Doubleday Anchor, New York, 1961, p. xiii.

7 Goffman, Ibid., p. 12, further suggests that these institutions are '. . . forcing houses for changing persons; each is a natural experiment on what can be done to the self'. We see that by depriving each person of the accoutrements of his prior status which he employed in his former life such as clothing, hair-style, personal possessions and freedom of association, ISKCON temple life attacks a neophyte's self-concept (identity) directly. Once broken this identity can be reconstituted by the conversion process.

8 Russ Rueger, 'Postscript to a Bum Trip', *Human Behaviour*, Vol. 2, No. 11, November 1973, p. 64.

9 Bhaktivedanta is called Prabhupāda by his devotees.

10 David G. Mandelbaum, 'The Study of Life History: Gandhi', *Current Anthropology*, Vol. 14, No. 3, June 1973, p. 180.

11 Erving Goffman, op. cit., p. 20.

12 In most cases the devotee has little or no contact with the swami. But they worship his pictures, read his books and listen to his tape-recorded sermons daily.

13 Victor Turner, *The Ritual Process,* Aldine, Chicago, 1969, p. 95.

14 Ibid., p. 95.

15 Mary Douglas, *Purity and Danger,* Routledge & Kegan Paul, London, 1966.

16 *Harynama* is literally translated from Sanskrit as 'holy name'.

17 A. C. Bhaktivedanta, *The Bhagavad Gītā As It Is,* Collier Macmillan, London, 1968, p. 122.

James A. Beckford

5 *Two Contrasting Types of Sectarian Organization*

Religiosity, Religion and Religious Organization

Dominant among the themes that have occupied the attention of sociologists of religion in the West in recent decades has been the importance of elucidating the 'internal' or 'personal' dimensions of religiosity. In different ways Lenski,[1] Fukuyama,[2] and Glock and Stark[3] have all devised procedures for analytically decomposing personal religiosity into a number of distinct dimensions for which measurable indicators could be found. Their discovery of some unexpected changes in the patterned interrelationships between the dimensions in the questionnaire responses of large samples of American church-goers led to the view that a novel form of denominationalism was emerging in the USA. Consideration of somewhat different evidence also convinced Bellah[4] that a fairly uniform 'civil religion' was replacing the former diversity of Protestant and Catholic doctrines and ideologies.

For reasons unconnected with these alleged transformations of the internal composition of beliefs among American Protestants, a few sociologists with insight into the condition of the Christian religion in a broader context, began at roughly the same time to write about religion from a different, but no less one-sided, point of view. In particular, Berger and Luckmann[5] popularized the view that the formal, institutional vehicles of Christianity had ceased to serve a useful purpose and had actually begun to hinder the expression of 'genuine' religiosity. Their argument implied that only the personal, interior cultivation of religious sensibility was appropriate for contemporary social conditions. In other words, the allegedly irreducible functions of religion as a cognitive and emotional bulwark against the terrifying threat of existential chaos were said to require satisfaction in contemporarily appropriate ways. The prescription, according to Berger and Luckmann, was for a highly interiorized, individual-oriented kind of faith for which institutional forms of expression were both unnecessary and unhelpful.

In these and many other less celebrated contributions to the

70

sociological analysis of contemporary Christianity in the West the impression has been created that 'religion' is to all intents and purposes synonymous with 'religiosity'. Doubtless these insights into the purely personal aspects of religion are vitally important for an adequate understanding of the place that some forms of religion are coming to occupy in modern societies. But they illumine only one, albeit major, facet of the total phenomenon. It is trite but nonetheless necessary to insist that this approach should ideally be supplemented with analysis of such 'outdated' topics as the *social organization* of contemporary religious groups. For even granted that the personal dimensions of religious faith are nowadays the focal point of theological and sociological interest, questions regarding the effects of this situation on the structure and dynamics of traditional religious organizations still merit attention.

For although the locus of 'genuine' religion is said to have shifted from groups and organizations to individual minds, it does not follow that methods of sociological analysis should treat the new phenomenon as if it had no extra-individual implications. Nor is it the case that the so-called 'invisible religion' exhausts the range of possible expressions for contemporary religion. Indeed, a fact that has often been overlooked in the current fascination for styles of personal religion is that it is precisely the groups which still insist upon the supposedly out-dated authority of 'external' or 'handed down' religious beliefs which are at the moment apparently enjoying the highest rates of membership-increase in the USA and Britain.[6]

A pressing task is therefore to elucidate the organizational aspects of religious initiatives that are both central and marginal to the transformations already outlined. How have religious organizations responded to the interiorization, if not de-institutionalization, of religious faith? What has been the fate of religious organizations that have deliberately combated the apparent swing towards invisible religion? The answers to these questions may then suggest ways of tackling a more general methodological question. What is to be gained from a study of the social organization of religious bodies in the modern world?

The method of approaching these tasks will be to examine in a deliberately one-sided fashion the *organizational* aspects of two religious bodies which stand in interestingly anomalous relations to the interiorizing and de-institutionalizing trends of some contemporary Christian groups. A well-known and well-established group—Jehovah's Witnesses—will be compared and contrasted in relevant respects with a relatively new and developing group—the Unified Family.[7] The analysis of their respective forms of organization and of their implications for their respective patterns of development will be sharpened by the application of J. D. Thompson's perspective on organizational dynamics.[8]

Brief Characterization of the Watch Tower Movement and the Unified Family

Jehovah's Witnesses subscribe to, and publicly proclaim, a set of Christian ideas about the alleged conformity of human history with God's 'plan for the world'. They learn these ideas from literature disseminated by the Watch Tower Bible and Tract Society whose world-wide headquarters is in New York. 'The Society' also equips Witnesses to teach its ideas systematically to people outside the movement, and its form of organization is therefore deliberately designed to promote the maximum 'outreach' attainable within the limits imposed by available resources. Jehovah's Witnesses are expected to display very high levels of commitment to the Watch Tower Society's goals and values, and their conduct is subject to rigorous controls, at all levels of the organization's hierarchy. Local congregations of rarely more than two hundred Witnesses act as worshipping units, as outlets for communication from the movement's small number of powerful elite-administrators, and as centres for the organization of unrelenting proselytism in their geographical territories. The relative purposefulness of the Watch Tower organizational design accounts in large measure for the extraordinarily high rates of growth in Witness recruitment in very many parts of the world, but the same feature is also indirectly responsible for high rates of turnover among mature recruits. On balance, however, the movement's numerical strength continues to grow at a rate unmatched by almost any other Christian movement of comparable size.

The Unified Family is the popular name for a syncretistic religious movement which originated in South Korea in the 1950s under the proper title of the Holy Spirit Association for the Unification of World Christianity. In the space of two decades its founder, chief apologist, supreme administrator and messianic leader, Sun Myung Moon, has become the spiritual guide of hundreds of thousands of followers all over the world. The following is presently concentrated in South Korea and Japan, but energetic proselytism in the USA[9] and Europe has also reaped impressive recruitment rewards within the last six years. There are now about two hundred committed followers in Britain, most of whom live in special 'family-centres' around the country. Some work full-time for the 'Family', others have retained at least part-time secular occupations but are committed to donating all their earnings to each family-centre's pool of common resources. The available evidence indicates that there is probably an equal number of non-resident sympathizers.

Moon's teachings are an esoteric blend of messianism, millennialism and Buddhist philosophy. Recruits are required to master the intricacies of the 'Divine Principle' as enunciated by Moon, and to devote their lives to the wider dissemination and appreciation of their master's wisdom. Like the Jehovah's Witnesses, Unified Family members are expected to display exceptionally high levels of commitment to the movement's values and goals. Further parallels between the two groups can be seen in the stringency of controls exercised over members' conduct, in the requirement that unquestioning obedience be accorded to the commands of superiors in the organizational hierarchy and in the claims that they both represent the exclusive agency of divine forces in this world during its 'last days'.

It must be added that these similarities between the two groups conceal some sharp differences. The biblical literalness of the Witnesses, for example, contrasts with the more eclectic outlook of the Unified Family, and the latter's manipulation of many Oriental symbols gives its whole ideology a greater flexibility than Watch Tower ideology could ever aspire to. Indeed, the Unified Family might appear to instantiate the allegedly growing popularity of 'interiorized' religion, whereas Jehovah's Witnesses have traditionally shown little concern for such personal matters, preferring instead to concentrate their energies on proclaiming the imminence of Christ's physical victory over the forces of Satan on Earth.

Problems of Religious Organizations

In spite of doctrinal differences, both the Watch Tower movement and the Unified Family, as organizations, face common problems in ensuring an uninterrupted supply of human and material resources for the processes which mark their distinctiveness. If they are to continue 'processing' people, increasing the number of people for 'processing' and propagating the necessity or benefits of their 'processes', certain requirements must be met. In short, conditions of irregularity or uncertainty in the supply of resources must ideally be controlled. In J. D. Thompson's terminology this amounts to establishing the organization's independence from its task-environment. Work organizations achieve this result by a variety of tactics : entering into contractual agreements with suppliers of raw materials; eliminating competitors; etc. The more successful an organization becomes in controlling its task-environment, the more likely it is to achieve the operative goals of its 'dominant coalition', that is, the members of an organization who happen to exercise most power at any given moment and are therefore in a position to make and implement strategic choices.[10]

But voluntary associations (and especially religious organizations in the West) are widely believed to be incapable of achieving great success in this direction, because they remain vulnerable to uncontrolled fluctuations in their environment. They cannot be assured of a constant supply of members, resources and 'markets' for their products. This situation is said to be a consequence of an 'enrolment economy', a situation in which the survival and vitality of an organization are dependent on (a) the continuing voluntary participation of members, (b) their unceasing readiness to contribute financially, and (c) their willingness to abide by organizational rules and conventions. The exigencies of an enrolment economy therefore oblige organizational leaders to adapt their programmes to suit the desires of the majority of members and to avoid any actions which might diminish the level of voluntary finance or commitment. Organizations with an enrolment economy have very little opportunity to achieve independence from their task-environment and in order to maintain recruitment are frequently constrained to carry out programmes which deviate sharply from their 'charter goals' and the goals of their 'dominant coalition'.

The full effects of an enrolment economy can be clearly seen in, for example, the power that local Methodist congregations in the southern USA are able to exercise over local ministers' attempts to implement denominational policies on racial integration[11] or in the on-going attempts by local branches of the YMCA to adapt their services to suit the changing requirements of their clientele.[12] But the dominant coalitions of some religious organizations have devised ways of combating these forces and of preventing them from diverting members from pursuing the 'official' objectives. This can only be achieved, however, if the objectives can be explicitly defined and unambiguously operationalized. Since the Watch Tower movement and the Unified Family are dominated by leaders whose main objectives seem to be the continual increase in numbers of recruits, volume of literature-sales and extent of public awareness of their programmes, both organizations are potentially capable of overcoming the problems of an enrolment economy. The next two sections will describe separately their respective, and very different, attempts to achieve this end.

Mass-movement Features of the Watch Tower Organization

There is a certain degree of symbolic congruence between the Watch Tower movement's doctrinal rigidity and its organizational structure. The congruence also extends to the unquestioning acceptance that Jehovah's Witnesses are officially expected to show towards its teachings and the passive legitimation that they are encouraged to accord to its authority structure. The notion of absolute truth is equated with the view that only one human organization can possibly embody it. Not surprisingly, unchangeableness is believed to characterize both the truth and its 'earthly vessel'. It follows that people who accept the group's teachings and internalize the concomitant values are for the most part willing to obey orders issued by the holders of legitimate authority within the organization. The authority structure is both hierarchical and inflexible; relationships between leaders and followers are normally conducted on a legalistic and formal basis.

The formality of the Watch Tower organization is matched by its impersonality. In theory, each individual Witness is related to the central organization solely as a subscriber to the literature that it publishes. The concept of membership is said to have no validity—Jehovah's Witnesses merely subscribe to, and disseminate, literature. And in many respects the practice bears out the theory : local congregations enjoy no 'constitutional' autonomy; regional groupings have only minimal significance apart from administrative convenience; and 'horizontal' relationships among Witnesses are deliberately subordinated to the dominantly 'vertical' dimension of authority relations. The Watch Tower movement therefore approximates quite closely in form to that of a 'mass' organization.[13]

These mass-movement features are essential for its capacity to avoid the trammels of an enrolment economy. Independence of its task-environment is partially achieved through the monopolization of its followers' interests and social attachments, through their unmediated relationship as individuals with the organization's centre, through the predominantly downwards direction of communication in the organization, through the unremitting obligation on followers to sell as much literature and recruit as many newcomers as possible, and through the exercise of all decision-making power by a very small, isolated elite. In combination, these characteristics help to account for the Watch Tower movement's ability to mobilize the Witnesses efficiently and, in turn, to avoid the most debilitating aspects of an enrolment economy : instability of long-term plans, short-term adaptations to members' wishes and gradual departure from 'charter goals'. The main reason why the Witnesses have escaped these problems is that mass-mobilization has over the past thirty years produced a secular, upward trend in the number of new recruits, the volume of literature-sales and the extent of public awareness of Watch Tower teachings in all parts of the world. These achievements have undoubtedly strengthened the power of the elite and the organization's material position in two important respects : (a) central sources of income from property and literature-sales now probably outweigh the amount of voluntary donations from individuals, and (b) as long as the number of new recruits continues to exceed comfortably the number of losses, the leaders can afford to impose their own objectives on the movement without fear of jeopardizing all social support. The avoidance of the worst feature of an enrolment economy is therefore dependent on the continuing success of mass-mobilization, but, as will be seen later, success cannot be completely guaranteed.

Community Intensity in the Unified Family

Belief in the literal truth of Sun Myung Moon's writings is an essential qualification for full fellowship in the Unified Family, but correctness of knowledge or interpretation is generally considered less important than the capacity to use them in heightening one's own spiritual achievements. The texts are recited and discussed in group sessions, not as an end in itself, but as an inducement to members to improve the quality of their spiritual life. This instrumental or facilitative aspect of the sacred canon is congruent with a degree of flexibility and (superficial) spontaneity in Unified Family meetings. A logic of congruence also seems to require a low-profile organization within which individuals may feel relatively free and unconstrained in their apparently self-directed efforts at spiritual perfection. Thus, Unified Family members in Britain usually have a very meagre idea of the organizational structure of the world-wide movement and a weakly articulated conception of the distribution of officers and authority in their own country. Certainly, Unified Family leaders are at pains to disguise the skeletal structure of their organization and to play down in public its importance. They prefer to propagate the view that all relationships in the group are personal, warm and basically unstructured in any hierarchical sense. 'Togetherness' is therefore a key component of the group's ideology, but it actually masks the reality of sharp differentials in the distribution of power and authority.

The appearance of informality is cultivated in the family-centres where fully committed members are permanently resident. The experience of communal living is an essential context for the practice of spiritual exercises and for the exercise of 'give-and-take' relationships of 'love' which reflect a person's progress towards the stage of spiritual perfection. In fact, there is no formal recognition of membership to anything wider than a family-centre, for consciousness of participation in an international movement is highly developed but not formally signified. Separation from other primary-group attachments is an important pre-requisite for fellowship, and members spend nearly all their time in the close company of fellow-members. 'Horizontal' relations are therefore predominant, and (as in Western monasticism) the full realization of personal abilities is believed to take place only when the individual is utterly immersed in the confessing community.

These communal arrangements enable the Unified Family movement to escape most of the constraints of an enrolment economy through a deliberate policy of isolating and insulating its followers against the pull of competing forces. The leaders are relatively free from the need to accommodate the wishes of members because the probability that the latter will withdraw if they become dissatisfied is reduced by their lack of alternative 'plausibility structures'.[14] The positive counterpart to insulation and isolation is, of course, the dependence on community that most members develop in the course of full-time residence in a family-centre. In combination, the negative and positive forces directed at members are successful in retaining at least a central core of committed adepts who can be relied upon to attract a slowly growing number of new recruits. The turn-over rate among recruits is not high enough to prevent a small increase in the size of the core membership and a larger increase in the size of the transient membership.

Partial independence from the organization's task-environment and from the trammels of an enrolment economy are secured for its leaders by three factors : (a) the submissiveness and high commit-ment-level of core members are a guarantee against the risk of losing all members in protest against unpopular programmes; (b) the continuing commitment of core members entails a steady source of income for the community from their part-time or full-time secular occupations and from their sales of Unified Family litera-ture to the public, as well as a regular supply of new recruits from proselytizing activities; (c) as long as members continue to prose-lytize as energetically as the leaders expect, there will be a supply of new recruits whose own money and enthusiasm will in turn guarantee the organization's survival in a basically unchanged form. The dominant coalition is thereby enabled to pursue its own object-ives without distraction from the potentially incompatible desires or aims of the rank-and-file members. What is more, the recent success of recruitment campaigns in Britain must have boosted the leaders' confidence that an organization based on intense com-munity living can be efficiently adapted for extensive proselytism.

Differential Concomitants of Organizational Types

The argument has so far attempted to demonstrate that within the class of religious groups conventionally labelled 'sects' there is con-siderable variation in the structure of organization. Even within the sub-class of sects which actively seek to mobilize their followers in methodical proselytism, there can be sharp differences in organiza-tional form. The solution to problems of an enrolment economy (and all that this implies in the way of environmental uncertainties) may take forms as widely divergent as the impersonal, mass-move-ment of Jehovah's Witnesses and the intensely communal structure of the Unified Family. The choice of organizational 'style' is linked by an opaque 'logic' of congruence with each movement's teachings and ideology. The heuristic usefulness of this approach to contem-porary forms of sectarianism remains, however, to be more com-pletely demonstrated. This can be achieved by an analysis of the multifarious aspects of the two sects which follow from, or are at least associated with, their type of organizational structure.

I(a) Firstly, *the pattern of problems and difficulties faced* by the Watch Tower movement and the Unified Family in the implementation of policy can be shown to vary with their respective forms of organization. On the one hand, the mass-mobilization of Jehovah's Witnesses and the relatively impersonal texture of personal relations in their local congregations are largely responsible for their extremely high rates of membership turnover. A closely associated difficulty is the tendency for Witnesses who fail to fulfil quotas for evangelistic 'service-work' to become apathetic about their faith in general and to constitute a kind of peripheral membership which is mobilizable only on special occasions. The very existence of the peripheral group (if the local officers fail to suppress it) may elicit apathy among the active members.

(b) On the other hand, the communal organization of the Unified Family hardly allows even *the possibility* of a peripheral membership. Instead, the intensity of group-pressures among family-centre residents precipitates total crises of faith and commitment on the part of those who begin to deviate from the approved norms of belief or conduct. The regular sessions of mutual criticism are particularly important in this respect, for they aggravate latent dissatisfaction and drag it into the open. Similarly, the consequences of withdrawal for the individual are severe because of the almost total isolation from alternative sources of social support. The ultimate fear of Unified Family leaders seems to be that whole communities could defect or be shattered by traumatic internal disruption. Consequently, one of the most important functions of leadership at both national and international levels is to keep in close communication with all family-centres and to remain alert to the earliest signs of incipient trouble. Evidence from Britain shows that leaders have been quick to expel people perceived as potential or actual sources of disruption.

In part, of course, the differential patterns of internal problems are also a function of the total size of each movement and the size of each local unit. When Watch Tower groups were mainly small, their principal problems resembled those of the present-day Unified Family in so far as they concerned personal relations and doctrinal divisiveness, but increasing size produced significant changes in the nature and locus of the problems.[15] It seems unlikely, therefore, that the Unified Family could retain the family-centre as a basic organizational unit if it were to attract thousands of members in Britain.

II(a) A second concomitant of organizational structure is *the type of evangelistic or proselytizing strategy*. The absence of cohesive intermediary groupings in the Watch Tower movement between mass and elite levels and the existence of a clearly articulated hierarchy of executive positions combine to facilitate the exercise of unitary control over Jehovah's Witnesses' activities. They are frequently mobilized, therefore, in publicity campaigns and constantly at work in routine evangelism/sales work. Moreover, these activities are highly co-ordinated at all organizational levels in order to achieve optimum impact on the public. But this is largely made possible by the organization's centralized decision-making process, the bureaucratic chain of command, and the circulation of mass organs of communication.

These organizational conditions impose constraints on the character of Watch Tower evangelism. For the mobilization of so many part-time evangelists could be positively harmful to the movement's cause unless they were strictly limited in the scope of their activity. Thus, they are trained only to distribute literature and to engage members of the public in set-pieces of conversation. The interaction between Witness and audience is therefore highly structured in advance and delimited in the acceptable scope of its content. In this way, mass-mobilization entails relatively few risks that the evangelists would be dissuaded from their views by persuasive antagonists. It also means that members of the public are only rarely engaged in intensive discussion : the interaction is more commonly a face-to-face confrontation between totally dissimilar points of view. But the Witnesses' main objective is to arouse interest (hostile or friendly) and to deposit items of Watch Tower literature which are expected to convey the group's basic arguments. The best results for this mass-movement are therefore achieved not by intensifying each evangelist-audience relationship but by maximizing the number of transient salesman-customer relationships. Impersonal literature is the initial instrument of proselytism.

(b) By contrast, the principal strategy of Unified Family proselytizers is to invite prospective sympathizers to spend at least a weekend in residence at a family-centre to sample some of the flavour of communal living. The whole arrangement is designed to intensify as quickly as possible the relationship between evangelist and audience and to demonstrate practically the alleged benefits of 'New Age' living.[16] This can, of course, only be achieved if the movement is not seen to be a highly structured or impersonal organization with a 'mass' membership. The nature of Unified

Family teachings and the communal structure of its local groups therefore require (by a logic of symbolic congruence and instrumental rationality) a proselytizing strategy which highlights personal and communal relations : The Witnesses' customer is replaced in the Unified Family by a client.

An allied aspect of the Unified Family's personalistic strategy is that it permits a wider range of tactics than does the Watch Tower version. The sale and distribution of propaganda are not less important to the Unified Family than to the Witnesses but they are supplemented by other possibilities. The more intensive and longer lasting socialization/indoctrination of Unified Family members prepares some of them for more arduous and responsible types of proselytism such as public lectures, the organization and administration of various 'front organizations' and the infiltration of non-Unified Family groups. Only professional employees of the Watch Tower movement would be allowed to tackle such tasks, but as will be seen from what follows, the range of tactics is severely limited for them.

III(a) A complex relationship of mutual reinforcement links organization, ideology, proselytizing strategy and the nature of each movement's (loosely-termed) *'political'* involvement. The Watch Tower movement is closed to most sources of external influence and, in turn, makes little attempt to operate through the conventional channels that condition public opinion. Since it regards 'this present wicked system of things' as irremediably doomed to imminent destruction, it very rarely proffers reformative proposals but prefers to remain aloof from direct involvement in the political process. This tactic is clearly consistent with the mass-movement structure which serves to mobilize all followers in sales campaigns but to discourage them from broaching profound conversations with the public about the details of political events. The indifference-to-the-world which characterizes the Witnesses' political outlook calls for proselytizing strategies which direct their audience's attention away from this-worldly affairs and on to allegedly next-worldly considerations. These tactics can be implemented in a simpler form of organization than is demanded by the relatively more highly differentiated tactics of the Unified Family.

(b) The Unified Family is also effectively insulated against most sources of external influence, but its teachings on the subject of human perfectibility and the conditional perfection of its members are consonant with an 'involved' political outlook. The group's organization is well adapted to reformism : it is relatively flexible yet cohesive; communal living induces homogeneous views among the members; and the large proportion of full-time evangelists creates the opportunity for diverse activities.

In Britain it therefore articulates its conservative brand of reformism (e.g., the restoration of capital punishment; arms for policemen; expulsion of communists from government service, etc.) through a variety of 'front organizations' in schools, universities and the popular entertainments world. It also lobbies political parties, circulates political propaganda and occasionally seeks to infiltrate the meetings of other organizations in order to propagate its own views. The search for prestige that the front organizations conduct could be interpreted as a further attempt to attain a degree of independence for the organization from its task-environment. For prestige may confer power, and such power could then be enjoyed by the organization's leaders in independence from their followers. But central control over the front organizations, which is absolutely essential for the success of such a scheme, may become more problematic if the membership continues to grow.

IV(a) Limitations of space permit consideration of only one more concomitant of differential organizational structure, and this concerns the *social characteristics* of each group's members. In accordance with its other mass-movement features, the Watch Tower movement in Britain attracts followers from a wide variety of social backgrounds and contains very little evidence of patterned differences among its participants. Its formality, bureaucratic impersonality and indiscriminately universal evangelism systematically reduce the likelihood that its appeal would be strongly felt in only a narrow segment of society. For other reasons, a few socio-economic groups are underrepresented among Jehovah's Witnesses, but the representation of age-groups and sexes is roughly proportional to their numerical strength in the wider society.[17]

(b)   The Unified Family, in contrast, not only conducts its proselytism selectively but also recruits from narrow and distinctive strata in British society. It directs propaganda at young people and it recruits almost exclusively from this age-group. Certainly, these are the people who are most likely to be attracted to communal living and collective work. The higher age of leaders helps to reinforce their authority and to legitimize the paternalistic form of leadership that characterizes authority relations at all organizational levels. It follows from the fact that most British members are younger than twenty-five that the vast majority of them are single but, providing that the marriage is solemnized by Sun Myung Moon in one of his celebrated multiple wedding ceremonies, there is no doctrinal reason why a married couple should not live together in a family-centre. The socio-economic status of members is quite varied, although an underlying bi-polarity between middle-class students or educational drop-outs and unskilled youths is definitely visible. Finally, males heavily outnumber females among members and (even more heavily) among leaders.

Conclusion

While no theoretical advantage could be gained from trying to assess the relative degrees of causal independence of factors such as ideology and organizational structure, it is instructive to see how they both bear upon the choice and the consequences of particular strategies for overcoming problems common to all organizations. Thus, two religious sects with similar objectives have been shown to employ contrasting types of solution to the problems of an enrolment economy—one by adopting mass-movement strategies; the other by fostering an intensive form of community. Although they are at vastly different stages of development they are both able to recruit new members at a time when most religious groups are suffering serious membership losses. In this respect, then, their strategies must be adjudged to be successful. This raises the intriguing possibility that the cultural appropriateness of a religious movement may have as much to do with its form of organization as with its set of teachings. The medium is certainly an important part of the message.[18]

There is indirect support for this view in E. K. Francis's[19] account of the process of instrumental adaptation that occurred in Christian monasticism. Changes in the organizational structure of religious orders were shown to make sense in the light of changes in their socio-cultural context, but all types of order have survived into the present-day. This indicates that innovations may respond to the conditions of a particular historical juncture but that once institutionalized they may survive into vastly different periods. It is incidentally interesting to note that versions of these two basic strategies have also been adopted by the same organization at

different historical junctures. Thus, the Bruderhof alternated between inward- and outward-looking phases ('creative withdrawal'
and 'outreach') in response to a complex of internal and external
factors.[20] These findings have two major implications for the arguments described in the opening section of this essay about the movement towards the so-called interiorization of present-day religion.
The first, and substantive, point is that even if this trend is actually
taking place in the manner described, it should not be divorced in
analysis from the contemporary popularity of such 'externalizing'
or practical religious phenomena as the Watch Tower movement
and the Unified Family. For they represent two diverse illustrations
of deep-rooted organizational traditions in Christianity which have
persisted into an age when new forms of religion have tended to
occupy the centre of the stage. The second, and methodological,
point is that the current vogue for analysing religious phenomena
exclusively in terms of beliefs, ideas and values (which may at first
glance appear to be well-suited to an age of 'invisible religion') is in
danger of obscuring a large number of organizational factors which
can throw considerable explanatory light on all religious movements.
To ignore religious organization in any sociological study of religion
is to leave out of consideration a most important set of constraints
on all human behaviour.

NOTES AND REFERENCES

1 Gerhard Lenski, *The Religious Factor*, Doubleday, New York, 1961.

2 Yoshio Fukuyama, 'The major dimensions of church membership', *Review of Religious Research*, Vol. 2, Spring 1961, pp. 154–161.

3 Rodney Stark and Charles Y. Glock, *American Piety: The Nature of Religious Commitment*, University of California Press, Berkeley, 1968.

4 Robert N. Bellah, 'Civil religion in America', *Daedalus*, Vol. 96, Winter 1967, pp. 1–21.

5 Peter Berger and Thomas Luckmann, *The Social Construction of Reality*, Doubleday, New York, 1966; Peter L. Berger, *The Social Reality of Religion*, Faber & Faber, London, 1969, (published in the USA under the title *The Sacred Canopy*, Doubleday, New York, 1967); Thomas Luckmann, *The Invisible Religion*, Macmillan, New York, 1967.

6 R. W. Bibby and M. B. Brinkerhoff, 'The circulation of the Saints: a study of people who join conservative churches', *Journal for the Scientific Study of Religion*, Vol. 12, No. 3, 1973, pp. 273–283; D. M. Kelley, *Why Conservative Churches are Growing*, Harper & Row, New York, 1972.

7 See Choi Syn-Duk, 'Korea's Tong-il movement', in S. T. Palmer (ed.), *The New Religions of Korea*, Transactions of the Korea Branch of The Royal Asiatic Society, XLIII, 1967, Seoul, pp. 167–180; Mark Cozin, 'A Millenarian Movement in Korea and Great Britain', in Michael Hill (ed.), *A Sociological Yearbook of Religion in Britain*, No. 6, S.C.M. Press, London, 1973, pp. 100–121; James A. Beckford, 'A Korean evangelistic movement in the West', in *The Contemporary Metamorphosis of Religion?*, Acts of the 12th International Conference on the Sociology of Religion, The Hague, 1973, pp. 319–335.

8 James D. Thompson, *Organization in Action*, McGraw-Hill, New York, 1967.

9 See John Lofland, *Doomsday Cult*, Prentice-Hall, New Jersey, 1966.

10 See John Child, 'Organisation structure, environment and performance: the role of strategic choice', *Sociology*, Vol. 6, No. 2, 1972, pp. 1–22.

11 James R. Wood and Meyer Zald, 'Aspects of racial integration in the Methodist Church: sources of resistance to organizational policy', *Social Forces*, Vol. 45, No. 2, 1966, pp. 255–265.

12 Meyer Zald, *Organizational Change: The Political Economy of the YMCA*, University of Chicago Press, Chicago, 1970.

13 For other aspects of its 'Mass-ness', see Werner Cohn, 'Jehovah's Witnesses as a proletarian movement', *The American Scholar*, Vol. 24, Summer 1955, pp. 281–298; James Beckford, *A Sociological Study of Jehovah's Witnesses in Britain*, unpublished Ph.D. thesis, University of Reading, 1972.

14 Peter Berger, op. cit., 1969.

15 See Alan T. Rogerson, *A Sociological Analysis of the Origin and Development of the Jehovah's Witnesses & their Schismatic Groups*, unpublished. D. Phil. thesis, University of Oxford, 1972.

16 James Beckford, op. cit., 1973.

17 See James Beckford, op. cit., 1972.

18 For confirmation of which, see J. H. Scalf, M. J. Miller and C. W. Thomas, 'Goal specificity, organizational structure and participant commitment in churches', *Sociological Analysis*, Vol. 34, No. 3, 1973, pp. 169–184.

19 E. K. Francis, 'Towards a typology of religious orders', *American Journal of Sociology*, Vol. 55, March 1950, pp. 437–449.

20 John Whitworth, 'The Bruderhof in England: a chapter in the history of a utopian sect', in Michael Hill (ed.), *A Sociological Yearbook of Religion in Britain*, No. 4, S.C.M. Press, London, 1971, pp. 84-101.

Roy Wallis

6 Societal Reaction to Scientology:
A Study in the Sociology of Deviant Religion[1]

Models

Scientology is a controversial new religious movement.[2] Unlike most traditional forms of sectarianism, Scientology accepts many prevailing cultural values and standards. Its deviance lies in the rejection of the 'facilities . . . culturally provided for man's salvation . . .'.[3] Among the many contemporary deviant forms of religion, Scientology appears to have become something of a *bête noire*, an object of special attention in the mass media, the courts, and national legislatures. Although it shares characteristics with other forms of sectarianism—Christian Science, Jehovah's Witnesses, Soka Gakkai,[4] etc., it has as they have not, been the subject of government inquiries in five states to date. Scientology has been portrayed publicly as 'an evil cult',[5] and a 'serious threat to the community'.[6] Laws have been passed prohibiting its practice in three states of Australia, and aliens were prohibited from entering Great Britain to pursue its study. The normatively pejorative and stigmatizing terms which have been employed to describe it and the relative severity with which Scientology has been treated suggest that this movement might fruitfully be examined from the theoretical perspective of the sociology of deviance.

The nature of the debate surrounding Scientology, and some of the rhetoric that has appeared during its course, suggest that at times Scientology has been viewed in a manner approaching *moral panic*. Stanley Cohen has defined moral panic as 'A condition, episode, person or group of persons [which] emerges to become defined as a threat to societal values and interests; its nature is presented in a stylized and stereotypical fashion by the mass media. . . .'[7] Drawing on Neil Smelser's definition of panic, we may add that it can be understood as involving a collective sense of immediate, powerful, but ambiguous threat to deeply held norms or values, for the preservation of which it is seen as urgent to take some action.[8]

This paper is specifically concerned with the question of the relationship between the development of Scientology and the reaction which it received from the surrounding society, particularly the mass media and agencies of the state. This area, of the relationship between deviance and societal reaction, has been an important focus of endeavour in recent sociology of deviance, and three simplified models of the nature of this relationship may be extracted.

The first model, which we can refer to as the *classic model*, relates deviance and societal reaction as a simple matter of unidirectional causation :

Deviance   ➤   Societal reaction

Deviance on this view is essentially unproblematic. It lies in the infringement of social norms which are consensually held. Deviance develops as a result of processes internal to the deviant and in due course provokes reactions of disapproval from conforming groups and individuals, and the mobilization of agents of social control.

This view informed most early speculation and theorizing concerning criminality. Criminals were held, due to differences of physiology, psychology or early life-experience to have some differentiating characteristic(s) which led them to violations of the law. The reaction of agents of social control was seen as a relatively straightforward process of identifying and processing norm violators, and hence the accounting procedures and official statistics generated by social control agents could be employed by social scientists with some conviction that they reflected more or less directly occurrences of deviance in the 'real world'. This view of the nature of the relationship between deviance and societal reaction has tended to be the 'official' view. It generalizes the account of this relationship typically held by agents of social control, moral entrepreneurs and the mass media. The assumptions upon which this model rests, however, have come under considerable criticism during the last fifteen years from proponents of the second model.

We can refer to the second model as the *labelling model*. Since what I am seeking to do here is to erect three models for heuristic purposes, rather than to characterize accurately the way this perspective has generally been employed, I shall draw it in extreme terms, ignoring particularly those sociologists who combine, or draw no distinction between, this model and the following one, and create a distinction where they would not.

Deviance on this view is seen as essentially problematic. Social norms and values have at best sub-cultural rather than general cultural acceptance, and infringements of norms are regular and widespread. Deviance is therefore a characteristic attributed to another, or a label imputed to him, which he is led to accept by public degradation and stigmatization, and coercive control. In Becker's oft-quoted words :

> . . . *social groups create deviance by making the rules whose infraction constitutes deviance* and by applying those rules to particular persons and labelling them as outsiders. . . . The deviant is one to whom the label has successfully been applied; deviant behaviour is behaviour that people so label.[9]

In its more extreme formulations, this model relates deviance and societal reaction as a similarly simple matter of unidirectional causation, but in the reverse direction to the classic model :

$$\text{Societal reaction} \quad \longrightarrow \quad \text{Deviance}$$

Such an extreme formulation is not altogether a 'straw man'. Lemert, for example, states that : '. . . older sociology tended to rest heavily upon the idea that deviance leads to social control. I have come to believe that the reverse idea, i.e. social control leads to deviance, is equally tenable and the potentially richer premise for studying deviance in modern society',[10] and this model is evident in David Cooper's notion of schizophrenia, which he defines as : '. . . a micro-social crisis situation in which acts and experience of a certain person are invalidated by others for certain intelligible cultural and micro-cultural (usually familial) reasons, to the point where he is elected and identified as being "mentally ill" in a certain way, and is then confirmed (by a specifiable but highly arbitrary labelling process) in the identity "schizophrenic patient" by medical or quasi-medical agents.'[11]

In order to define or dramatize the normative boundaries of society, moral entrepreneurs and social control agents select from among a range of available norm-violators those suitable for labelling. On some accounts, the labelling model provides a conspiracy theory of deviance-generation. A 'victim' is selected who is 'scapegoated' by others and forced into a deviant role, more or less coercively, from which he may not be permitted to escape. Appeal is frequently made to this model by those identified as deviant, as an account of their own situation.[12]

The third model can be referred to as the *deviance-amplification model*. This model, elaborated initially by Leslie Wilkins to account for gang delinquency,[13] has since been employed to explain among other things, the development of 'Mods and Rockers' as social problems,[14] and the nature of the social reaction to drug-taking.[15] In its simplest form the deviance-amplification model suggests the possible sequence :

1 Initial deviation from valued norms
                    leads to
2 Punitive reaction
                    which leads to
3 Further alienation of the deviants
                    which leads to
4 Further deviation
                    which leads to
5 Increased punitive reaction
                    which leads to 3 . . . etc,

in an amplifying spiral.

Cohen discusses this process as it affected the identification of the Mods and Rockers as a social problem and the subsequent attempts to control them.

Minor acts of rowdy and irritating behaviour at a seaside resort during Easter Weekend 1964 were exaggerated and distorted enormously by the press, which presented the incidents as episodes of uncontrolled vandalism and violence. The media reports were instrumental in the creation of a stereotype accepted and reinforced by social control agents on subsequent occasions. Future bank holiday weekends were viewed with fearful anticipation by residents, businessmen and police in seaside communities, leading to a propensity to over-react to the behaviour of the young people. The latter in turn were attracted to the resorts in increased numbers by the possibility of a repetition of the previous incidents, and identified themselves with one of the two stereotypical factions portrayed by the media.

The inevitable friction between police and Mods and Rockers was further dramatized in the media and by the courts, and sanctioned by heavy fines and some cases of imprisonment. De-amplification, Cohen suggests, finally set in as a result of the severity of social control. Potential deviants were 'frightened off or deterred by actual or threatened control measures. After being put off the train by the police before arriving at one's destination, and then being continually pushed around and harassed by the police on the streets and beaches, searched in the clubs, refused service in cafés, one might just give up in disgust. The game was simply not worth it . . . the amplification stops because the social distance from the deviants is made so great, that new recruits are put off from joining.'[16]

The models of the relationship between deviance and social control outlined above are suggested as competing hypotheses to account for developments in the relationship between Scientology and society. While empirically rather than normatively directed, they have clear implications for the attribution of responsibility for the process, and those involved therefore tend to have an interest in promoting one theory rather than another. The Scientologists themselves are clear that model two best characterizes their brief history :

> To understand why the Church of Scientology ever needed stiff internal discipline in the past to defend a perimeter against over-whelming odds—it is necessary to look at the situation which existed at those times, *which forced the Church to develop policies to handle outside threats.* Which came first, the strict internal ethics policies, or the threat which they were designed to cater for?[17]

The implication here and elsewhere is that Scientology has been the victim of a concerted campaign sponsored by the World Federation for Mental Health because of Scientology's 'forthright' stand against 'psychiatric atrocities' :

> An analysis of 21 years of attacks shows a very plain pattern. First, several extremely vicious newspaper and magazine articles are published. Investigation by Church officials has shown these often to be commissioned articles. Reprints or copies are then made of these articles and are sent to every government or private agency which might be in a position officially or unofficially to censure or take action against the Church. After a period of time in which several articles have been sent, these agencies then receive a letter basically expressing the following: 'See how public opinion is against this group. Don't you think something should be done?'[18]

The moral entrepreneurs and social control agents involved appear to accept model one as typifying the process. In the absence of explicit commentary to this effect, we can perhaps accept their statements against Scientology and appeals for action to be taken regarding it, as implying the view that Scientology caused and was responsible for the reaction that resulted. In opposition to both these views I shall argue that model three most adequately characterizes the process that developed.

Becker and others have stressed that social problems are in part at least a consequence of *moral enterprise*. Some individual or group of individuals must generate public concern and mobilize public opinion or the opinion of legislators and law enforcers that 'something needs to be done' about the object of concern.[19] This moral enterprise may be exhibited by any number of individuals and agencies, variously motivated. Gusfield has described[20] how the Woman's Christian Temperance Union originally formed part of the general progressive, humanitarian movement for social reform in the late-nineteenth and early-twentieth centuries. Its adherents were members of socially dominant groups whose secure social position permitted them to feel sympathy for the plight of immigrant workers, and led them to organize to seek the conversion of individual drinkers.

After the repeal of Prohibition, the WCTU found itself in a changed situation. Abstinence was no longer a norm of the dominant middle class. As drinking became increasingly acceptable, the total abstainer became a figure of ridicule, and the WCTU lost its upper-middle-class members. The movement increasingly adopted an attitude of moral indignation and a policy of coercive reform towards drinking as lower-middle and lower-class members found their values repudiated by the upper and middle classes.

Dickson offers a persuasive account of the role of the Bureau of Narcotics in the passage of federal legislation against marihuana,[21] suggesting that the primary motivation was to improve the position of the Narcotics Bureau as a bureaucratic agency in a period of declining appropriations. Generating anxiety about marihuana use was a means of impressing upon the public and Congress that the Bureau was an important agency which should be maintained, even expanded.

The generation of moral panic may therefore be motivated in some cases by status anxiety or bureaucratic insecurity, or 'empire-building'. It may, of course, also arise from a sincerely felt conflict of values. Whatever its sources, the mass media are typically central to its propagation. As various studies have suggested, the operation of the mass media is to some extent constrained by commercial

D

objectives. Fulfilment of these objectives may lead to exaggeration and distortion in the presentation of news concerning 'social problems'.

> The mass media operate with certain definitions of what is news-worthy. It is not that instruction manuals exist telling newsmen that certain subjects (drugs, sex, violence) will appeal to the public or that certain groups (youth, immigrants) should be continually exposed to scrutiny. Rather there are built-in factors ranging from the individual newsman's intuitive hunch about what con-stitutes a 'good story', through precepts such as 'give the public what it wants' to structured ideological biases, which predispose the media to make a certain event into news.[22]

The media typically build upon labels imputed to individuals and groups, elaborating a stereotype which will render the phenomenon intelligible and 'predictable' to the readership in terms of general cultural images.

The Reaction to Scientology

Until the 1960s, Scientology had rated public attention in the mass media only sporadically, and then on only a local scale. When it first emerged as a lay psychotherapy, Dianetics, in the early 1950s, it was roundly criticized by medical men as yet another 'mind healing cult',[23] and by established psychiatrists and psychologists as a 'serious menace to public health'.[24] These attacks were undoubtedly to some degree responsible for the collapse of its brief mass popularity[25] and permanently coloured the already jaundiced view of organized medicine, psychiatry and the press held by its founder, Ron Hubbard.

From the late 1950s, Scientology, as the movement had by then become, impinged increasingly upon public attention. In 1958 the US Food and Drug Administration (FDA) seized and destroyed 21,000 tablets of a compound known as Dianazene, marketed as a preventative and treatment for radiation sickness, by an agency associated with the Washington Founding Church of Scientology, on the grounds that they were falsely labelled.[26] While this action passed largely unnoticed by the press it resulted, in conjunction with internal problems of defection by leading figures in the movement, in a tightening of the internal security of Scientology, most evident in the appearance of 'security checking'.[27] Somewhere around this time the US Internal Revenue Service also began taking an interest in the tax-free income of the Washington Church, later revoking its tax-exempt status.

In 1960 the movement received unfavourable publicity as a result of activities of the headmistress of an East Grinstead private preparatory school who was devoting a brief period each day to carrying out Scientology exercises on her pupils.[28] Most of these exercises involved simple, repetitive and rather innocuous commands such as 'stand up', 'sit down', etc., or communication exercises such as the teacher saying 'hello' and the children replying 'all right' for a few minutes. The exercise that led to the press outburst involved the pupils following the directions : 'Close your eyes. Concentrate. Now imagine you are dying. Imagine you are dead. Now you have turned to dust and ashes. Now imagine you are putting the ashes back inside yourself.' The press reports referred histrionically to these periods as 'Death Lessons'.[29]

After investigating a device, the E-meter, employed to monitor changes in the spiritual state of the individual in auditing, during 1962, the FDA again raided the premises of the Founding Church of Scientology in Washington early in 1963 to seize examples of the E-meter and associated literature.[30] Unlike the occasion in 1958, the FDA clearly saw this as an opportunity for exhibiting their importance as agents of the public interest, meriting the appropriations they received. The raid was accompanied by considerable publicity, the press, it was said, having been forewarned.[31]

Senator Edward Long, no friend to the FDA, described this raid later when reporting on the investigations of the Senate Subcommittee on Administrative Practice and Procedure :

> . . . recent hearings before the Subcommittee on Administrative Practice and Procedure exposed certain activities of the Food and Drug Administration to be disgraceful and completely contrary to the protective guarantees of our Constitution. Perhaps the most shocking of these exposures involved the raiding of a premises here in the nation's capital. This raid was reminiscent of a bygone era when large numbers of Federal and local law enforcement officials set upon centers of gangland activity. True to form, this recent raid was preceded by intelligence from an FDA spy planted on the premises. In authentic Hollywood style, FDA agents and marshals descended on private property while local police roped off the street and held back the crowds. Press reporters and photographers accompanied the agents while they ran through the premises, banged on doors, shouted and seized what they viewed as incriminating evidence.[32]

The FDA seizures gave Hubbard cause to reaffirm the attitude of his organization to the press : 'The reporter who comes to you, all smiles and withholds [sic], "wanting a story", has an AMA instigated release in his pocket. He is there to trick you into supporting his preconceived story. . . . The story he will write has already been outlined by a sub-editor from old clippings and AMA releases.'[33] In the subsequent suit, the FDA charged that :

> . . . the labeling for the E-meter contains statements which rep-resent, suggest and imply that the E-meter is adequate and effect-ive for diagnosis, prevention, treatment, detection and elimination of the causes of all mental and nervous disorders and illnesses such as neuroses, psychoses . . . arthritis, cancer, stomach ulcers, and radiation burns from atomic bombs, poliomyelitis, the common cold, etc., and that the article is adequate and effective to improve the intelligent quotient . . . which statements are false and mis-leading. . . .[34]

The seizure action led to the first serious press attention to Scien-tology in ten years in America. Much of it was hostile and supported the FDA action. The Scientologists, however, reacted with con-siderable indignation, subsequently referring to the FDA with an uncharacteristic sense of irony as 'an agency behaving as a sort of cult, with an almost fanatical urge—to save the world'.[35] The years following the FDA raid were a period of increasingly severe internal control within Scientology and of extreme hostility toward those the Scientologists believed were attacking them.

The FDA raid was reported throughout the English-speaking world, and in the state of Victoria in Australia it added fuel to a debate which had been taking place in the mass media over Scien-tology. In Victoria, Scientology had been under observation for some years by the Mental Health Authority and the Australian Medical Association. A statement to the press by a Dr Dickson, medical secretary of the Victorian Branch of the Australian Medical Association, in 1960 led to a sharp attack by Hubbard : 'We are having Dickson investigated for anti-social background, and if it ever comes to a court case, we'll ruin him.'[36] The Report of the Board of Inquiry into Scientology in Victoria recounts similar attempts by the Melbourne Hubbard Association of Scientologists International (HASI) to 'muzzle' critics of Scientology. The Rev. Dr L. Rumble, also in 1960, replied on the radio to a request for advice on Scientology by recommending that the inquirer have nothing to do with it. His reply was also published in *The Tribune*, a Catholic weekly. This provoked letters from HASI officials which accused Rumble of having 'allied yourself further with international subversive communism', suggested that he was 'seeking to profit by the sickness and troubles of man . . .', and threatened Dr Rumble that he too 'would be investigated'.[37] Hubbard also attacked the British Medical Association later that year :

> With what amazed surprise we viewed the recent attack upon us by the British Medical Association. With their hands caked with blood they sought to point a grisly finger at us and to bring down upon us the wrath of the government they claimed they controlled. Folly, thy name is medicine. . . . I have found that the British Medical Association in England . . . has encouraged its doctors to spread vicious lies about us via their patients.[38]

During the following five years Scientology received a great deal of unfavourable publicity in Victoria. The Melbourne newspaper *Truth* attacked the movement in a series of feature articles. In November 1963 the Hon. J. W. Galbally, in a speech to the Legislative Council of the Parliament of Victoria, alleged that Scientology was being used for blackmail and extortion and had seriously affected the mental well-being of undergraduates at Melbourne University. On 26 November, 1963, Mr Galbally introduced a *Scientology Restriction Bill* seeking to provide that fees should not be charged for Scientology services. Shortly thereafter the Victoria government agreed to establish a Board of Inquiry into Scientology.

The Hubbard Association of Scientologists International (HASI) in Australia initially co-operated with the Board of Inquiry but withdrew its representatives in November 1964. The Report published in 1965 was a devastating indictment of the movement. Anderson, the architect of the Report, there formulated a number of phrases which were to be quoted throughout the world :

> Scientology is evil, its techniques evil, its practice a serious threat to the community, medically, morally and socially; and its adherents sadly deluded and often mentally ill.[39]

> The appeal of Scientology is at times deliberately directed towards the weak, the anxious, the disappointed, the inadequate and the lonely. . . .[40]

> The principles and practices of Scientology are contrary to accepted principles and practices of medicine and science, and con-

stitute a grave danger to the health, particularly the mental health of the community.[41]

Scientology is a grave threat to family and home life.[42]

Anderson claimed to have 'been unable to find any worthwhile redeeming feature in Scientology. It constitutes a serious medical, moral and social threat to individuals and to the community generally,'[43] and described Scientology processes as having a 'brainwashing effect'. One disinterested commentator observed of the Report that it 'betrays a considerable lack of the objectivity and detachment necessary for proper scientific evaluation of evidence. The language is often highly emotive, and argument proceeds by the use of debating devices rather than by the scientific method.'[44]

The immediate result of this Report was the passage in December 1965 of the *Psychological Practices Act* (1965) which banned the practice of Scientology, use of the E-meter unless a registered psychologist, and provided for the seizure and destruction by the Attorney General of Scientological documents and recordings.

Shortly after the withdrawal of the Scientologists from the Victoria Inquiry, Hubbard promulgated a series of swingeing 'ethics' policies, enforced by Ethics Officers, an internal security force. A series of 'Conditions' were established which signified something approximating the state of grace of an individual or organization. Ethics Officers had the power to assign individuals to a 'lower condition', which had penalties attached; for example:

ENEMY—Suppressive Person Order. May not be communicated with by anyone except an Ethics Officer, Master at Arms, a Hearing Officer or a Board or Committee. May be restrained or imprisoned. May not be protected by any rules or laws of the group he sought to injure [i.e. Scientology] as he sought to destroy or bar fair practices for others. May not be trained or processed or admitted to any organization.[45]

The Condition of Enemy also carried, until 21 October, 1968, the further penalty of 'Fair Game', defined as follows:

May be deprived of property or injured by any means by any Scientologist without any discipline of the Scientologists. May be tricked, sued or lied to or destroyed.[46]

This penalty attached to anyone declared a 'Suppressive Person'

(SP). A large number of Scientologists were expelled between 1965 and 1968, many of whom were declared to be suppressive persons.

Another important policy was that concerning 'disconnection'. Someone connected to a Suppressive Person was held to be a 'Potential Trouble Source'. To continue in Scientology, such an individual was required to 'handle' the source of suppression or 'disconnect' from it. Handling was never clearly defined, but appeared to mean reforming the suppressive individual concerned.[47] If 'handling' was of no avail, the Scientologist was obliged to disconnect from the SP, that is, to cut off all communication or contact after declaring an intention to do so in writing. This policy led many Scientologists to disconnect from former friends, relatives, or even sometimes total strangers whom they believed to be 'suppressive' (i.e. hostile to Scientology).[48]

It was not until 1965 that Scientology began to appear systematically in the British press. The first coverage indicated in *The Times Index* is for the report of the Australian Inquiry and Hubbard's subsequent threats to sue the Victoria Government. Shortly after, a number of other British newspapers discovered Scientology to be newsworthy. All cited the Victoria Report at length.[49] In January the *News of the World* reported a young Scientologist's disconnection from her mother.[50] In February, Lord Balniel, M.P., then Chairman of the National Association for Mental Health, asked whether the Minister of Health would initiate an inquiry into Scientology in Britain, referring in his question to the findings of the Anderson Inquiry.[51] The Minister replied that he would not, but the question itself roused the Scientology leadership to an apparently furious reaction. In a series of documents issued in February 1966 Hubbard outlined a policy to be followed in the face of proposals to investigate Scientology.[52] The basic principle of this policy was to investigate the critics of Scientology and expose their past 'crimes' with 'wide lurid publicity'.[53] A Public Investigation Section was established to pursue this end. In March *The People*, under the headlines 'One man Britain can do without . . .', published the story of a private investigator recruited by the Scientology organization to advise on setting up this section.[54] Lord Balniel, it appears, was to be the first to be investigated.

Other newspapers developed these themes. The *Daily Mail* proved to be one of the movement's severest critics, publishing a front-page story in February which challenged Hubbard's credentials,[55] and in August, the story of Karen Henslow, a schizophrenic who had been working at Saint Hill Manor, the head-

quarters of the movement, and had been returned to her mother's
home one night in a deranged state.[56] This case became a *cause
célèbre* when Peter Hordern, M.P. for Horsham, referred to it in
the House of Commons in the adjournment debate on 6 March,
1967.[57] Geoffrey Johnson Smith, M.P., also spoke, referring to the
'. . . many open-minded people in the town of East Grinstead, whose
judgement on matters of this kind one can trust, [who] are seriously
disturbed by the activities and objectives of this organization. . . .'[58]
The Minister of Health, Kenneth Robinson, in his reply referred to
a resolution sent to him by East Grinstead Urban District Council
in December 1966 expressing 'grave concern' about Scientology and
its effects on the town and its people. Liberal reference was made
to the Anderson Report and Mr Robinson concluded of the Scientologists :

> What they do . . . is to direct themselves deliberately towards the
> weak, the unbalanced, the immature, the rootless and the men-
> tally or emotionally unstable, to promise them remoulded, mature
> personalities and to set about fulfilling the promises by means of
> untrained staff, ignorantly practising quasi-psychological tech-
> niques, including hypnosis. It is true that the Scientologists claim
> not to accept as clients people known to be mentally sick, but
> the evidence strongly suggests that they do.[59]

During 1967 reports continued to appear concerning discon-
nections, and the growth of Hubbard's private fleet, the Sea Org.[60]
The Sea Org was '. . . specifically designed and intended to safe-
guard the organization of Scientology against opposition'[61] and
marked a further tightening of social control within the movement.
Reactions to the Scientologists in the area of their headquarters had
not improved and the East Grinstead U.D.C. refused planning permission for extensions to their premises. The ensuing inquiry by a
Ministry of Housing Inspector in July 1968 gave an opportunity
for Scientology's neighbours to voice their feelings. The Scientologists were accused of accosting people in the streets, boycotting
East Grinstead shops and services, visiting local schools in an attempt
to give instruction in Scientology to pupils, bringing foot-and-mouth
disease to the district, and allowing 'a mentally deranged member
of your establishment' to range at large over a neighbouring bar-
rister's estate.[62] That these accusations had little to do with the
subject of the inquiry seems to have been the view adopted by the
Minister of Housing who permitted the Scientologists' appeal
against the U.D.C. in a decision finally rendered in 1969.[63]

In July 1968, Mr Robinson announced in a statement to the House of Commons that during the previous two years the Government had 'become increasingly concerned at the spread of Scientology in the United Kingdom'.

> The Government are satisfied, having reviewed all the available evidence, that Scientology is socially harmful. It alienates members of families from each other and attributes squalid and disgraceful motives to all who oppose it; its authoritarian principles and practices are a potential menace to the personality and well-being of those so deluded as to become its followers; above all its methods can be a serious danger to the health of those who submit to them. There is evidence that children are now being indoctrinated.[64]

The Government had therefore decided to take action to 'curb the growth' of the movement in Britain. Scientology organizations would no longer be recognized as educational establishments for the purpose of admission of foreign nationals; Scientologists would therefore no longer be eligible for admission to the UK as students and no extensions to entry or work permits of foreign Scientologists would be allowed. Thereafter up to June 1971 some 145 aliens were refused admission to Britain to study or work at Scientology establishments.[65]

In 1969 Acts were passed banning the practice of Scientology in the states of South Australia and Western Australia,[66] and a petition was presented to the New Zealand Parliament asking for an Inquiry into, and Government action against the movement there.[67] In South Africa, Scientology had been criticized in Parliament during 1966 and in 1968 became the defendant in an action for defamation initiated by Dr E. L. Fisher, the M.P. most active in parliamentary criticism of the movement, who had been libelled in a Scientology publication.[68] In the USA the FDA won a decision ordering the destruction of the seized E-meters and in the same year, 1967, the tax-exempt status of the Washington Church of Scientology was revoked.

In the face of fierce criticism in the press and various national parliaments, the Church of Scientology in November 1968 promulgated a *Code of Reform*, including:

1 Cancellation of disconnection as a relief to those suffering from familial suppression.
2 Cancellation of security checking as a form of confession.

3 Prohibition of any confessional materials being written down.
4 Cancellation of declaring people Fair Game.[69]

The Church of Scientology claimed that these reforms were a response to public criticism of the practices concerned. This action was too late, however, to prevent the British Government establishing an Inquiry into Scientology in January 1969[70] and the South African Government in April.[71] By mid-1968, however, the severe British Government action against Scientology had begun to cause some doubts to appear about the justifiability of these actions. Questions were raised as to why Scientology had been singled out for such treatment when various other cults and sects which seemed to behave in a similar fashion were not.[72] M.P.s questioned the logic of banning people 'coming to this country to study something which we now admit we know so little about that we have to set up an inquiry.'[73]

The New Zealand Commission of Inquiry reported in June 1969 in mild tones, recommending no changes in legislation and observing that if Scientology kept to its Code of Reform there should be 'no further occasion for Government or public alarm. . . .'[74] Such a finding must have been heartening to the Scientologists, who further modified their practice in October 1970 by dropping the various penalties which attached to the assignment of an individual to a 'lower condition'.[75]

In 1969 the Scientologists also scored a success in the United States, when they appealed against the decision of a federal jury in 1967 in favour of the FDA, which had directed that seized E-meters and literature should be destroyed. The US Court of Appeals reversed this decision in February 1969 on the ground that the Founding Church of Scientology had made out a *prima facie* case that it was a bona fide religion and that the E-meter was related to its religious dogma, and therefore not subject to the Court's condemnation.[76] The FDA retained the items seized, pending a decision on appeal. In a final action seeking condemnation of the E-meter in 1971, the federal judge ruled that the E-meter had been misbranded and its secular use condemned, but that it might continue to be used in bona fide religious counselling if labelled as ineffective in treating illness.[77]

The Report of the British Inquiry conducted by Sir John Foster was published in December 1971. This Report also contained passages of undoubted comfort for the Scientology organization. Among these, Sir John observed that he disagreed:

profoundly with the legislation adopted in both Western and South Australia, in turn based on part of that adopted in Victoria, whereby the teaching and practice of Scientology as such is banned. Such legislation appears to me to be discriminatory and contrary to all the best traditions of the Anglo-Saxon legal system.[78]

He advocated the establishment of a Psychotherapy Council to control practitioners of psychotherapy, whose ranks Scientologists should be allowed to join provided they could satisfy the Council's requirements. The Report also argued that it was wrong for the Home Secretary to exclude foreign Scientologists when there was no law against the practice being carried out by their British colleagues.

The South African Commission of Enquiry reported in June 1972 and also recommended the passage of legislation to provide for the registration and control of psychotherapists, to make illegal 'disconnection', 'public investigation', 'security checking' and similar Scientology practices, and to control psychological testing, and the dissemination of 'inaccurate, untruthful and harmful information in regard to psychiatry and the field of mental health in general'.[79] Assuming the implementation of these recommendations, the Commission held that 'no positive purpose will be served by banning the practice of Scientology as such.'[80]

In Australia it would appear that an attitude of increased tolerance for Scientology has begun to prevail. The electoral victory of the Labour Party resulted in the registration of the Church of the New Faith, a Scientology organization, as a recognized denomination for the purposes of the *Marriage Act*, authorizing its nominated personnel for the lawful solemnization of marriage.[81] In May 1973 the Western Australian *Scientology Act*, and in March 1974 the South Australia Scientology (Prohibition) Act, were repealed.

The Moral Crusaders

Those who have filled the ranks of the anti-Scientology crusade have fallen into a number of discrete categories, with distinct motivations for involvement:

1   state agencies—such as the FDA in America and the Mental Health Authority in Victoria;

2 doctors and psychiatrists (and to a lesser extent ministers of religion) and their professional bodies;

3 disgruntled ex-Scientologists;

4 relatives of Scientologists;

5 neighbours of Scientology establishments;

6 Members of Parliament;

7 the press.

While one would not wish to impugn the motives of any of those involved in demanding action against Scientology, it is clear that however righteous their moral indignation, such a crusade had functional consequences for each group. Characterizations of Scientology as a 'fraud', 'brain-washing', 'hypnosis', 'quackery', etc., served to legitimize attitudes adopted by the crusading groups and individuals, and their demands for social control of the movement. Several of these groups experienced a direct conflict of interest between the movement and themselves. Doctors and psychiatrists have persistently attacked Dianetics and Scientology, tending to resent Scientology's therapeutic claims particularly in fields in which they had themselves experienced little concrete success, such as severe psychological disorder. They also scorned the brief unorthodox training of its practitioners in comparison with their own lengthy and arduous process of qualification. State agencies appear sometimes to have seen in Scientology an opportunity to impress legislators and the public with their zeal for the public protection, and their importance as recipients of public funding.

Former Scientologists and relatives of members may sometimes have seen in stigmatization and government action against the movement a means of self-justification. If Scientology was a form of hypnosis or brain-washing, then this could justify and explain their involvement in, and devotion of considerable resources to, a movement which they now repudiated. Similarly relatives could explain the involvement of spouses or children in the movement as a result of fraud or brain-washing and thereby excuse what might otherwise have been conceived as a failure on their own part that their relatives were led to join such a movement. Some of Scientology's neighbours in East Grinstead appear to have found the presence of the movement in a respectable middle-class township a source of irritation and embarrassment.

The press and Members of Parliament have an institutionalized interest in taking up a moral crusade of concern to customers or constituents. The two M.P.s active in the British criticism of the movement were the M.P. for East Grinstead and the M.P. for a neighbouring constituency, Horsham. The press found sensational copy in Scientology and the allegations made about it, and as Young has pointed out :

The mass media in Western countries are placed in a competitive situation where they must attempt constantly to maintain and extend their circulation. A major component of what is news-worthy is that which arouses public indignation. Thus the media have an institutionalized need to expose social problems, to act as if they were the personified moral censors of their reader-ship.[82]

Reality Conflict

Scientology confronts the conventional world with a deviant reality of massive proportions. Unlike a belief-system such as spiritualism, it does not merely add another layer to existing reality, with only marginal implications for conventional life.[83] Rather, it offers a total *Weltanschauung*, a complex meaning-system which interprets, explains and directs everyday life by alternative means to conven-tional, common-sense knowledge. Particularly in the area of the psychological life of man, it offers a radically competing theory to those prevailing in orthodox scientific circles and those which look to them for the authority for their beliefs.[84] The somewhat pre-carious status of the sciences of the person, and the therapeutic arts dependent, upon them, has led their practitioners to be particularly sensitive to belief-systems and practices which challenge their authority. Orthodox psychological healing practices have managed to secure no more than a tenuous claim to public legitimation as possessors of some unique professional expertise.[85] Like many radical belief-systems, and in this respect no more than early Christianity, Scientology also presented a competing claim to the loyalty typically owed to the family. Unlike early Christianity, how-ever, Scientology emerged in an era when the family had become a particularly fragile institution,[86] and its claim to a higher loyalty under some circumstances was thus peculiarly threatening.

A further important feature of Scientology's challenge to prevail-ing reality lay in its ambiguous status.[87] Western conceptions of religion grounded in the Christian experience identify religious institutions and practices in terms drawn from that tradition and its vicissitudes. Religious institutions are discriminable from secular institutions. The boundaries between church, business, science, and to a lesser extent psychotherapy are relatively clearly drawn. Scientology infringed these boundaries, and, refusing to recognize any necessity of occupying one category rather than another, behaved in ways characteristic of them all. It was thus a source of cognitive anomaly and psychological anxiety.[88] Since it behaved as a business as well as a religion (and that of a singularly alien form) many argued that its religious claim must be purely 'a front', and Scientology 'a con'.

Scientology's challenge to conventional reality remained unimportant while the movement itself was insignificant. However, there are indications that during the late 1950s and early 1960s, Scientology began to grow rapidly. Figures cited during the American tax case indicate that the income of the Washington Church almost doubled between 1956 and 1957.[89] The Victoria Report shows a steady growth from 1958 to 1963:

Income of Scientology Organizations in Melbourne[90]

Year ended 30 June	£
1958	12,150
1959	30,500
1960	47,075
1961	57,640
1962	71,977
1963	54,071

The Foster Report indicates that in Britain, the movement's income roughly doubled every year between 1965 and 1968.[91]

Scientology was clearly having a considerable impact, recruiting individuals away from conventional reality. Moreover, the individuals recruited were not by any means *marginal* in conventional terms. Many were prosperous; businessmen and professionals were converted as well as the less successful.

For some, particularly Anderson, Scientology's conflict with conventional reality was a *moral* affront. The Victoria Report reverberates with Anderson's indignation that anyone could believe such a 'weird idea',[92] such 'nonsense',[93] so much that was 'entirely contrary to conventional learning and experience',[94] 'irrational and perverted'.[95] He appears to have found it perverse and indeed 'incredible that a witness with such high academic qualifications, could voice such nonsense . . .'[96] and was forced to conclude that

Hubbard's followers were 'deluded',[97] or in the grip of 'some inescapable compulsion'.[98] How otherwise could one account for the fact that apparently rational men could come to hold such bizarre and alien beliefs, than that they were 'hypnotized' or 'brainwashed'? Scientology posed a threat not only to the precarious domains of psychological treatment and family life,[99] but to the fabric of conventional reality itself.

Discussion

Since its earliest days, Scientology has been an authoritarian movement with only one source of authoritative definition of reality: its founder, Ron Hubbard. The debacle of Dianetics in the early 1950s convinced Hubbard that two major dangers threatened the survival of his organization—attacks from outside the Scientology community inspired by medical and psychiatric interests, and threats from within, in the form of heresy, 'individualism', and schism. Both these perceived dangers need to be considered to understand the movement's development.

In the late 1950s and early 1960s, the gradual growth of the movement and its quasi-therapeutic claims brought it to the attention of a variety of state and professional agencies. In the pursuit of largely bureaucratic ends, the FDA in America, the Medical Health Authority in Victoria, AMA, BMA, APA, etc., maintained a certain surveillance over Scientology, and occasionally issued public comment upon it. This led to defensive and offensive action by the Scientology organization in response. Critics were attacked and internal security tightened. The FDA raid in 1963 seems to have been at least in part a public relations exercise when its handling and press coverage are compared to the 1958 seizure. It inevitably led to further alienation from and hostility towards the state, press, and professional bodies for what was felt by many Scientologists to be, and characterized by its leadership as, religious persecution.[100]

It was, however, the developments in Victoria which led to an international moral panic. There, press, medical and psychiatric agencies, professional bodies and disgruntled former Scientologists joined forces to promote government action against Scientology. The grounds for such action—alleged blackmail, extortion and adverse effects on the mental health of local university students—were generally unsubstantiated by the Anderson Inquiry.

However, Anderson's Report presented, often in emotive terms, a highly negative stereotype of the movement. It instituted a *moral passage* in public designations of Scientology, leading to a transformation of the prevailing stereotype. The former conception of the movement as a relatively harmless, if 'cranky', health and self-improvement cult was transformed into one which portrayed it as 'evil', 'dangerous', a form of 'hypnosis' (with all the overtones of Svengali in the layman's mind) and 'brain-washing'. The symbolization of the movement rested largely on the *putative* features of its deviation, i.e. 'that portion of the societal definition of the deviant which has no foundation in his objective behaviour.'[101] Much play was made of Scientology practices which were *likely* to be harmful to mental health,[102] the *'potentiality* for the misuse of confidences',[103] and activities which were *'potentially* very dangerous to the mental health of the community'.[104] Exaggeration and distortion appear throughout the Report, probably the most notorious example of which occurs where Anderson asserts that he realized he had observed a woman being 'processed into insanity', when nine days after a demonstration auditing session in which she had participated, she was admitted to a mental hospital.[105]

The Anderson Report provoked not only a legal ban on Scientology in Victoria, but a reaction in many other English-speaking countries. In 1966 Scientology became the subject of a question in the House of Commons, as well as numerous unfavourable press reports, many of which drew directly upon Anderson's rhetoric and stereotyping. Hubbard was also requested to leave Rhodesia where it appears he may have hoped to settle.[106] In 1967 Scientology came under the scrutiny of the Ontario Committee on the Healing Arts.[107] The process described by amplification theorists began accelerating :

> . . . when society defines a group of people as deviant it tends to react against them so as to isolate and alienate them from the company of 'normal' people. In this situation of isolation and alienation, the group . . . tends to develop its own norms and values which society perceives as even more deviant than before.[108]

What Scientologists regarded as their 'persecution', experienced at a personal and not merely an organizational level, resulted in the rapid development of a severe sense of alienation from the surrounding society, and the development of new norms conceived to be essential for the movement's survival, although regarded by the conventional society as further evidence of Scientology's deviance. This alienation is evident in passages such as the following :

> Scientology regards ordinary society as something akin to [a] dense jungle of intrigue, lies, confusion, illness, violence and sudden death covered with a thin social veneer of mildness.[109]

This sense of alienation and imminent threat led to increasingly severe policies of internal control and led the leadership to draw further away from contact with the society, geographically as well as symbolically, with the creation of the Sea Org, a fleet of vessels manned by totally committed followers, on the flag ship of which, Hubbard now resides. Scientologists began to take what they construed as defensive action by more vigorous attacks on critics through legal actions, investigation for past 'crimes', and (whether as a matter of organization policy, or an excess of individual enthusiasm) acts which might be interpreted as designed to harass or silence critics of, or commentators on, Scientology.[110]

It should be stressed that the reaction of the movement was not purely to external attack. The measures taken by the leadership to tighten internal security were also to a considerable extent motivated by the threat of schism and secession. Since 1952 and the split between himself and the Hubbard Dianetic Foundation in Wichita, Hubbard had loudly declaimed against heretics and schismatics. The failure of the early Dianetics organizations he attributed to a communist-AMA inspired plot to create secessions.[111] In 1959 Hubbard's eldest son and a number of other leading figures in the movement had defected, some to establish more profitable independent practices outside the organization. In 1962 secessions occurred in the Johannesburg organization. In 1964 a Scientology follower, Robert de Grimstone, and his wife left the movement to establish Compulsion's Analysis, which later, much modified, became The Process, or the Church of the Final Judgement.[112] Press reports often conflated Scientology and The Process, an alliance the Scientologists found unflattering.[113] Late in 1964 and in early 1965 a former employee of the Scientology headquarters at East Grinstead widely circularized Scientologists concerning a new system he had invented, Amprinistics, which briefly attracted a considerable following away from Hubbard's movement and roused him to a vicious attack on the new system's leaders.[114] The ethics policies from 1965 on were as much a reaction to the threat of heretical and schismatic movements within its ranks, as to external attacks.

By 1968, however, Amprinistics had largely foundered, and the external threat had reached such proportions as to render a multi-national ban an imminent possibility. Moreover, there is some suggestion that the severe internal control measures may have caused a loss of committed membership. The only figures available are those for successful completion of the 'clearing course'. This was not developed in its current form until 1966, at which point it was the most advanced course available. It was later effectively demoted as a result of the introduction of even more advanced courses. (This should if anything have increased the number of students taking the course.)

Period	Number declared 'clear'[115]
March —December 1966	131
January—December 1967	475
January—December 1968	901
January—December 1969	774
January—December 1970	441
January—December 1971	385
January—December 1972	359
January—December 1973	383

With the announcement of clearing in 1966, recruitment to the clearing course expanded rapidly. The publicity that Scientology received during the early and middle 1960s drew new adherents to the movement, particularly among adolescents and young adults, attracted by the anti-establishment image which it was gaining. Recruitment to and completion of the clearing course increased through 1968, but then proceeded to decline, although it may have stabilized since 1971 or even have begun to increase again. Clearing is a relatively advanced stage of achievement in the movement's structure and indicates a level of considerable commitment. It is therefore not possible to say how lower-level training and auditing have been affected. Indeed, the only figures published by the movement suggest that in the United Kingdom, membership in Scientology has continued to increase rapidly.[116] Since it is quite unclear how these membership figures are calculated, it is difficult to be certain of their validity. Six months' free 'membership' is given to any inquirer who wishes it.[117] Hence membership clearly does not imply any high degree of commitment. But evidently, at the advanced levels, the rate of growth slowed after 1968 for several years.

One possible interpretation of these figures is that a process of de-amplification had begun during 1968. Publicity had become so unfavourable, and the internal regime so repressive ('puritanical' is the term preferred by the Scientologists themselves to describe this period) that new members were not being recruited at the same rate as during the early and middle 1960s, were becoming alienated from the organization earlier, or both. The gap between society and extensive Scientological commitment may have become too wide for many to cross. A 'field staff auditor' and former 'franchise operator' (i.e. a semi-autonomous practitioner of Scientology) confirmed that a considerable drop in recruitment had been experienced at least at the local level, following the Government statement in the House of Commons in 1968.[118] In an effort to correct this situation, perhaps, the Scientology leadership attempted a major modification in policy. Between 1968 and 1970 the severest social control measures were publicly dropped as part of a campaign to change the movement's image.

A *Policy Letter* issued in March 1969, for example, states :

We are going in the direction of mild ethics and involvement with the Society. After 19 years of attack by the minions of vested interest, psychiatric front groups, we developed a tightly disciplined organizational structure.

(. . .) We didn't know it at the time, but our difficulties and failures were the result of false reports put out by the small, but rich and powerful group of individuals who would deny man freedom.

Now that we know . . . we will never need a harsh spartan discipline for ourselves.[119]

Early in their history Scientologists had realized the advantages of being recognized as a religion.[120] They now saw the advantages of being regarded as a denominational rather than a sectarian form of religion. The stabilization and possible increase of recruitment to advanced courses suggests this policy may have been successful.

De-amplification appears to have occurred on the part of agents of control as well. In Britain and Australia particularly, commitment to 'freedom of thought' and 'freedom of religion' led to uneasiness concerning the severity of state action against Scientology, and a willingness to reconsider earlier, possibly precipitate decisions.

In the period after 1968 the organization opened its premises at East Grinstead on Sundays, invited doctors and ministers of all denominations to take courses and developed its social reform programmes, particularly publicizing its stand as a radical opponent to institutional psychiatry, and the drug rehabilitation scheme sponsored by the Church, Narconon.[121] The Church of Scientology therefore had open to it a strategy of de-amplification generally unavailable to the illicit drug-user or the delinquent. That is, to pursue a conscious attempt to change the stereotype which had grown up. Whether or not this strategy is successful, remains to be seen. During the period 1970–1973 Scientology has been the subject of a number of books and articles by former Scientologists and others which have continued to publicize its more deviant features.[122] In its reaction to its critics both in the courts and beyond them, there is some ground for believing that Scientology's denominationalization, its rapprochement with conventional reality, may be, as yet, only public-relations officer deep.[123]

Conclusion

The deviance-amplification model appears to be supported by the development of Scientology and the societal reaction to it. Initial deviation by this movement led to hostile societal reaction which in turn led the movement to adopt strategies of defence towards and attack upon its detractors, construed by the press and agents of social control as confirmation for their initial diagnosis. A set of generalized beliefs and a stereotypic characterization of the movement were formulated and disseminated by the mass media and moral crusaders, leading to a panic reaction issuing in changes in the law.

It should be stressed, however, that amplification is not a deterministic process. The Scientology movement chose to adopt an increasingly hostile stance in part as a consequence of internal processes, a need to cope with the emergence of heresy, defection, and the threat of schism; and in part as a consequence of the character of the movement's leadership. Ron Hubbard, it would seem, has never tolerated opposition with equanimity.

De-escalation appears to have occurred as a result of the severity of governmental action, and a decline in the growth rate of committed membership. However, this de-escalation may be primarily a public-relations exercise, since despite a considerable drop in moral panic and the severity of societal reaction, the movement continues to react to criticism and commentary in a manner which suggests a persisting alienation from conventional norms of behaviour in this area.

NOTES AND REFERENCES

1 My thanks are due to Drs Bryan Wilson, Sheila Mitchell, David Downes, Russell Dobash, and Stan Cohen, and the Guardian's Office of the Church of Scientology for comments on a draft of this paper. I also wish to record my thanks to the Editor and Librarian of the *News of the World* and the General Manager of Reuter for permitting me to use their libraries. I am also grateful to the Social Science Research Council for a grant in support of my research.

2 For accounts of the beliefs and practices of Scientology see Cyril Vosper, *The Mind Benders*, Neville Spearman, London, 1971; Robert Kaufman, *Inside Scientology*, Olympia, London, 1972; and my forthcoming monograph, *The Road to Total Freedom: A Sociological Analysis of Scientology*.

3 Bryan R. Wilson, *Magic and the Millennium*, Heinemann, London, 1973, p. 21.

4 For a comparison of Christian Science and Scientology, see Roy Wallis, 'A comparative analysis of problems and processes of change in two manipulationist movements: Christian Science and Scientology', in *The Contemporary Metamorphosis of Religion?*, Acts of the 12th International Conference on the Sociology of Religion, The Hague, Netherlands, August 1973. On the Jehovah's Witnesses, see Alan T. Rogerson, *A Sociological Analysis of the Origins and Development of the Jehovah's Witnesses and their Schismatic Groups*, unpublished D.Phil. thesis, Oxford, 1972. On Soka Gakkai, see John Wilson, *Soka Gakkai and Mass Society*, Stanford University Press, Stanford, California, 1970.

5 *The People*, 19 March, 1967.

6 Kevin V. Anderson, *Report of the Board of Inquiry into Scientology*, Government Printer, Melbourne, Australia, 1965, p. 1.

7 Stanley Cohen, *Folk Devils and Moral Panics*, MacGibbon & Kee, London, 1972, p. 9.

8 Neil Smelser, *Theory of Collective Behaviour*, Routledge & Kegan Paul, London, 1962.

9 Howard S. Becker, *Outsiders: Studies in the Sociology of Deviance*, Free Press, New York, 1963, p. 9.

10 Edwin M. Lemert, *Social Pathology*, McGraw-Hill, New York, 1951.

11 David Cooper, *Psychiatry and Anti-Psychiatry*, Paladin, London, 1970, p. 16.

12 Gresham Sykes and David Matza, 'Techniques of neutralisation', *American Journal of Sociology*, Vol. 22, December 1957, pp. 664–70; Miriam Siegler, Humphry Osmond and Harriet Mann, 'Laing's models of madness', *British Journal of Psychiatry*, Vol. 115, 1969, pp. 947–58.

13 Leslie T. Wilkins, *Social Deviance*, Tavistock, London, 1964, pp. 87–94, reprinted in W. G. Carson and Paul Wiles (eds.), *Crime and Delinquency in Britain*, Martin Robertson and Co, London, 1971, pp. 219–226.

14 Cohen, op. cit.

15 Jock Young, *The Drugtakers*, Paladin, London, 1971.

16 Cohen, op. cit., p. 202.

17 Anonymous, 'Attacks on Scientology and "attack" policies—a wider perspective', photocopy of manuscript, n.d., made available to me by the Church of Scientology, my emphasis.

18 Anonymous, *'Scientology: The Now Religion*; false report correction', mimeo, n.d., made available by the Church of Scientology.

19 Howard Becker, op. cit., Chapter 8.

20 Joseph Gusfield, *Symbolic Crusade*, University of Illinois Press, Urbana, Illinois, 1963; and 'Social structure and moral reform: a study of the Woman's Christian Temperance Union', *American Journal of Sociology*, Vol. 61, 1955, pp. 221–232.

21 Donald T. Dickson, 'Bureaucracy and morality: an organisational perspective on a moral crusade', *Social Problems*, Vol. 16, 1968, pp. 143–156.

22 Cohen, op. cit., p. 45.

23 'Poor man's psychoanalysis', *Newsweek*, 16 October, 1950, pp. 58–59, quoting Dr Morris Fishbein.

24 Martin Gumpert, 'The Dianetics craze', *New Republic*, Vol. 132, 14 August, 1950, p. 21.

25 Roy Wallis, *The Road to Total Freedom*, op. cit.

26 Food and Drug Administration, *Personal Communication*, 21 January, 1972.

27 On 'security checking' see Paulette Cooper, *The Scandal of Scientology*, Tower Publications, New York, 1971, Chapter 11.

28 *Daily Mail*, 29 November, 1960.

29 *Daily Mail*, 28 November, 1960; Cooper, op. cit., p. 102.

30 George Malko, *Scientology: The Now Religion*, Dell Publishing, New York, 1970, p. 75.

31 Evidence before the Senate Subcommittee on Administrative Practice and Procedure, reprinted in Church of Scientology, *The Findings on the US Food and Drug Agency*, Department of Publications World Wide, Church of Scientology, East Grinstead, 1968, p. 32.

32 Senator Edward Long, *Congressional Record*, 8 September, 1965. This description of the events was congenial to the Scientologists, who reprint it in Church of Scientology, *The Findings . . .*, op. cit., p. 27.

33 L. Ron Hubbard, *H[ubbard] C[ommunications] O[ffice] Policy Letter*, 14 August, AD [After Dianetics] 13 [1963] 'Scientology press policies', cited in Anderson, op. cit., pp. 200–201.

34 Cited in Malko, op. cit., p. 76.

35 Church of Scientology, *The Findings* . . ., op. cit., p. 3.

36 L. Ron Hubbard, *HCO Bulletin*, 15 June, 1960, cited in Anderson, op. cit., p. 132.

37 Ibid., p. 106.

38 L. Ron Hubbard, *HCO Bulletin*, 24 July, 1960, cited in Ibid., p. 131. I have so far been unable to trace any 'attack' by the BMA at that time.

39 Ibid., p. 1.

40 Ibid., p. 1.

41 Ibid., p. 2.

42 Ibid., p. 2.

43 Ibid., p. 2.

44 Terence McMullen, 'Statutory Declaration', manuscript originally delivered to a Joint Meeting of the Sydney University Psychological Society and the Libertarian Society in 1968—copy made available to me by Dr McMullen, but reprinted in *Whatever Happened to Adelaide?—A Report on the Select Committee on the Scientology (Prohibition) Act*, no publisher stated (The Church of Scientology), 1973, p. 50.

45 L. Ron Hubbard, *HCO Policy Letter*, 21 July, 1968, 'Penalties for lower conditions', cited in Sir John Foster, *Enquiry into the Practice and Effects of Scientology*, HMSO, London, 1971, p. 128.

46 Ibid., p. 129.

47 *Report of the Commission of Enquiry into Scientology for 1972*, Government Printer, Pretoria, South Africa, p. 131.

48 I have interviewed individuals who, on being declared in a Condition of Enemy, received over 200 'disconnecting' letters. Many were from people of whom they had never heard.

49 *News of the World*, 10 October, 1965; *The Sun*, 6 October, 1965; *Daily Mail*, 22 December, 1965; *The Times*, 6 October, 1965.

50 *News of the World*, 16 January, 1966.

51 *Parliamentary Debates (Hansard): House of Commons*, Vol. 724, 7 February, 1966.

52 Sir John Foster, op. cit., pp. 140–145.

53 Ibid., pp. 140–149; L. Ron Hubbard, *HCO Policy Letter*, 25 February, 1966.

54 *The People*, March 20, 1966.

55 *Daily Mail*, February 14, 1966.

56 *Daily Mail*, August 23, 1966.

57 *Parliamentary Debates (Hansard): House of Commons*, Vol. 742, 6 March, 1967.

58 Ibid.

59 Ibid.

60 *News of the World*, November 19, 1967.

61 *The Auditor*, 32, 1968, p. 2.

62 C. H. Rolph, *Believe What You Like*, Andre Deutsch, London, 1973, pp. 66–67; *The Times*, July 19, 1968.

63 *Daily Telegraph*, August 11, 1969.

64 *Parliamentary Debates (Hansard): House of Commons*, Vol. 769, 25 July, 1968.

65 Ibid., Vol. 820, 29 June, 1971.

66 Scientology Act, 1968—Western Australia; Scientology (Prohibition) Act 1968—South Australia.

67 *Report of the Commission of Inquiry into the Hubbard Scientology Organisation in New Zealand*, Government Printer, Wellington, New Zealand, 1969, p. 8.

68 *Report of the Commission into Scientology for 1972*, op. cit., p. 119.

69 Ibid., p. 153.

70 Sir John Foster, op. cit., p. v.

71 *Report . . . for 1972*, op. cit., p. 2–3.

72 C. H. Rolph, 'Why pick on Scientology?' *New Statesman*, 23 August, 1968, p. 220; Quintin Hogg, 'Political parley', *Punch*, August 14, 1968, pp. 230–231.

73 *Parliamentary Reports . . .*, Vol. 776, 26 January, 1969.

74 *Report . . . in New Zealand*, op. cit., p. 58.

75 Sir John Foster, op. cit., p. 128.

76 Malko, op. cit., pp. 76–77; *Psychiatric News*, March 1969.

77 *Washington Post*, July 31, 1971; *Denver Post*, August 14, 1971.

78 Sir John Foster, op. cit., p. 181.

79 *Report . . . for 1972*, op. cit., p. 232.

80 Ibid., p. 232.

81 *Commonwealth Gazette*, 15 February, 1973, p. 20.

82 Young, op. cit., p. 103.

83 On spiritualism, see Geoffrey K. Nelson, *Spiritualism and Society*, Routledge & Kegan Paul, London, 1969.

84 For descriptions of the theory and practice of Scientology, see Vosper, op. cit.; Kaufman, op. cit.; Anderson, op. cit.

85 Harold L. Wilensky, 'The professionalization of everyone?', *American Journal of Sociology*, Vol. 70, 1964, pp. 137–158, reprinted in Oscar Grusky and George A. Miller (eds), *The Sociology of Organisations*, Free Press, New York, 1970, p. 489.

86 Talcott Parsons, 'The American family: its relations to personality and the social structure', in T. Parsons and R. F. Bales, *Family Socialisation and Interaction Process*, Free Press, Glencoe, 1956, pp. 3–21.

87 Mary Douglas, *Purity and Danger*, Routledge & Kegan Paul, London, 1966.

88 This anxiety seems evident, e.g. from the almost audible sigh of relief uttered by the American Psychiatric Association when Scientology was legally

declared a religion in a federal court, and they could henceforth regard it as beyond their domain. *Psychiatric News*, Vol. 4, No. 3, March 1969, p. 2.

89 Founding Church of Scientology *v.* USA in US Court of Claims, Washington D.C., 1967, 'Brief for the United States'.

90 Anderson, op. cit., p. 38.

91 Sir John Foster, op. cit., p. 36.

92 Anderson, op. cit., p. 48.

93 Ibid., p. 59.

94 Ibid., p. 48.

95 Ibid., p. 12.

96 Ibid., p. 52.

97 Ibid., p. 51.

98 Ibid., p. 52.

99 One of the most persistent complaints against Scientology during this period was that it broke up families. I find little evidence to support this complaint.

100 This is the tenor of Church of Scientology, *The Findings* . . ., op. cit., e.g.

101 Lemert, op. cit., pp. 55–56.

102 Anderson, op. cit., p. 136.

103 Ibid., p. 1, my emphasis.

104 Ibid., p. 108, my emphasis.

105 Ibid., p. 135.

106 This is suggested in Christopher Evans, *Cults of Unreason*, Harrap, London, 1973, p. 85; *Daily Mail*, 14 July, 1966.

107 John A. Lee, *Sectarian Healers and Hypnotherapy: A Study for the Committee on the Healing Arts*, Queen's Printer, Toronto, Ontario, 1970.

108 Jock Young, 'The role of the police as amplifiers of deviance, negotiators of reality and translators of fantasy, [etc]', in Stanley Cohen (ed.), *Images of Deviance*, Penguin Books, Harmondsworth, 1971, p. 33.

109 Anonymous, 'Scientology ethics policies and handling of attacks on Scientology', photocopy of manuscript, n.d., p. 16, made available by the Church of Scientology.

110 Roy Wallis, 'Religious sects and the fear of publicity', *New Society*, 24, 557, 7 June, 1973; *The Observer*, 29 July, 1973; *Report* . . . *for 1972*, op. cit., p. 122.

111 AMA plot: L. Ron Hubbard, *Scientology: Clear Procedure*, Hubbard Communications Office, London, 1957, 'Introduction'; Communist plot: 'Charles Strickley', *A Synthesis of the Russian Textbook on Psycho-Politics*, referred to in Anderson, op. cit.

112 *Daily Mail*, December 8, 1965; *News of the World*, May 3, 1970.

113 *Sunday Telegraph*, July 17, 1966.

114 L. Ron Hubbard, 'Amprinistics', *HCO Executive Letter*, 27 September, 1965.

115 These figures were calculated from lists of clears published in *The Auditor*.

116 *Freedom*, 37, March 1972, p. 2.

117 This offer is made in most Scientology publications.

118 In an interview.

119 *HCO Policy Letter*, 7 March, 1969, as cited in 'Scientology ethics policies . . .', op. cit., p. 25.

120 Hubbard incorporated a Church of American Science in New Jersey in 1953.

121 *Freedom*, various issues.

122 Vosper, op. cit.; Malko, op. cit.; Cooper, op. cit.; Kaufman, op. cit.

123 E.g. a move by the Scientologists to commit Vosper and a newspaper editor to jail was described by a High Court judge as a deliberate attempt 'to try to stifle any criticism or inquiry into their affairs', *Daily Telegraph*, 4 March, 1972. See also the references cited in note 110.

John Mckelvie Whitworth

7 *Communitarian Groups and the World*

My argument in this paper is that, despite the much bruited flowering of communal and communitarian groups in North America (and to a lesser extent in Europe) in the six or seven years after 1965—a movement which is now rapidly waning, but which was ecstatically hailed by many writers as 'the dawning of a new age' and as signifying the 're-tribalization of youth'—the life-chances of communitarian groups in western industrial societies are extremely slim. By the life-chances of communitarian groups I imply the chances of the members of such groups successfully main-taining and promulgating the particular form of intentional com-munity or alternative society which they believe is institutionally and morally superior to western capitalistic society.

This is a broad thesis, and some qualifications are necessary. First, in view of the fact that in some quarters such an argument might appear to be over-pessimistic and reactionary, it is worth pointing out that to discuss the difficulties attendant upon the construction of alternative societies does not necessarily imply total satisfaction with the dominant social arrangements and styles of life.

Second, and more substantively, I intend to restrict the primary focus of my discussion to communitarian groups; that is, to those groups which regard economic communism as, if not the funda-ment, then at least an intrinsic part of the ideal social structure. However, I feel that those very aspects of modern industrial societies which militate most strongly against the survival of communitarian groups are also likely, perhaps even more likely, to prove to be significant threats to the survival of non-communitarian, communal groups.

Third, I do not intend to attempt to catalogue past or con-temporary communitarian movements to analyse the reasons for their specific successes or failures.[2] Rather I will concentrate my discussion on those general aspects of what, for want of a better term, may be called the 'social climate' of western industrial societies which I feel are likely to have an adverse effect on the maintenance and promulgation of communitarian groups.

These points and qualifications aside, I shall now outline the mode of argument of this paper. I intend to provide a preliminary typological distinction which serves to illustrate conceptually the two main types of communitarian groups whose members strive to establish radically divergent institutional forms in some considerable degree of isolation from the surrounding society. Subsequently, in order to provide some empirical historical illustration, I shall outline the history of one extraordinarily long-lived and complex communitarian group (the Shakers), and will pay particular attention to the range of external social factors which in the nineteenth century influenced, impeded and finally stultified the group's development. Finally, I will examine several conceptually distinguishable aspects of western industrial societies which I believe adversely affect the life-chances of contemporary communitarian groups.

Introversionist and Utopian Communitarian Groups

So far I have referred to communitarian groups in the broadest sense without mentioning the fact that the nature and implications of such groups' rejection of the external society may vary widely, and that the ideological justification of this rejection (if a coherent or articulated justification exists) may be cast in a religious or secular mould. In order to isolate what I feel are the two most thoroughgoing forms of communitarian rejection of the world, I will now refer to what is certainly the most far-reaching and inclusive conceptual formulation in regard to religious sects.

In two articles Wilson[3] described the sect as a religiously oriented institution which tends towards totalitarianism and is committed to maintaining a high degree of separation from other religious bodies and from the external society in general. From this broad characterization Wilson developed a typology of sects which he argued was at least potentially applicable to the analysis of both Christian and non-Christian sectarian groups, and which I feel is useful in distinguishing the orientation of some non-religious protest groups.

Wilson based his classification on the various types of mission and closely associated responses to the world exhibited by sectarian gnostic, conversionist, thaumaturgical, reformist, introversionist groups. He distinguished seven sub-types of sect—the adventist, and utopian types. Here I will discuss only the introversionist and utopian types, under which I feel most historical and contemporary religious or secular communitarian groups can be subsumed.[4]

The members of religious introversionist groups regard themselves as having a mission to cultivate and deepen their spirituality, and so seek to avoid contamination by the world. Typically such groups are little concerned with orthodox eschatology, but the Holy Spirit is believed to be manifested to the individual member in and through the gathered fellowship of the sectarians. In consequence, high value is placed on communalism, and the desire to escape the world may lead an introversionist group to intensify their isolation by embracing full communitarianism, usually in conjunction with a move to the geographic fringes of settled society. Recruitment in such sects is almost entirely internal, they are almost completely indifferent to social reform, to other religious groups and to persons in the world, all of whom are regarded with at most some measure of pity as being 'tainted with perdition' and hence to be avoided.[5]

The great majority of the communitarian ventures spawned in North America in the aftermath of the 'student revolts' and more general social and moral disaffection of the late 1960s were secular in orientation (at least initially) and overwhelmingly introversionist in their response to the world. To use their own phraseology, the predominantly youthful members of these groups sought to 'drop out' of what they perceived to be the materialistic, sterile, impersonal, life-destroying culture of their parents, and to 'drop in' to a purer, 'more meaningful' and often relatively untrammelled and rising subsistence farming, and sometimes engaging in small-scale unregulated social world. Typically such groups attempted to retreat from the wider society and to 'tune in to reality' by prac-craft manufacturing. Their members largely isolated themselves from any concerns save those of maintaining their communal lives and heightening the 'highs' which they variously derived (temporarily at least) from co-operation, fellowship, communion with nature, drugs, sexual freedom, their sense of moral superiority to the world outside, or any combination of these elements.

As regards the utopian sect, Wilson stated:

> Its response to the external society consists partly in withdrawing from it, and partly in wishing to re-make it in accordance with a better model. It is more radical than the reformist sect, potentially less violent than the adventist sect, and more concerned with social reconstruction than the conversionist sect.[6]

Wilson's characterization of the utopian sect was avowedly tenta-tive, and I should like to expand his description on the basis of my own research into three utopian sects.[7] In summary, the utopian sect is inspired by a detailed vision of human society transformed as a result of the abandonment of existing institutions and their replacement by those divinely revealed social arrangements which the sectarians believe can alone remove the corruption of the world.

Utopian sectarians believe themselves to be endowed with some measure of the power of the Holy Spirit, and they undertake the task of transforming the world in the expectation that their spiritual and physical endeavours will be rewarded and furthered by fresh outpourings of divine power, but they believe, or come to believe, that should they prove unworthy of God's confidence, His grace will be withdrawn from them. As builders working to God's blueprints, and as stewards of God's Kingdom on earth, they feel themselves to be subject, in a peculiarly intensive way, to divine scrutiny and injunctions. Every praiseworthy effort of the group and of the individual will be rewarded, every transgression punished, and the sectarians believe literally that the whole future of the world depends on their actions.

Although initially the sectarians' confidence in their capacity to effect the replacement of earthly institutions may be very great, the utopian vision is essentially gradualistic. The world is believed to be occupied by the forces of evil, and must be reclaimed piece by piece. To escape, and ultimately to put an end to the corruption of worldly society, the sectarians abandon the world to construct the embryo of the form of society which they believe is divinely ordained to spread throughout the earth. Once the nucleus of the ideal society is established, they regard themselves as divinely commissioned to proselytize, in the expectation that the superiority of their way of life will be readily apparent to all but the most depraved of men.

It is important to emphasize the distinction between the response to the world of the introversionist and the utopian sect. The introversionist sect is largely indifferent to the world and to the people in it. The members of utopian sects care passionately about the plight of persons suffering in the corrupt world and offer them a panacea—a world reconstructed according to the model revealed by God to His elect. Similarly, the secular utopian (Robert Owen and his American followers provide good examples) believes that men can be relieved of misery if only they are informed of, and will adopt, those 'rational' institutional forms which will effect changes in their behaviour and, ultimately, in their psychological dispositions.

Of the two, the utopian response is by far the most complex. Introversionists seek merely to retreat from the world; utopians retreat *pour mieux sauter*. They seek to institutionalize their social arrangements and then to announce their superiority to the world. The members of utopian groups believe that they have a dual mandate—to keep themselves as much as possible 'unspotted by the world' and to evangelize. In practice it is extremely hard for any group to maintain a position of what may be termed 'viable detachment' from the surrounding society, and even when such a position is temporarily achieved, repeated disconfirmation of the utopian hope of a rapid extension of the ideal form of society generally leads the sectarians to despair of overcoming the corruption of the world and (if the group does not immediately disintegrate) to adopt an increasingly introversionist position.

As indicated above, utopian groups retreat from the world to establish their ideal form of society in isolation from its corrupting influences, and it follows that, where social conditions militate against such a retreat and against the survival of introversionist groups, utopian groups are unlikely to survive even the teething stages of their development. I will return to this point below, but first will consider the history and development of the Shakers in order to illustrate how, even in the backwoods and frontier areas of nineteenth-century America, the external society impinged on this communitarian group, and was in part responsible for the decline of the Shakers' utopianism and their eventual recognition of the possibility of their group's complete extinction.

The Shakers and the World

The Shakers originated in England when, in 1747, led by Jane Wardley, the wife of a Lancashire weaver, some thirty persons broke away from the Society of Friends. The Wardley group, whose ecstatic manner of worship led them to be nicknamed 'Shaking Quakers' or 'Shakers', announced the imminence of the apocalyptic overthrow of worldly society, and proclaimed the continuing nature of divine revelation, which was believed to be manifested in prophecies which were usually accompanied by drastic physical seizures.

In 1758 the group was joined by Ann Lee, who had previously

worked in a variety of menial jobs, and who in 1762 married a blacksmith, Abraham Stanley. In four years Ann Lee bore her husband four children, all of whom died at birth or shortly after. As a result of these repeated tragedies, Ann Lee developed a horror of all sexual relationships and in 1772, whilst imprisoned for sabbath-breaking, she claimed to have had a vision of the original self-indulgent sexual act, which took place in the Garden of Eden, and which she believed resulted in the almost total corruption of mankind and its consequent estrangement from God.

After experiencing this vision, Ann Lee proclaimed herself to be divinely inspired to denounce sexual relationships as the source of all sin, and taught that only through celibacy could men hope to attain regeneration in this life and salvation in the next. Ann Lee quickly rose to prominence among the Shakers, and usurped the authority of Jane Wardley, who left the group.

Despite Ann Lee's ascendancy, the Shakers made few additional converts, and their public diatribes against carnality in general and the institution of marriage in particular engendered considerable ridicule and persecution. In 1773 Ann Lee reported receiving revelations urging the group to migrate to the American colonies, and prophesied that they would make large numbers of converts there. In consequence, in May of 1774, Ann Lee, her husband and seven other followers sailed for New York.

Ann Lee's husband deserted her shortly after the group arrived in America, and after some time the sectarians settled on a tract of land at Niskeyuna, close to Albany in New York State. For two years they engaged in subsistence farming and practised informal communism, until in 1780 a number of converts were drawn from among the persons who had been 'excited' by a religious revival at New Lebanon, a town in the vicinity of Niskeyuna. Fired by evangelical enthusiasm, Ann Lee and two of her original followers travelled throughout New York and New England and in the course of two years made perhaps a thousand scattered converts, but, weakened by persecution and her evangelical labours, Ann Lee died in September 1784.

The early English and American Shakers were united by their admiration for Ann Lee (whom they believed to be the female counterpart of Christ, the person entrusted with the revelations which were to usher in the final dispensation of human history into an informal, charismatic, largely unstructured fellowship. They believed that celibacy offered the only road to salvation; in the continuance of divine revelation as manifested in ecstatic prophecy;

and violently condemned the world's toleration of sexual relations, within marriage or without.

In the last fifteen years of the eighteenth century and the first quarter of the nineteenth, under the successive leaders of the sect, James Whittaker, Joseph Meacham and Lucy Wright (the latter two being American-born converts), Ann Lee's charismatic legacy was routinized, and full communitarianism was established as the fundamental organizational principle of the Shaker Church. Celibate communitarianism was eventually justified and sanctified by historical exegesis and an elaborate theology.

Joseph Meacham, who had been hailed by Ann Lee as her 'first-born son in America', was primarily responsible for the codification and rationalization of Ann Lee's diverse prophecies and strictures, and in 1788 he commenced the 'gathering' of the sect, organizing the scattered sectarians into eleven communities, whose affairs were regulated by an hierarchical, sexually dualistic authority structure presided over by the self-recruiting Central Ministry at New Lebanon.

Persons wishing to join the sect were required to subscribe to a membership covenant in which they acknowledged that the Shaker Church was the only true dwelling place of the Spirit of God on earth. On entering the Junior Order of their society, converts were required to dedicate their labour to the group without any expectation of recompense should they decide to leave. Converts were expected to struggle to progress through the hierarchy of the sect, and eventually, if judged to be sufficiently developed in their moral and spiritual qualities, became members of the full, Church Order of their society, on entry to which they formally and irrevocably donated any property which they might possess to the sect.

Within the individual societies the members lived in celibate 'families' composed of both males and females, but all relations between the sexes were subject to extreme regulation and scrutiny. Indeed, virtually every aspect of the lives of the individual Shakers was hedged about by incredibly detailed rules which were believed to be of divine provenance, and which were designed to foster the qualities required of the regenerate man—celibacy, humility, selflessness and subordination.

Meacham insisted that the Shaker communities were the nuclei of God's Kingdom on earth, and that they were designed to replace all existing forms of human society. Their expansion was however declared to be dependent upon the spirituality and sustained evangelical efforts of the sectarians. The Shakers were to establish and

E

maintain their societies as standing examples of the perfection of the regenerate life, and were to labour to intensify their spirituality in order to merit that measure of power of the Holy Spirit which would enable them to overthrow the corruption of the world.

In 1797, after the gathering of the first societies was completed, the Shaker testimony was 're-opened to the World', and in the wake of the Great Kentucky Revival of 1799–1805, several new societies were established in the then frontier territories of Kentucky and Ohio. By 1812 the group had a total of some three thousand members, by 1825 upwards of four thousand and a peak of somewhat less than six thousand members was reached in the decade 1840–50.

Being celibate, the Shakers were of course entirely dependent on external recruitment to maintain and expand their societies, and although the total membership continued to increase until about 1850, few mass conversions were made after the first decade of the nineteenth century, when the south-western societies were established.[8] In the decade 1837–1847, the leaders of the sect conducted a prolonged internal 'revival' in the course of which numerous spiritual communications were received by supposedly divinely inspired 'instruments' or mediums within the societies. These spiritual communications condemned the spread of behavioural laxity and spiritual apathy among the sectarians, and promised that, once the Shakers had purified themselves and re-dedicated themselves to the task of building the Kingdom of God on earth, huge numbers of converts would flock to the sect.

This prolonged period of purification (in the course of which evangelical activities were almost entirely suspended) certainly purged the sect of many disgruntled or lukewarm sectarians. However, when the Shakers 're-opened' their testimony in 1848, they made very few converts, and the zeal of the majority of the sectarians dwindled rapidly, while the leaders of the group, the Central Ministry at New Lebanon, increasingly concerned themselves with devotional matters and greatly relaxed the former vigilance of their control of the economic and spiritual affairs of the subordinate societies.

After a decade of stagnation, the American Civil War caused much disruption in the affairs of the south-western societies, and in the 1860s and '70s the stark facts of institutional and numerical decline became impossible for the sectarians to ignore. The Shakers became increasingly dependent upon hired labour to cultivate their estates, land was leased or sold outright to 'the world's persons', standards of craftsmanship and ascetic practices were eroded, and the numbers of the group fell from approximately five thousand in 1860, to two thousand four hundred in 1875.

In the decades after the Civil War, as the atrophy of the sect's culture and the failure of its evangelism became glaringly apparent, the Central Ministry remained aloof and apathetic, but two divergent schools of thought—the 'progressives' and the 'conservatives'—emerged among the small, articulate and highly literate minority of Shakers who sought to revitalize the sect.

The progressive sectarians argued that, as the most spiritually enlightened group on earth, the Shakers should stand in the vanguard of reform, and should offer their wisdom and allegiance to all those worldly groups which sought to alleviate not only the spiritual and moral, but also the material, condition of mankind. The conservative Shakers scorned the progressives and insisted that the failure of Shaker evangelism was due to the insidious worldly influences which had permeated the sect, and so had sapped it of its spiritual power. The conservatives insisted that, rather than seeking the sympathy and recognition of the world, the Shakers should purify themselves behind the bulwarks of their societies, and should rely on God and the example of their ascetic renunciation of the world to preserve, and possibly eventually to expand, the Shaker Church.

The literary arguments and personal antagonisms between the leaders of the two factions were bitter, but neither side succeeded in checking the decline of the sect. On the one hand, the progressive Shakers failed to influence or attract the members of reform-oriented movements. On the other, the conservatives failed to influence the majority of the ageing sectarians who in the last decades of the nineteenth century appear to have adopted a position which may be termed 'apathetic introversionism', and who eschewed earlier ascetic practices, and sought comfort for the disappointment of their utopian hopes in their private devotions and the mundane satisfactions of their ordered, tranquil and economically secure lives.

With the deaths of the leading figures of the progressive and conservative groups in the early 1890s, the Shakers appear to have resigned themselves to the non-fulfilment of their earlier hopes of transforming the world into the celibate Kingdom of God, and to the possibility of the complete extinction of their group. By 1910 there were approximately a thousand persons left in the sect and many societies had been closed. A few converts were made in the twentieth century, but they appear to have acted primarily as housekeepers or companions to the venerable sectarians, and today, while the world's people avidly seek to acquire Shaker artifacts and preserve Shaker buildings, only a handful of the sectarians remain alive.

The above history of the Shaker sect is an extremely simplified and necessary backdrop for consideration of the variety of external factors which influenced the development of the group, and which may be divided, in conceptual terms at least, into geographic, political and broader socio-cultural factors.

The systematization and elaboration of the doctrines of the sect occurred concomitantly with the intensive evangelism in which the Shakers engaged for some years after the New Lebanon revival and in the first decades of the nineteenth century. Initially at least, the violence of the Shaker missionaries' denunciations of worldly institutions and their success in winning converts from the orthodox denominations aroused much hostility and violent persecution. The missionaries were frequently mobbed, and the sectarians generally were variously accused of heresy, secret carnality and attempting to break up families in order to gain converts and land. Far from dampening the Shakers' ardour, persecution appears to have invigorated them, and to have convinced them of the 'overcoming power' of their testimony against lust, pride and selfishness.

The persecution suffered by the sectarians was generally short-lived, and over time the Shakers won the respect of the majority of their neighbours for their diligence, honesty in business matters and their religious sincerity, but the tolerance eventually shown to the sectarians by the world's people brought problems in its train.

As indicated above, the utopian sect attempts to establish itself in a position of 'viable detachment' from the surrounding society, and seeks to maintain its ideological distinctiveness and internal purity while actively seeking converts. In the case of the Shakers, by the end of the period of internal revival in 1847, the areas around both the north-eastern and the south-western Shaker colonies had lost many of their earlier backwoods or frontier characteristics, and maintained a relatively settled population. Familiarity with the doctrines and life-styles of the Shakers bred among their neighbours not contempt, but tolerance or indifference, and the sectarians were regarded at worst as harmless eccentrics, who performed a useful service by offering refuge and solace to distressed individuals.

In the decades after the Civil War, the few converts who joined the sect were predominantly mature or elderly women, many of whom appear to have been motivated as much by a desire for tranquillity and economic security as by religious conviction. Such persons entered the sect not as did the majority of the earlier converts in an atmosphere of revivalistic excitement, but more soberly and deliberately, after having gained some knowledge of the advantages and disadvantages of life in the Shaker societies.

The original group of Shakers who settled at Niskeyuna enjoyed almost complete isolation from their neighbours and freedom from the demands of government, but with the rapid expansion of the sect in the forty years after 1780, the Shakers were forced to come to terms with the demands of the state in regard to such matters as the formal contractual basis of their communities, taxes and military service.

In 1795, as a result of legal actions brought by apostates, the group's original oral membership covenant was put into writing and signed by all converts, and this written covenant was subsequently modified five times, each time being strengthened in the light of prior legal proceedings and also brought into accordance with worldly notions of justice and equity. The Shakers did not vote, and at least until the Civil War they held themselves aloof from political discussions and controversies, but they compromised their separatist principles to the extent of paying whatever taxes were demanded of them. In addition, until their pacifism was legislatively recognized, they also paid militia levies and sums in lieu of the military service of their members. By 1833 these successive compromises with 'the world of damnation' had been theologically rationalized, and the sectarians' position was summarized in one of their hymns:

> I've listed for Christ, I have taken the oath,
> If Caesar should call me, I cannot serve both.
> I'll follow my captain, his call is divine,
> If Caesar should sue me, I'll pay him his fine.[9]

The Shakers' enforced accommodation to the demands of the external society and the decline in the novelty of their doctrines and way of life indubitably contributed to the failure of their evangelism after the internal revival, but a more important contributing factor was the change in the religious and broader intellectual climate of the United States which occurred in the middle decades of the nineteenth century.

In the 1820s, in the main theatres of Shaker evangelical activity, decades of intensive religious revivalism had generated an intellectual mood which writers of the time termed 'ultraism'. This term denoted a state of mind in which every manifestation of religious fervour or of moral concern was interpreted as the work of the Holy Spirit, and as presaging the imminent and total collapse of sin before the power of God.

The general depression of the American economy in the period 1837–1844 caused the concerned middle classes of the cities of the eastern seaboard to withdraw their financial support from the many itinerant backwoods preachers who had fostered the revivalism which was virtually endemic in remote rural and frontier areas, but even before the onset of the depression, many persons had begun to despair of curing social evils through mere exhortation and invocation of the power of the Holy Spirit. With the recovery of the American economy the rural areas of New York and New England became more prosperous, fewer religious revivals occurred, and the middle classes increasingly turned their attention to practical attempts to abolish such specific evils as prostitution, slavery and intemperance and to tackle the new, or newly realized, problems arising from the influx of immigrants to the urban slums.

In consequence, when in 1847 the Shakers emerged from their period of purificatory retreat, their hopes of rapid expansion were brutally disappointed. The impact of evangelical failure was severe, and the majority of the sectarians simply 'abandoned the world' to its own sinful devices, and concerned themselves with devotional matters and with the practical affairs of their societies.

After the Civil War, the progressive Shakers attempted to latch on to the dominant conception that the United States stood in the vanguard of evolution and progress, and proclaimed themselves to be the persons best qualified to guide worldly reformers and the march to human redemption, but they made no specific, detailed, practical proposals for bringing about the reforms they desired. The radical perfectionism which characterized American society after the Civil War was intensely pragmatic and activist. God was certainly held to be on the side of America, and American institutions were frequently said to be inspired by the Holy Spirit, but the extension of these institutions and the removal of social evils was recognized to be dependent on the deliberate, cumulative and calculated actions of men. In such an intellectual climate, the claims of the progressive Shakers—members of a declining, celibate and rural sect who spoke in the tones of the earlier and now totally discredited apocalytic ultraism—were dismissed as irrelevant or totally ignored.

By the end of the nineteenth century, the Shakers had come to share the fate of the many introversionist communitarian groups which had sought to preserve 'island societies' in what had once been isolated frontier areas. They were regarded by the world as quaint and archaic survivals in the midst of an increasingly urban, materialistic and individualistic society. The Shakers themselves took their decline philosophically and proclaimed that the sect (whose early members had condemned social reforms as merely serving to shore up a corrupt society) had been a 'centre of good influences' and had provided a demonstration of the viability of economic communism and of the joys of human fellowship.

Communitarian Groups in the Modern World

The preceding discussion of the history of the Shaker sect and of some of the external factors which contributed to its decline is intended to provide a comparative basis for consideration of those aspects of western industrial societies which I feel militate most strongly against the persistence and expansion of contemporary communitarian groups. I shall consider these geographic, political and wider socio-cultural factors separately, but must emphasize that the employment of such conceptual distinctions does rough justice to reality, and that any attempt to establish a radically divergent alternative society is likely to be beset by a host of complexly interlocking problems.

As has already been indicated, the vast majority of contemporary communitarian groups have adopted a retreatist position *vis-à-vis* western industrial society. To the best of my knowledge no truly utopian group—one committed to the concrete task of transforming the whole world into an ideal form of society—has emerged in recent years, presumably because the same factors which inhibit the development of contemporary introversionist groups also inhibit the initial retreatist phase of utopian colony building.[10] The members of contemporary introversionist groups regard western industrial societies as inherently corrupt (most are secular in orientation and see this corruption as being caused by the very nature of capitalist society, rather than as symptomatic of man's estrangement from God), and as destructive of man's 'true' potential for fellowship and self-realization. The members of such groups seek to live in a high degree of independence from the materialistic world and to shun the contamination of the cash nexus; but today independence from the influence and claims of the dominant culture is increasingly hard to achieve.

Nineteenth-century American communitarian groups were able to take advantage of free or cheap, but nevertheless fertile land on which to establish themselves (often for some decades) in a high degree of isolation and independence from the wider society of which they were formally a part, but with the advance and eventual 'closure' of the frontier, even they found themselves encapsulated by, and subject to the corrosive influences of, the society which they despised and sought to renounce.

The brute fact facing contemporary introversionist groups is that many, but not all, of the avenues of geographic escape have been sealed. Large areas of easily cultivated and fruitful land are almost completely unavailable, and as a result the majority of recently founded agriculturally based North American communes have been established on marginal land in such states as New Mexico and California and in Canada in the interior of British Columbia.[11] Locations like these certainly provide physical isolation, but the successful cultivation of marginal land requires agricultural skills of an order which few of the youthful communards (who are predominantly drawn from urban bourgeois backgrounds) possess, and sustained physical efforts of a kind which they often seem reluctant to exert. Typically, agricultural communes attract considerable numbers of summer residents, but the onset of winter usually drives all but the most hardy or committed back to the materialistic snares of central heating and supermarket shopping.

In this connection some mention should be made of the existence of large numbers of urban communes whose members have frequently 'been through the farming trip' but whose verbal denunciations of capitalistic industrial society are often just as vehement as those of the rural communitarians. Many urban communes possess resounding and inspiring names, but consist of only a handful of persons sharing a house and pooling their economic resources. In every case financial considerations, whether the members of the communes are rentiers living on their incomes, wage-earners, manufacturers of craft objects or recipients of welfare payments, put the urban communards in a position which is hardly convincingly independent of the cash nexus.

Since the nineteenth century the scope and complexity of the bureaucratic apparatus of the state and the demands it makes on, and the provisions it makes for, its citizens have increased enormously, but even in the nineteenth century communitarian groups were forced to comply with certain basic governmental requirements. In the case of the Shakers, by the end of the first quarter of the nineteenth century the compromises which the group had made with the demands of government (as manifested at the local and the national level) and the conflicting pressures of theological conviction and expediency had led the sectarians into a highly ambivalent position. Thus in many of their hymns and chants they proclaimed their loyalty and gratitude to the American nation for its tolerance of their unorthodox creed, while condemning the moral condition of the American people and the basic institution of marriage.

The majority of contemporary communitarians indulge in blanket condemnations of the American state and of its most cherished institutions (often as vehemently but less articulately than did the Shakers), but the demands of that state remain inexorable. As a result, any communitarian group which attracts a relatively large number of converts is likely to have to reconcile itself to a number of governmental impositions and to be subject to scrutiny by the police and other official agencies. Thus conscription for the Vietnamese War led many American communards to emigrate to Canada, where those who had entered the country illegally often led furtive and harassed existences.

The fiscal demands of the modern state have little impact on those communitarians who eke a living from subsistence agriculture, but the members of those groups whose ideology (or simple reaction against middle-class norms) prompts them to consume illegal drugs or to neglect the formal education of their children, render themselves subject to bureaucratic admonition or legal proceedings. In such circumstances it must be extraordinarily hard for the persons concerned to retain their conviction that they have broken free from the constraints of the 'straight' world and established a genuinely alternative society.

Of course, for some time at least, many small communitarian groups may escape the attention of the various official agencies of the bureaucratic apparatus (and it must be remembered that probably more than 90 per cent of contemporary communes have a population of less than twenty persons), but I feel that the provisions which the modern state makes for its citizens also tend to inhibit lasting commitment to the arduous task of establishing an introversionist alternative society, let alone a utopian nucleus of a new world order.

Most of the persons converted to the Shaker faith in the early decades of the nineteenth century, who often suffered persecution, ridicule and total estrangement from their friends, appear to have been primarily motivated by sincere religious convictions, but it is possible that other considerations also overtly or subliminally influenced their decisions to join the sect. For example, the sexual dualism of the Shaker authority structure offered women from even the humblest backgrounds access to positions of sanctified power and prestige which scarcely existed in the external society. Sexually disappointed or impoverished persons could also find a degree of emotional and economic security in the Shaker societies which may have outweighed (even if only temporarily) those attractions of worldly society which in any case were largely beyond their reach.

In addition, the fact that on becoming full members of the sect individuals consigned their property irrevocably to the group, may have led many (particularly elderly) persons whose faith was dwindling to keep up at least the outward appearances of conviction, lest they be expelled into a world which offered them little but the prospect of loneliness and poverty.[12]

In contrast, in contemporary societies a host of reform oriented institutions or movements exist to exert pressure to remove perceived injustices or inequity, and basic welfare programmes have freed individuals from the harrowing realities of complete destitution or even starvation. As a result, the 'costs' and risks of 'dropping out' of communitarian ventures have been considerably reduced, and many individuals appear to have constructed a 'career' out of living in a variety of communes, most of which collapse or dissolve a few months after their establishment.

Finally, I should like to turn to consider briefly some extremely broad and inevitably overlapping aspects of the 'social climate' of western industrial societies (taking as above the United States as the paramount example), which I feel in the long term restrict the life chances of communitarian groups, even though they appear to have been responsible for the widespread flowering of such ventures in recent years. First, I intend to touch on the implications of the development (largely engendered by the mass media) of what I shall term a widespread but largely unarticulated sociological awareness, and second, will consider some characteristics of the counter-culture which developed primarily among college-educated youth in the late 1960s.

In comparison with the nineteenth century, contemporary

American society is remarkable for the number of options which are open to its inhabitants and for its tolerance of divergences from the theoretical norms of the middle- or aspirant middle-class mass of its population. Many contemporary Americans, especially the young, possess at least a rudimentary kind of sociological awareness in that they have some knowledge of the past and present diversity of human cultures and institutions; have some conception of the essential artificiality and the at least potential mutability of social arrangements; and realize that they have the capacity to exercise a large number of choices of companions, careers and life-styles. However, this very awareness of the somewhat arbitrary nature of many parts of the social structure and the range of choices available, in combination with the high degree of cultural estimation placed on individualism, renders it extremely hard for an individual to make one definite choice, one definite binding commitment, whether it be to a style of dress, a neighbourhood or a spouse.

In this sense, Durkheim's prediction that anomie could be expected to become 'the disease of modern life' has been fulfilled. The anonymity and impersonality of life in modern cities, the dilemmas of freedom intimated above and the pervasive feeling of many individuals that they are at the mercy of forces which they do not fully understand, have generated a widespread hunger for 'truly warm, meaningful relationships', and have led many young people to a form of romantic identification with various types of 'noble savage' figure or to reject the dominant society more radically by dropping out into the kind of alternative communities here discussed.

The problem is that the very persons who seek to establish alternative communities or communitarian groups are those who have suffered most from anomie and the associated dilemmas of choice, and who also frequently possess some knowledge (usually gleaned from the mass media or the 'underground press') of a range of communal or communitarian ventures. Theoretically such knowledge of the variety and vicissitudes of past and contemporary alternative societies may provide a feeling of continuity and, in a sense, of tradition, and so may be intellectually bracing, but in practice it is likely to have a dampening effect on enthusiasm and commitment.

To put the matter bluntly, I feel that it is harder for an individual to devote his life to establishing an alternative form of society which he recognizes is similar to many previous social experiments, than it is for him to devote his life (as did the early Shakers) to establishing what he believes to be the unique prototype of a new world order.

Quite frequently members of contemporary communitarian groups who have lost their initial (often quasi-mystical) enthusiasm, discuss their adherence to the particular group as being but one part of their 'growth experience', thereby implying that their commitment to the venture is temporary. The presence of many such restless and permanently dissatisfied individuals in the counter-culture from which today's communitarian groups largely derive their members, goes far towards explaining the fact that many groups have a turn-over rate of three-quarters of their population each year.

In terms of the present discussion, the salient characteristics of the members of the amorphous and evanescent counter-culture which developed in the 1960s were their glorification of geographical mobility and transitory social, spiritual and intellectual experiences; a measure of yearning for the supposed joys of the rural life; contempt for established authority or for authority of any kind; and their extremely high valuation of individualism and of quests for individual self-realization.

As Kanter has perceptively indicated,[18] the key to an understanding of much of the counter-culture lies in the word 'trip', which in ordinary language means a short, return journey. The members of the counter-culture might describe themselves as being on a drug trip, a sex trip, a celibacy trip or an organic food trip, but however deeply committed they might believe themselves to be to the particular trip which they were on, their phraseology implied that their commitment was temporary, and that they were likely to embark on another (and often almost completely contrasting) trip within a short period of time.

Such persons appear to have constituted the majority of the population of recently founded communitarian groups, and in conversation and in print they frequently extolled the joys of communitarian living—the 'commune' or 'tribal' trip. However, the commitment of the majority to communitarian ventures was ephemeral and, once the hardships of subsistence agriculture or the difficulties arising from communal living became intense, they readily declared communitarianism to be a 'bum trip', and often moved on enthusiastically to dip into other ventures or life-styles—to 'get into' revolutionary politics, eastern mysticism, craft manufacture or even in some cases to embrace 'the establishment trip'.

The counter-cultural contempt for authority and glorification of individualism as manifested in 'doing one's own thing' led to the establishment of hundreds of unregulated or avowedly anarchistic communes, most of which dissolved as soon as their members

realized that their individual paths to self-realization were conflicting or mutually exclusive.

Certainly, all long-lived communitarian groups have possessed a
unifying belief-system, but with extremely few exceptions that
system was a religious one. The Shakers and other religious communitarians did not regard themselves as entering into a social
contract with each other as consenting individuals, but rather
believed that they were collectively endowed with a mandate from
God to establish an ideal form of society on earth. In these cases
divine revelation and commission (usually coupled with the expectation of heavenly rewards) justified their sacrifices and physical
efforts, and the employment of severe mechanisms of social control
which were believed necessary to cultivate the qualities thought to
be appropriate for God's servants on earth.

The position of secular communitarians (who form the vast
majority of recently established groups) is different. In many cases
persons who had come to realize that total individual freedom and
a complete lack of regulations spelt disaster for communal living
perceived the need for a unifying ideology and an associated normative system and (sometimes quite literally) sat down to construct or
adopt one. In this sense the communards entered into a true social
contract with each other, but a contract without external or supernatural legitimation.

The problem arising from the adoption of such a contract is that
the persons who subject themselves to it also know themselves to be
its artificers. As a result, when an individual or group of individuals
feel themselves to be unduly restricted by the normative system and
associated sanctions which they have devised, there is little to stop
them attempting to change the terms of the contract to suit their
convenience. The life span of such groups is likely to be, and in
the case of recently formed communes has proved to be, extremely
short.

In conclusion, I feel that urbanization, the claims and provisions
of the modern bureaucratic state and aspects of the 'social climate'
of western industrial societies render the life-chances of introversionist communitarian groups, and even the 'birth-chances' of
utopian groups, extremely small. In sociology (as in virtually any
other discipline) to make unqualified sweeping statements is of
course simply to give hostages to fortune. A number of recently
founded introversionist groups (especially those few with a religious
orientation) may survive for several generations, and such long-
established groups as the Hutterites and Bruderhof are not likely

to wither away rapidly, although they are likely to become defensive ethnic enclaves, subject to much the same erosive pressures as are North American Indian reservations.

Those countries of the world which are dominated by totalitarian ideologies offer virtually no prospects for the emergence or survival of deviant groups committed to establishing alternative societies, but possibly introversionist and utopian communitarian groups may arise and flourish for a time in those areas of the Third World where tribal affiliations are breaking down, religious conceptions or styles of thought persist, and it is possible for dedicated groups to win a high measure of freedom from the claims of a tolerant, weak or indifferent state.

NOTES AND REFERENCES

1 See for example Ron E. Roberts, *The New Communes*, Prentice-Hall, New Jersey, 1971.

2 Rosabeth Moss Kanter, *Commitment and Community*, Harvard University Press, Cambridge, Massachusetts, 1972, provides a detailed analytical discussion of 'commitment building mechanisms' in a wide variety of past and contemporary communitarian groups.

3 B. R. Wilson, 'An analysis of sect development', *American Sociological Review*, Vol. 24, 1959, pp. 3–15, and 'Une typologie des sectes . . .', *Archives de Sociologie de Religion*, Vol. 16, 1963, pp. 49–63.

4 Of course it is possible that some of the 'individuals' of other types of sect may, temporarily at least, adopt communitarian forms. Thus the members of an adventist sect may separate themselves from the world to await its destruction, or gnostic sectarians may form themselves into an isolated and supposedly especially enlightened enclave. Nevertheless, adventist retreatism is usually short-lived, and gnostic communitarian groups (and others) are subject to the external erosive forces discussed below.

5 The Hutterites provide perhaps the best-known example of a contemporary introversionist sect.

6 Translated from Wilson, op. cit., 1963, p. 55.

7 See John Mckelvie Whitworth, *God's Blueprints*, Routledge & Kegan Paul, London, 1975.

8 The Shakers adopted a considerable number of children, but most of them left the sect on attaining maturity.

9 Philos Harmoniae, *A Selection of Hymns and Poems . . .*, published by the Shakers, Watervliet, Ohio, 1833, p. 31.

10 Some writers have dwelt on the idea of building up a kind of federation of communitarian groups linked by modern telecommunications, but no

practical steps appear to have been taken, and the idea remains in the realm of counter-cultural wishful thinking.

11 Few recent communitarians appear to have considered the possibility of emigrating to such sparsely populated countries as Paraguay (which provided a haven for the Bruderhof and some Menonite groups), perhaps because of their disapproval of the politics of the ruling groups of these countries.

12 The Shakers usually gave small sums as quittance money to persons who left the sect amicably, but stressed that these payments were given out of generosity rather than as a result of any legal obligation.

13 Kanter, op. cit., p. 167.

PART THREE

Sectarianism and Near-Sectarianism in the Secular Domain

Barry Sugarman

8 Reluctant Converts:

Social Control, Socialization and Adaptation in Therapeutic Communities

Introduction[1]

In this paper we shall present some material dealing with a type of intentional community or total institution that displays many similarities to those groups more commonly included in the sociology of sects. Our subject will be the so-called 'Concept Houses' or therapeutic community drug dependence treatment programmes, located mainly in the contemporary USA.[2]

The similarities to which we refer include : the total dedication to moral and spiritual improvement of members; the use of public confession and mutual criticism; the elimination of privacy; the hierarchy of authority based on moral and spiritual superiority; the procedures for mortification of deviants and for periodically generating states of ecstatic love and joy within the group.[3]

On the other hand, there are some significant differences. The usual symbols of supernatural entities and scripture are both absent, either in Christian or any other form. More important yet, the recruitment of members for Concept Houses takes place long before conversion. If the decision to enter a group is seen as resulting from a combination of pulls or attractions to the group and pushes or repulsions from one's prior situation[4] then the typical Concept House recruit compared to the typical new sect member is less attracted to the group *per se* and more repelled by his prior situation. The Concept House is also a rehabilitation community. This implies that the problems of social control and socialization in this kind of therapeutic community are far greater than in the average sect, although the basic function of each type of group for its established members and basic operating structures are remarkably similar.

Although the main source of recruitment for Concept Houses is among people with 'drug problems'[5] we must dispel immediately two common misconceptions. Firstly, the problems of physical addiction and withdrawal from drugs present no problem within the Concept House.[6] What does cause difficulties is the lack of prior commitment to the values of this group or preparation for this new style of life, and also certain 'dope-fiend personality traits' such as impulsivity.

Secondly, we must dispel any notion that medical procedures or personnel play any significant part in these groups. Indeed it is a central feature of Concept House doctrine that 'drug problems' are merely symptomatic of more basic personality problems and that the only reason for membership in a Concept House is to work on the basic problems themselves. The structure of the Concept House is alleged to facilitate this process of self-improvement. Individual responsibility is preached within a context of strong group pressures to follow certain avenues to self-improvement.

One large theoretical assumption is made here. Along with O. H. Mowrer,[7] we assume that mental health and morality are aspects of the same central concern, as are psychology and religion. The common concern is with human happiness and integrity, or people's search for satisfying ways to live. On the level of social organizations and movements, we see that Concept House therapeutic communities share this focal concern with many religious sects, as well as some political-ideological movements and educational movements.

We are dealing with social movements focused on defining and teaching new meaning systems and normative systems, including methods for coping with social situations and for handling emotional states. The movement under scrutiny in this paper requires full-time residence under stringent social controls for a period of one to two years. The ideal end product of this learning process is a person viewed by movement leaders as not only superior to the person who entered, but also superior in significant ways to the average member of society. The patterns of living embodied in the social structure of the Concept House are clearly differentiated from those of the secular society, as we shall see. Yet the fundamental values are related clearly to submerged ideal values of that society, as we shall also see.

In this paper we shall not attempt to translate our findings relating to therapeutic communities into the conceptual framework of the sociology of religion. Rather we shall present and interpret these findings in terms of general sociological and social psychological concerns, our perspective being that both specialities (the sociology of sects and the sociology of therapeutic communities) need to be related to general sociological theory as much as they need to be related to each other.

The term 'Concept House' designates a type of residential programme for the treatment of drug addicts, based on the model of Synanon, the California-based community founded in 1958 by Charles Dederich. Formerly an active member of Alcoholics Anonymous (AA), he adapted some of their basic principles while adding some important new ones.[8] Originally Synanon catered to hard-core drug addicts and aimed to return them eventually to the outside society. Now the Synanon resident population is well over a thousand and includes a large proportion of 'life-stylers', mainly middle-class people who have chosen to live in Synanon because they like the life-style.[9] Thus, it has changed its emphasis from rehabilitation in the direction of becoming a utopian community. Although a large but undocumented percentage of residents leave, the goal of Synanon leadership is now life-long residence.

Before this change of policy occurred the message that Synanon had apparently found a way to cure drug addicts reached a few professionals in this field and government funds were obtained for other programmes based on the Synanon model. Daytop Village was opened in 1963 and the Phoenix House programme in 1966. Both are located in New York State and both depended for their initial success on former Synanon residents serving as staff. Since then a third and fourth generation of Concept Houses has arisen, each founded and staffed by products of earlier houses. Today the number of Concept Houses is probably in the hundreds and covers most of the USA.[10] (These programmes are known generically as 'Concept Houses' and the term 'the Concept' designates the common philosophy and approaches of these communities.[11])

We shall take it as given that the Concept House has been quite effective in helping former addicts to modify substantially their life-style. Although research in this area leaves much to be desired, there is some clear evidence that programmes of this type not only modify a number of psychopathological traits during treatment but also reduce the incidence of arrest among drop-outs as well as graduates.[12]

Inside the Concept House: Social Control & Socialization

The Concept House is typically staffed by former addicts who have come up through the ranks of this programme themselves, with one man invariably as the head of a hierarchical structure. The group resembles a patriarchal family or a boarding school run by the prefects. There is a strong group spirit, definite discipline and many bonds of friendship and concern among members.

The Concept House is a species of therapeutic community (TC), which may be defined as a group of people who come together in order to bring about changes in themselves through a co-operative group process.[13] All forms of the TC strive to create among members a culture in which there is mutual help and trust, together with strong social pressures to conform to the official norms of the group. Concept Houses differ in certain ways from other species of TC. Most important is the fact that their staff rarely have professional credentials but they do have experiential authority—they have 'been through it' themselves. Also, the enforcement of rules is much stricter in the Concept House than in other TCs.

Unlike many other kinds of TC and many other kinds of drug rehabilitation programme, the Concept House demands complete abstinence from drugs immediately upon entry and from then on. The notion exists here that the drug addict can only change his pattern of life by making a *complete break*, giving up drug use, former associates, and all ties with his former life upon entering the Concept House. There he finds himself in a group composed entirely of others in a similar situation, though at different stages of progress—not addicts (or deviants) any more but ex-addicts and devotees of the Concept way of life. This emphasis on the complete break is also found in Alcoholics Anonymous (AA) and comes to the Concept Houses from AA via Synanon.

BASIC STRUCTURE

The Concept House operates as an organization separated by high social boundaries from the outside society. It partakes of many of the features of both the total institution[14] and the utopian community.[15] With more or less severity the new member is stripped of his possessions and former social identity, assigned the status of a low-ranking new member and indoctrinated into a set of teachings which involves the rejection of one's former ('negative') way of life and the upholding of a new set of 'positive' values. The effort to realize these new values and the reassessment of one's own identity is what all members are supposed to have in common, other differences between them being minimized in order to emphasize these common aims, their common humanity and basic similarities.

The 'treatment' offered in the Concept House cannot be specified in terms of a few techniques because it entails the attempt to socialize its members into a *total* new style of life. As explained by Concept House leaders, members have essentially failed in their emotional and moral development and the Concept House serves them as a substitute family for their second attempt at growing up. This family is an all-encompassing or total institution, admitting few areas of privacy and demanding high degrees of control over the conduct of its members. At the same time it offers the chance to enjoy warm concern and friendship from one's fellows there.

BOUNDARIES

The Concept House has a high boundary separating it from the outside society, a boundary that implies many restrictions on the behaviour of residents and stringent requirements for acceptance as a resident. Acceptance into the group requires overt assent to the question : 'Do you wish to change your former ways of behaviour and outlook?' It is not assumed that he is entirely sincere, but he must talk and act as if he were. Should he fail to conform to the rules of the group he may be expelled. Quite often members choose to leave rather than accept the consequences which fall to those who violate the basic rules of the group.

The most striking symbol of the boundary is perhaps the 'prospect chair'. This is where the prospect seeking admission is required to wait; where the resident who wishes to leave is expected to sit and think over his decision; and where a resident is placed when he is felt by staff to be making no effort and is under consideration to be expelled. A person sitting on the chair is poised at the boundary between the Concept House and the outside society, either on his way in or on his way out.

Within the boundary, a resident is subject to all the rules and restrictions of the house, not allowed to come and go at will, nor to have communication with people outside the house without permission.

'Splittees' are barred from access to the house and its residents. The most impenetrable boundary separates them from their erstwhile comrades. They are seen as having betrayed the group and those who tried to help them and as having threatened the motivation of others by their leaving. They are not allowed to visit the house—unless they are formally seeking reacceptance by sitting on the chair and then are usually subjected to a mortifying 'general meeting' of the whole house.

IDEOLOGY

New members are soon indoctrinated with the basic beliefs of the Concept. It is affirmed that addicts *can* change their way of life (and the presence of the older residents seems to prove it) but only given a great deal of mutual help. The help ones gives to a fellow member, it is said, benefits not only the recipient but also the donor; and even the newest novice is capable of giving some significant help to a fellow member.

In very forceful terms the prospect or the new resident is told that *he* is responsible for what he does and that he cannot blame it on unloving parents, negligent teachers, a corrupt society, or any of the usual culprits. These indictments may all be true but to focus on them gives him a 'cop out' or excuse not to try to change himself. The former addict in a Concept House is required and helped to redefine drastically himself and his situation.

The psychological theory of the Concept holds that the addict uses his drugs to withdraw from situations he finds difficult. This is his basic coping strategy, used in preference to confronting the situation realistically.

He does this because he feels inadequate about his abilities and himself. His behaviour reinforces and confirms his fears.[16] The problem is to get him out of his vicious cycle. Instead of the standard approaches to the addict, either punishing him for his addiction or pitying him for it and babying him (which again tend to reinforce the addict in his behaviour), the Concept House offers something different. It offers unambiguous feedback on his behaviour with insistent demands that he change it. It removes his habitual escapes : no drugs or alcohol (no 'chemical highs') are permitted and great efforts go into ensuring that no opportunity is given for smuggling contraband into the house or for using it undetected. The other 'cardinal rule' of all Concept Houses forbids any use of violence, which is also a common escape from reality-oriented problem-solving.

Drug addiction is held to be only the symptom rather than the real, underlying problem. What the person has to learn to change is his way of dealing with problem situations : specifically to learn to face them realistically rather than running away from them. A corollary of this position is that people who are not drug addicts but who run away from problems they should face up to and who have an inadequate self-image may benefit equally from a Concept House experience.

SOCIAL ORGANIZATION

The sharp dichotomy between staff and inmate norms, typically found in prisons, mental hospitals and reformatories, is not present in the Concept House. Through its policy of selection and rigorous social control it keeps those residents who are not prepared to conform away from positions of influence in the group and constantly pressures them to change or leave.

The day in a Concept House usually begins with a morning meeting for all residents, a ritual which serves several functions. One is to focus everyone's mind on their common goals. This is aided by the solemn reading of the house's philosophy, which is commonly the first event. Another function is to point out instances of bad conduct (often with a confession by the culprit) and to sermonize about the reasons why it is deemed important to avoid such behaviour. Announcements of an administrative nature are made and there is general participation in some humorous and light-hearted group activities before the meeting ends and everyone goes to their respective jobs within the house.

Work responsibilities are organized into departments (kitchen, service crew, etc.), each with its hierarchy of supervision. Everyone has a job within this structure except for some of the most advanced residents in the 're-entry' phase of treatment who have outside jobs or go to school on the outside. All the work necessary to the running of the house is done by residents—cooking, cleaning, repairs, building conversion. Only certain highly technical jobs are done by outsiders. None of this work is 'occupational therapy'; it is all clearly necessary to the comfort and well-being of the group and hence meaningful to those who do it.

Work is one aspect of treatment. A resident is taught that high standards of work performance are demanded, but that when he is distressed he can ask to be excused from work for a while in order to talk with an older resident. No two persons, including addicts, have the same personality problems but certain ones come up again and again : giving orders, taking orders, making 'pull-ups', discussing feelings, relating to members of the opposite sex, speaking in public, doing certain kinds of jobs. Concept House policy is to move people around to different jobs quite frequently so as to expose them to a great range of different situations. Of course, this creates some problems with continuity and re-training but there are methods for dealing with these problems in this non-bureaucratic structure.

Authority is attached mainly to a hierarchy of formal statuses based on the work structure : house directors, co-ordinators, heads of departments. A further authority structure attaches to seniority within the house. Thus newer residents are supposed to respect more senior ones and to comply with their requests or orders. Seniority does not constitute a totally ascriptive base of status, however, for residents are sometimes formally deprived of their right of seniority as a result of bad conduct.

On the interpersonal level feedback is recognized to have a paramount importance. In Concept jargon it is generally known as 'confrontation'. On a one-to-one level residents are supposed to 'confront' each other whenever one of them thinks that another is doing something wrong or is feeling 'messed up'. This one-to-one approach is frequently enough to put the matter right, especially when it comes from someone who is liked and trusted. It takes place between peers, between older and newer residents (mostly, but not exclusively, from older to newer), and between staff and residents. The term 'confrontation' does not indicate a style of interaction that is basically aggressive or hostile. Essentially it indicates conversation of a non-trivial kind, where each person 'puts it all up-front'.

This one-to-one interaction can be the basis for close friendship to develop. Residents are taught that they are expected to make efforts in this direction. 'Who have you started to get close to?' they will be asked. Typically, the kinds of people who find themselves in a Concept House have not previously been successful in making friendships based on mutual honesty and concern. Concept House norms emphasize the importance of 'being for real' as opposed to 'phony' or presenting oneself in ways that one thinks will impress the other person. These norms also emphasize the importance of *responsible* concern between friends. This requires a resident to confront his friend if he thinks the latter is acting foolishly; that is to tell him what he honestly thinks—even though the friend may not welcome that at first. It may also require the resident to inform staff or other senior residents about the conduct of another resident or about his suspicions. This 'honour code' is taken very seriously. Those who conform to it are publicly praised and anyone who complained about being exposed would have to do so in secret and would risk having that complaint reported. Someone making such a complaint would be told that he had revealed how much he had to learn before he could hope to be a responsible and 'together' person.

Confrontation and conversation throughout the day on an informal basis is a most important part of treatment. Encounter groups or confrontation groups are also an important medium of treatment. Two main functions are served by these groups; they provide for controlled release of hostility and verbal aggression and they are the setting for confrontation with intense social pressures for honesty and change.

The group sometimes begins with one person hurling a torrent of angry abuse at another member of the group. The latter may become angry and reply in kind. Someone comes in with the question, 'What actually happened?' Then the one who initiated the exchange is supposed to give a calm and objective statement of his complaint. Other members of the group act as cross-examiners and jury, probing to get at the truth and restraining any further outbursts of anger. The encounter group is also used for individuals to talk about 'what is happening with them', their difficulties and achievements, their goals and doubts. Group members provide advice, support, encouragement, and share experiences.

It is impossible to explain the dynamics of the group without taking account of the social setting in which it operates. First, the members are living under a great deal of strain and the encounter serves them as a safety valve for the feelings that arise.

Second, members of the group work and live together (unlike the members of a more typical therapy group), so that many of the stresses in each person's life arise directly out of his daily interaction with the other persons in his encounter group. These problems can be examined in concrete detail. In most situations there is someone in the group who has a fairly impartial viewpoint, since he sees how both parties act but is not involved in the current dispute.

The third point about the dynamics of the group concerns the motivation to participate. It is quite simple: all residents must attend and must actively participate. The more vigilant members of the group encourage, goad, or bully the silent ones into contributing.

SOCIAL CONTROL

The mechanisms through which social control is maintained in the Concept House are among its most impressive features. We must try to explain how this unusually high level of conformity is possible—conformity to an unusually stringent set of norms by persons formerly characterized by extremely uncontrolled behaviour. A large factor in the explanation will be the wide range of positive and negative sanctions which are used.

The word 'punishment' is carefully avoided and all negative sanctions are defined as 'learning experiences'. Usually, when a negative sanction is imposed on a resident, he is called before a number of senior members and peers to be told in no uncertain terms what he has been doing wrong (feedback). The 'learning experience' (sanction) he is given is carefully tailored to the nature of his problem, and its whole purpose (he is told) is to help him improve, not to punish.

One reward is promotion to more responsible jobs within the house. Conversely job demotion (which is not at all infrequent) is one of the more severe learning experiences. On entering the Concept House a resident gives up many rights that are taken for granted outside. These become 'privileges' that can be earned by good conduct.

Negative sanctions are easy to see and many can be catalogued. There are 'pull-ups' (e.g. 'Who left the lights on in the closet?'). For more serious offences a 'haircut' will be given in which the offender will have to listen to several of his peers and staff shout their displeasure with his conduct in very pungent terms. He is not allowed to respond, though later he may talk to them individually and he can take the matter to a confrontation group.

Among the other severe and infrequent learning experiences is the wearing of a cardboard sign around the neck that carries a pertinent message, such as 'I am a baby. I cannot control my feelings. Please help me,' or carrying around a symbol of one's dereliction, for example, a light-bulb for someone who persistently leaves lights on. All these sanctions have the additional function that they act as reminders to other residents to avoid the same mistakes.

These learning experiences are harsh but they are used only when more gentle methods have failed. Embarrassment in front of peers is the common feature of all 'learning experiences' and the slow-learning resident is made to feel foolish for what he has done. This is, in part, a system of aversive conditioning. Yet, as we shall see below, the dynamics of learning experiences in this context can go far beyond the conditioning model.

The resident will not be shunned after receiving a 'learning experience'. On the contrary individual residents will ask to talk about what he did to deserve it. The effect on the deviant himself seems to be strong but we should not forget about the effects on those who administer the haircut or other sanction. It is very hard for them, especially for the friends of the deviant. However, it helps them to reject that part of their former selves that they are criticizing in the deviant, and it makes it virtually impossible for them to commiserate with the recipient later about the 'unfairness' of the house.

The culture of the Concept House contrasts sharply with prevailing practices in outside society. There it is most common for deviants to be avoided and criticized behind their backs. This way they have no pointers to help them change the behaviour which is disapproved of and may be unaware of the offence they are giving. They are punished by avoidance and ostracism without having a fair chance to change the offending behaviour. In the Concept House 'bad rapping' someone behind his back is a serious offence. They must be confronted so that they have the benefit of clear feedback, which they need for both informational and motivational uses.

Concept Houses have been very successful in preventing the development of an inmate culture whereby residents connive to subvert staff objectives. Older residents generally put themselves out to 'pull in' the newcomers, to be friendly to them, acquaint them with the ways of the Concept, and to talk over problems. Residents are told to 'act as if' they are the kind of people they want to become and to 'act as if' they believe in the rules of the house. Clearly then, the level of conformity observed is well beyond the level of actual commitment and this creates an 'Asch effect' on residents[17]—the illusion that the rest of the group is unanimous, an illusion to which they themselves contribute *vis-à-vis* other residents.

Some social control mechanisms clearly function also as feedback mechanisms and as part of the treatment process, for example 'pull-ups', 'haircuts', and 'learning experiences'. All are formalized kinds of confrontation, which goes on all the time in informal ways. For the most part, these confrontation techniques are used in a setting where most residents feel that others care about them—

although these efforts sometimes fall short—and only this makes it possible for them to put up with the rigours of the regime we have described.

Adaptation to the Larger System

What we have described thus far is the Concept House seen as a therapeutic community. We have not yet looked at the relationship between the TC and the larger society—except to note the higher boundary that separates the two.

ECONOMIC FACTORS

Although Concept House residents are much more productive and self-sufficient than their counterparts in jail or hospital, substantial inputs of economic resources from outside are necessary. Staff salaries, rent, food and other supplies, telephones, medical expenses, upkeep of vehicles, etc., must all be paid for. The cost of keeping one person in a Concept House for one year is approximately $5,000. Neither the client nor his family is usually in a position to contribute significantly towards this. In any event Concept Houses do not usually request such payments. The main source of cash funds is the government.

The budget of even a small Concept House has to be around $100,000, and some are over $1 million per year. Bureaucratic structures for accounting, record-keeping and *control* of activities which incur costs have been grafted onto the TC structure already described. This is required by government funding agencies and, in a free enterprise system with several Concept Houses available for funding in many areas, they have reluctantly seen the necessity of compliance.

Personnel other than the indigenous clinical leadership mentioned above have of necessity been added. Records experts, proposal writers familiar with government agencies, and above all business managers who impose restraint on spending and require careful records, make their appearance. They alter the balance of power, the patterns of decision making, and create strains, as staff who have come up through the ranks and have hitherto ruled the roost have to make adjustments.

The other major form of fund-raising consists of soliciting donations of cash and goods from individual members of the surrounding community, especially from businesses. This approach is known in the Concept House movement as 'hustling', a term jokingly borrowed from the junkie culture where it refers to all manner of devices, usually dishonest, used by the resourceful junkie to raise money for his next fix.

Hustling or community relations (as it is more politely known) is justified in several ways, aside from the sheer survival need to raise extra contributions. It is said to be good for the residents who learn how to hustle honestly, how to deal with unfamiliar types of people, to weather the disappointments, and to enjoy the satisfactions. It is said to be good for the outside community since they learn about the drug problem in their midst and become involved in a meaningful response to it.

There is probably an element of truth in both assertions. It is not irrelevant that the present US tax laws permit someone who donates either cash or goods to a recognized charity (which includes probably all Concept Houses) to deduct it from his taxable income. In the case of goods donated, the value placed upon them can be inflated, so that it actually costs the donor little or nothing, after tax. Many donors do not even avail themselves of this option, while some exploit it to write off entire outdated and unsaleable inventories of goods.

RECRUITMENT AND POLITICO-LEGAL FACTORS

The Concept Houses have built up to their present position on the basis of the punitive American drug laws. Mere possession of certain drugs is a crime. Despite recent developments towards softening the attitude to marijuana, introducing methadone maintenance, and sometimes permitting 'treatment' as an alternative to punishment through civil commitment laws, the situation remains basically unchanged.

Many applicants come to Concept Houses because the courts will otherwise send them to jail. This is the essence of the situation that permits Concept Houses to stay in operation, continuing to draw recruits, despite the rigour of their demands. Even so, dropout rates are high. At best, 30 per cent are lost in the first month after admission and a total of 60 per cent in the entire first year. (Figures for Marathon House.)

Since the introduction of methadone maintenance programmes, which represent a much easier alternative, and since the over-expansion of Concept Houses, a more competitive situation has developed. Both individual clients and agencies (such as probation departments) which make referrals can now be more selective. Partly in response to this, partly due to the increasing maturity of staff, some Concept Houses have begun to moderate some of their demands, to be more flexible in the way they are applied, and to be more self-questioning about the need for certain features that have become traditional.

There always have been 'volunteer' residents in Concept Houses, though it is impossible to know how many of these have been motivated by fear of eventual arrest and imprisonment. If it becomes harder to get clients in fear of legal sanctions Concept Houses may have to turn increasingly to volunteers and perhaps more towards people with 'presenting' problems other than drug dependence. They have always maintained that there was no real difference anyway. As clients of different backgrounds become attracted, it may also become advisable to modify certain features of the programme for this reason. Younger persons with less 'hard-core' drug histories are already being seen. Programmes specializing in young clients are also emphasizing a more flexible approach.

BASIC CULTURAL VALUES

The ideology of the Concept House movement has enabled it to make certain allies who are no friends of each other. Some quite conservative law enforcement representatives are supporters because they like the tough, no-nonsense discipline in this approach. At the same time some liberals are attracted by the communal nature of the movement and its emphasis on mutual concern and individual authenticity. In this strange way the Concept House movement straddles values that have been considered far apart, though both lie at the roots of western civilization. The work ethic and personal responsibility ethic worshipped by the early Puritans and their Victorian descendants are, for the first time, combined with the 'love thy neighbour' ethic of the early Christians.

It must be emphasized that the alliances just indicated only involve certain elements of the conservative and liberal camps— only those conservatives who have a genuine concern for people and only those liberals who are open to the need for a structured framework (including sanctions) for communal living. Repressive conservatives and anarchist liberals are outside such alliances. Likewise, the linkages we suggested between the Puritan values of work and responsibility on the one hand, and the early Christian values of altruism and unconditional love on the other, require qualification.

In the main, Concept Houses understand 'love' to mean *conditional* love. The effusions of ecstatic love among members in Concept Houses tend to occur through formally structured occasions such as the all-night encounter group or the marathon (thirty-hour) group. Loving feelings surge up among those who have been truly involved in this structured experience. This is not to say that one person loves another *because* the other has performed outstandingly in terms of group expectations. Rather, that dedicated involvement in this situation, structured to require self-revelation, leads automatically (under favourable conditions) to an upsurge of loving feelings between participants. Individuals who are perceived as not having acted appropriately (not being 'open') would not feel or be the focus of these feelings. This is not due to anyone's conscious intention to punish or exclude them. It simply would not normally happen.

The Puritan ethic of personal responsibility and activism,[18] with an emphasis on the individual's obligation to struggle to overcome all obstacles in his path rather than accepting them fatalistically, has been a central theme in western civilization and a dominant one in American history. Over time, however, this ethic of activism has been redefined in purely materialistic terms. In the Concept House personal responsibility and the obligation to seize control of one's destiny is defined in humane terms. Here the main emphasis is on improving oneself as a human being—learning to be more honest, caring, thoughtful, and public spirited. In this sense the spirit of the Puritans has been brought closer to the spirit of the early Christians.

THE CRISIS IN AMERICAN SOCIETY

In an America wracked not just by the recent crises of Watergate and Vietnam but by deeper and older troubles, of which these are perhaps only symptoms, there is a great yearning among thinking people for explanations and remedies. Some choose to see their explanation in internal enemies and dissidents and their remedies in further repression of deviant groups (like drug addicts).

American society has been torn by the crises of the Vietnam War and the Watergate scandals. Yet these troubles are symptomatic of more profound problems in this society. Philip Slater[19] has suggested that there is a basic despair among older middle-class Americans

F

related to their dim realization that the way of life they have embraced has committed them to chasing an ever-receding goal of happiness. Older pleasures, related to long-standing friendships, membership in a stable community, the enjoyment of simple pleasures not mediated by TV, have generally been abandoned in favour of a highly competitive, individualistic chase after ever greater material rewards. The loathing of so many middle-aged middle-class Americans for 'hippies' and other youthful dissenters, Slater sees as indicative of how very bitter this disappointment tastes.

Criticism of American society is no recent fad, though it has come to a focus in a so-called 'counter-culture'.[20] The other side of the counter-culture coin can be seen in the search for forms of experience or consciousness that are more authentic, real, or in some way more satisfying, than those provided in 'square' American culture. Hence, we find the enormous interest in sensitivity groups, meditation, drug experiences, mind-control techniques, etc.[21] To some of the people involved in such concerns the Concept House has been and should be of great interest.

One may suggest that these same basic problems, outlined above, contribute also to the existence of the drug abuse and delinquency problem among the youth of middle-class America.

At least two programmes have produced plays depicting the Concept House experience, presented by residents and graduates, which have been widely performed. Through its community relations and Open Houses every Concept House has attracted a number of friends and hangers-on. So, although enclosed behind high boundaries, the Concept House movement is tied in to the larger society in significant ways. Not only are there instrumental connections through which the Concept Houses draw money, goods, and recruits from the outside society. There are also cultural connections through which this movement is related to some of the root values in American society.

RECYCLING PEOPLE VS. THE ALTERNATIVE SOCIETY

In most Concept Houses there is provision for 'graduation' usually after about two years of residence and when senior staff feel confident that the resident has matured to the point where he can be trusted to make his own decisions in a 'responsible' way. After this point he is no longer subject to the supervision of the house. The graduate who works for a Concept House is, of course, subject to its control as his employer. That is different. He or she is a 'recycled' person free to participate in the outside society as desired.

The Concept movement has always been torn between two conflicting directions or goals : rehabilitation agency or utopian movement (alternative society). Synanon has opted decisively for the latter, after straddling both for a while. Daytop—up to the 'Big Split' of 1969, when David Deitch resigned as Executive Director—took a posture *vis-à-vis* the outside society of a missionary or social change agency, dedicated to challenging and trying to change some of the basic values and institutions of the established society.[22] The later Daytop, Phoenix House, Marathon House and most other Concept Houses today define their goals as falling somewhere between those of a traditional rehabilitation agency and those of a low-key utopian movement.

Most Concept House staff maintain that the Concept House operates by principles that are morally superior to those found in most segments of society today and that the honesty, responsibility and loving concern which are taught and practised (however inadequately) in the Concept House are not merely rehabilitative techniques but principles of a better way of life. This is the utopian element. It does not mean, however, that residents are pressured to stay and work within the movement. They have a choice and those who wish to work in the Concept must pass an evaluation process to see whether they have the desired qualities.

For those graduates who work outside the Concept House movement their affiliation with former peers and former staff is now optional. For many, perhaps most, of these it becomes quite tenuous within a year after graduation. They keep in touch with one or two former peers and return for a graduation or social event once or twice a year. If they need help in finding a job or getting a scholarship for college they will contact staff. Otherwise, they may or they may not. This at any rate has been Marathon House's experience. The intense involvement for two years seems to become defined, soon after graduation, as a transitional life-experience, analogous again to that of the family. It is profoundly important to one at the time. After a certain point one outgrows it and loosens the ties but remains cognizant of the value of having had that experience (possibly while still resenting certain things that happened).

In the earlier years of the Concept House movement most graduates did take jobs within the movement. That was a time of rapid expansion and a shortage of qualified staff. It was also the time of greatest enthusiasm and idealism within the movement.

Currently, a significant proportion of graduates from Concept

Houses are taking employment outside the movement. At Marathon House, 55 per cent of all graduates to date are working in conventional jobs unrelated to any drug programme and the proportion is higher among the more recent graduates. Thus they have to come to terms with the discrepancy between the rigorous standards of morality they have learned and the realities of the outside world. Their situation then becomes somewhat similar to that of the person who has had a strict religious upbringing but works among non-believers and only meets his co-religionists occasionally. There is, however, no equivalent to the weekly religious service for the Concept House graduate.

Conclusion

Concept Houses began as highly autonomous groups, operating behind high boundaries and dealing with the outside society for strictly limited purposes only. Their mission they defined as providing an environment in which people who had led 'negative' and worthless lives could change their direction and become 'positive'.

It is significant on more than one level that the leaders of these groups had only recently achieved this same change in their own lives. This made them more effective leaders and at the same time by being leaders they reinforced themselves in the changes they had made for themselves. To these early leaders the sense of status in being part of a new and momentous social movement was important. Generally they lacked the kinds of vocational skills or other social assets that could have earned them this kind of prestige in any other way and most of them were sufficiently unsure of themselves to have serious doubts about whether they could 'make it' in conventional roles in conventional society. Indeed Synanon for much of its history has taught its formerly addicted residents that they *cannot* 'make it' in this way. By now, though, there are plenty of examples to disprove this to Concept House graduates, and it seems that there are significant numbers of them who prefer to make their lives outside the community that gave them a new life, adapting the new values they have learned there as well as they can to the conditions of life in modern society. In part, the sociology of sects is the sociology of how people drop out of the dominant institutions of society, and how they drop into an alternative. The sociology of therapeutic communities can be seen in a similar way.

However, as we have just seen, the drop-outs may decide to drop back in again some time later. This is perhaps easier to see in the groups studied here, since they always had more connection with goals of rehabilitation, than is the case with sects or similar groups such as 'hippies'. Yet these groups too may be performing a more important function than is generaly realized, as a temporary haven or socialization agency for people who will shortly rejoin the main stream of society. Whether they leave feeling that they have out-grown their haven or that they made a mistake in choosing it, they are undoubtedly changed by the experience. In the life-long struggle to define the meaning of one's life, they have surely moved along significantly, thanks to their experience in a group whose entire *raison d'être* is to create meanings within their own essentially limited but indisputably powerful structures. The analysis of such structures and how they function is a realm in which, until very recently, sociologists scarcely dared to tread.[23]

NOTES AND REFERENCES

1 The author of this paper is employed by Marathon House, one of the Concept Houses analysed here. Hence, he is clearly not a detached observer. Whether this is more of an asset or a handicap for the purposes of this research, only the reader can judge.

2 Several examples of this kind of community can be found in England too, notably Alpha House in Portsmouth and Phoenix House in London.

3 Benjamin Zablocki, *The Joyful Community*, Penguin Books, Baltimore, 1971.

4 L. Brill, *The De-addiction Process*, Charles C. Thomas, Springfield, Illinois, 1972.

5 We use quotation marks around the term 'drug problem' to emphasize that this is a socially defined condition. Those whose drug-use patterns are socially unacceptable tend to be punished and perhaps pressured into entering a treatment programme such as those described here. At the same time recruits are more self-motivated and enter because they themselves are suffi-ciently unhappy about their current lives to seek a way of changing.

6 When seeking admission, 'prospects' are warned that no drugs are permit-ted in the House and advised to taper off and stop their usage before entry. Those who do not do this for some reason go through 'cold turkey' with-drawal without medication. This takes several days of rest and presents no serious problem, despite the contrary impression held by the lay public. They have been grossly misled on this subject. Two main factors are involved: addicts over-dramatize their suffering in order to get more medication, or at

least pity, but that only works with 'squares', not with the former addicts in charge here; and the social situation here is supportive ('you can make it') though not pitying and the person withdrawing is part of a friendly group—rather than being alone in a cell or isolation ward.

The discomfort of withdrawal is described as being comparable to a bad case of 'flu. Only for the rare barbiturate addict is medication medically necessary.

7 O. H. Mowrer, *The Crisis in Psychiatry and Religion*, Van Nostrand, Princeton, New Jersey, 1961; idem, *Morality and Mental Health*, Rand McNally, Chicago, 1967.

8 D. Casriel, *So Fair a House*, Prentice-Hall, New Jersey, 1963; R. Volkman and D. R. Cressey, 'Differential association and the rehabilitation of drug addicts', *American Journal of Sociology*, Vol. 66, 1963, pp. 129–142; L. Yablonsky, *Synanon: The Tunnel Book*, Penguin Books. Baltimore, 1965.

9 National Institute of Mental Health, *Directory of Narcotic Addiction Treatment Agencies 1968–1969*, NIMH, Washington, 1970.

10 David A. Deitch, 'Treatment of drug abuse in the therapeutic community', in *Technical Papers of the Second Report of the National Commission on Marijuana and Drug Abuse*, Appendix, Vol. IV, 1973, pp. 158–175.

11 M. Bennett, 'The Concept: an answer to addiction? New York City's attempt to treat drug addicts through existential encounter', *Washington Monthly*, May 1969, pp. 51–62; M. A. Shelley and A. Bassin, 'Daytop Lodge—a new treatment for drug addicts', *Corrective Psychiatry*, Vol. 11, 1965, pp. 186–195; B. Sugarman, 'Daytop Village: a drug cure co-operative', *New Society*, April 1967, pp. 526–529; idem, 'Evaluating drug treatment programs', *Drug Forum*, Vol. 3, 1974; Deitch, op. cit.

12 Barry Sugarman, *Daytop Village: A Therapeutic Community*, Holt, Rinehart & Winston, New York, 1974.

13 Maxwell Jones, *Social Psychiatry*, Tavistock Publications, London, 1952; idem, *Beyond the Therapeutic Community*, Yale University Press, New Haven, Connecticut, 1968.

14 Erving Goffman, *Asylums*, Doubleday, New York, 1961.

15 Rosabeth Moss Kanter, *Commitment and Community*, Harvard University Press, Cambridge, Massachusetts, 1972.

16 D. Casriel & G. Amen, *Daytop: Three Lives*, Hill & Wang, New York, 1971.

17 Solomon E. Asch, *Social Psychology*, Prentice-Hall, New Jersey, 1952, Chapter 16.

18 F. Kluckhohn and F. Strodtbeck, *Variations in Value Orientations*, Row, Peterson, Chicago, 1961.

19 Philip Slater, *The Pursuit of Loneliness*, Beacon Press, Boston, 1970.

20 T. Roszak, *The Making of a Counter Culture*, Doubleday, New York, 1969.

21 K. Back, *Beyond Words*, Russell Sage Foundation, New York, 1972; A. Weil, *The Natural Mind*, Houghton Mifflin, Boston, 1972.

22 Barry Sugarman, *Daytop Village*, op. cit.

23 Data for this analysis come from three summers spent as a participant-observer (two at Daytop Village and one at Marathon House), two summers as a residential staff member (one at Marathon House and one at Alpha House, Portsmouth, England), two years as senior staff member at Marathon House, an examination of the published literature, visits to other programmes, and interviews with persons familiar with other programmes.

Roger O'Toole

9 Sectarianism in Politics:
Case Studies of Maoists and De Leonists

Notions of 'secular' and 'political' religion are not new to sociology, but until recently discussions of them have tended to be macro-sociological in focus.[1] Scholars have located and analysed secular counterparts of established national churches or to Roman Catholicism but have shown less interest in the 'secular counterparts' of the multifarious religious sects so richly investigated and documented.[2] This paper suggests that analysis of the sectarian disposition in 'non-religious' contexts has consequences for the study of both politics and religion. It is based upon investigations of two 'Marxist' political sects : The Internationalists and the Socialist Labour Party, which are active in Toronto, Canada.[3]

The Internationalists

The Internationalists are the members of a political sect founded in Canada in the 1960s and formally dedicated to making a revolution in accordance with the Thought of Chairman Mao Tse-tung.[4] Essentially Maoists in the style of the individuals portrayed in Jean-Luc Godard's film, *La Chinoise*, they are mainly university students from middle-class backgrounds. While their ideology may be summed up by their declaration that they 'uncritically and loyally follow Chairman Mao',[5] the Internationalists also owe allegiance, though of a less formal kind, to the founder of their sect, a Punjabi intellectual resident in Canada. In order to understand this sect, as much attention has to be paid to the thought of this man, Hardial Bains, as to the Thought of Chairman Mao.[6]

INTERNATIONALIST IDEOLOGY AND THE INDIVIDUAL

The writings of Hardial Bains provide material for uncovering the main base of Internationalist recruitment.[7] While claiming to represent the only true version of 'Marxism-Leninism-Mao Tse-tung Thought' their emphasis is decidedly upon *personal* rather than social change. The 'Necessity for Change' preached by Bains refers essentially to *self-change*, and the target of his writings is the young 'alienated' intellectual. To such an individual, this 'revolutionary teacher and . . . revolutionary in all aspects of his life'[8] reveals the way to find truth, serve others, and change the world by first changing himself. In this there is a striking resemblance to the philosophy of 'Moral Rearmament' preached by Frank Buchman's Oxford Movement as well as to Ron Hubbard's Scientology movement.[9] Emphasizing the worthlessness of 'Imperialist' culture, and the egotism, selfishness, hollowness and loneliness which he considers characteristic of modern society, the founder and leader of the Internationalists assigns to the young intellectual the historic role of changing the world. Bains appeals to the young intellectual by using a technique familiar to revivalist practitioners of 'old-time religion' : the inducement of an overpowering sense of personal guilt. This process may be explored by reference to Bains's concept of 'Fascist being' which is surely unique among 'Marxist' analyses of Fascism :

> The extreme form of egocentric is the I of the fascist, the fascist thinks that he is the only person alive. The egocentric I of the fascist is defined and qualified in terms of distinctions between him and the remainder of mankind. Fascism starts from a person's being, and it is important to go into the genesis of fascism and fascistic tendencies. When idealists talk of fascism they are usually referring to murderous crusades carried out as a result of social, political or religious dogmas . . . we would suggest that this is an easy definition of fascism, a comfortable rationalization which allows us to ignore the genesis of fascism within ourselves and within our society. . . .[10]

Bains asserts that man has within himself an evil egotistical presence, a 'Fascist being' which contaminates his true human nature. If man is to be changed, he must rid himself of this gnawing inner evil by a supreme act of will : a genuine dedication of himself to the seeking of the true and the good. Thus, just as the 'hellfire' evangelist harangues his congregation as reeking of sin, wallowing in evil, and requiring purification, so Bains presents the young intellectual with a vision of himself as an evil, selfish, degenerate social parasite ruled by his inner 'Fascist being'. 'Fascism' thrives, for Bains, when individuals accept the 'Anticonscious' Imperialist culture, and 'take for granted' a reality defined by the existing wider society. Thus, just as the religious sectarian may purify himself of the 'sin' which contaminates his soul, so the aspiring Internationalist must cleanse himself by conquering his inner 'Fascist being'.[11]

The individual's 'Fascist being' can be overcome, according to Bains, by an act of genuinely 'seeking truth' and an active attempt to understand reality. By replacing 'Anticonsciousness' with 'Consciousness', that is by perceiving 'reality' for the first time, the individual will then be able to transform himself *morally*. He will see 'Fascist being' and 'serving self' in their true light and will be aware of his moral duty to 'serve people'. Therefore, in the view of 'the founding member of the Internationalists [who] has consistently participated in all facets of the organization's development',[12] social change is initiated and engineered by intellectuals who, like himself, are willing to 're-make' themselves by escape from 'the historical crib'.[13]

THE CONVERSION PROCESS

Discussion so far has only considered the sect's literature without assessing its impact on individuals, but it appears that at least some Internationalists have experienced the classic conversion[14] implied in the notion of 'Necessity for Change'. Herbert Blumer states of the sect : 'In order to become a member, an outsider has to have a conversion experience—a moral transformation similar in character to that of the original members. The public confession is a confession of such an experience and is a sign that the individual is a member of the elect.'[15] Despite its doubtful general applicability, this assertion is appropriate in the case of the Internationalists for the group's periodicals proclaim the importance of the conversion process by publishing testimonials in which members relate how they learned to 'seek truth and serve people'.[16] The extracts below, from an Internationalist magazine, illustrate the sect's style of public confession[17] and demonstrate how one Canadian university student perceived his transition from a life of selfishness, idleness, debauchery and parasitism to a new, meaningful 'Conscious' existence in the sect :

I would like to make public the role of the Canadian Student Movement [the Internationalists] in *mobilizing me as an anti-imperialist force*. . . .

After having received my general B.A. degree, and realizing its basic worthlessness except in providing a passport to full-fledged membership in a meaningless rat race, I resolved to remain at university sponging off the government. . . . My time and consciousness were exhausted on an endless chain of pub nights, reading T. S. Eliot, James Joyce, Leonard Cohen, Modern Cinema, so-called anti-establishment folk-singers, and shopping for women. *My complete being was deeply entrenched in petty bourgeois culture.*

At the time I was confronted with friends enthusiastic over ideas developed from the Canadian Student Movement. . . . Attracted by their enthusiasm and resolve, I joined . . . a group they had formed. . . . The outlook which was the basis of my whole life *was totally exposed as a pro-imperialist, anti-people, bankrupt way of life.* Once exposed in a precise, rational manner this fact could not be denied, but an attempt could be made to ignore it. This I did *rigorously* with the result that the glaring contradictions of my way of life and the objective analysis of the facts exposed myself a [sic] powerful force of reaction. I was so deeply involved in the imperialist culture that a threat to it was considered a threat to my very existence. . . . I recognized the tremendous power of the anti-imperialist ideas backed up by undeniable logic and saw from my subjective bourgeois view that I had committed myself to launch something that would destroy me. This *schizophrenia* finally resulted in my running hard and fast . . . from the people of the movement [and] marked the beginning of a gluttonous consumption of bourgeois culture, drunken nights at the pub, frenzied parties; evenings spent in an effort to wrench the last drop of subjective enjoyment out of consuming my girl friend as a product. No activity was rejected which I felt could help me to forget the realization that my life was indeed entirely bogus, that I was an active reactionary, that my former, and my present life was unbearable and oppressive.

Whether I had consumed alcohol or not I had a continuous hangover from the consciousness that my life and existence were completely false. I had deserted the people who had exposed the bankruptcy of my bourgeois existence. . . . These pro-imperialist actions were the last desperate struggle of my reactionary culture. Their frenzied irrational nature reflected the inherent weakness of these forces. . . .

There were only two alternatives open to me. I could either become a conscious servant of reaction and imperialism or take a stand against imperialism. I could no longer bury my head in the sand.

At this crucial stage of my personal development I [attended] the historical Canadian Student Movement 'Necessity for Change' conference—I was in a precarious position. I wanted to take a stand against imperialism but I was overwhelmed at the enemy both within and without me. During the conference I not only became highly conscious of the nature of our enemy, Imperialism, and how it has penetrated to every level of bourgeois society—I also became aware of its weaknesses and of positive ways in which to fight it on the cultural front in the University. Through my own experience I know that it is impossible to ignore the imperialist forces. Once consciousness of them has been instilled, a stand must be taken : either a vicious reactionary position in which one continues to oppress the people for profit, or an anti-imperialist revolution to end the oppression of all the people of the World.[18]

The leading Toronto Internationalist presents a dramatic example of radical conversion in having undergone a transformation from a conservative 'playboy' student politician, and having decisively rejected his 'respectable' wealthy parents and his former associates since achieving 'Consciousness'.

MAINTENANCE OF COMMITMENT

A sect must not only gain converts but must maintain their commitment. Like religious sects, this political sect 'tends to dominate a large part of the life of its members',[19] demanding of them 'the whole of their lives'.[20] In being 're-born' into the sect the recruit is expected to place himself completely at its disposal, for only by so doing can he genuinely 'serve people'. The ideal relationship between the individual and the group in the Internationalists is expressed succinctly by the sect's founder : 'We must develop the material base of the organization so that the material base of the individual is always that of the organization. There must never be disparity between the two.'[21] He also declares : '. . . the development of the individual is irrelevant if it does not serve the political needs of the organization.'[22]

The Internationalists aim at building an organization whose members are equally and totally committed to it above all. They work to build a sect which will be the dominant fact in each member's life and which will be composed of persons who are alike because they each 'reflect' the organization. In order to gain and maintain members' total commitment, the Internationalists attempt to ensure that the individual is constantly involved in the activities of the sect, and continually reinforced, in its beliefs and attitudes, by other members. Such a situation is secured partly by the insistence that all activities which might claim a member's attention, and particularly his emotional investment, at the expense of his involvement in the sect, must be curtailed or terminated. Even familial ties, which might be expected to weaken a member's commitment, are subject to the supervision of the sect.[23] Thus, the sect member is subject to strong interpersonal pressure to conform to 'correct' beliefs, behaviour patterns, and even linguistic usage, so that the fact that he is, first and foremost, an Internationalist is sharply underlined. In the attempts to exercise a high degree of control over their members' lives, to persuade members to measure their own worth solely in terms of their utility to the organization, and to induce members to experience severe guilt whenever they believe they have proven inadequate, the Internationalists appear to have been largely successful.

Some sense of this may be gained from a consideration of the unusual homogeneity in attitudes and behaviour displayed by Internationalists. Lewis Coser has noted :

In addition to attempting to reduce to a minimum the outside social contacts of its members, and to encompass their total personality, the sect has a tendency to level off individually. A many-sided development of the personality of the member is likely to bring into play attitudes and thoughts which cannot be easily controlled.[24]

In developing members who 'reflect' the sect, the Internationalists are concerned to 'level' or standardize, and thus wage a constant war on 'individualism' and individuality. Internationalists tend to think and behave according to a distinctive, rather stereotyped pattern which makes them almost immediately recognizable to informed observers of radical political activity. In conversation, for example, to speak with one Internationalist is essentially to speak to all, as members of the sect characteristically repeat mechanically the same slogans, phrases and arguments with little or no individual creative embellishment. Their conversation is as stereotyped in its form as in its content for they not only write, but speak in a style of English apparently derived from Chinese propaganda publications. Internationalists develop a facility for speaking habitually in the same style as their writings. For example, the quotations from Internationalist publications reproduced below might well be direct quotations from recorded speech :

Mass Line is being born at a time when Marxism-Leninism-Mao Tse-tung Thought is gaining worldwide acceptance and the bright red banner of international proletariat [sic] is flying in a lofty manner. . . . All attacks from revisionists, neo-revisionists and neo-trotskyists will be resolutely countered.[25]

Mortally afraid of the Quebec people, arch-reactionary Richard Nixon dared not travel through the city of Montreal. Like a coward, he rushed into a helicopter from the airport, rushed back through the same means after a brief 'celebration' with reactionaries, CIA and FBI agents, US Imperialist lackey police in Quebec calling itself 'RCMP' and other evil gentry.[26]

Despite the criticism and ridicule to which Internationalists are subjected by their opponents for their use of 'stereotyped language', they take pride in its use and assert vigorously its importance as the 'scientific' language of 'the masses'.[27] Inculcation of rigid linguistic usage would seem to be important in the sect's efforts to eradicate individualism, but it might also be seen as a key element in maintaining the individual's identification with the sect in another way. As in many religious groups, the use of a distinctive, esoteric, and 'sacred' language may reinforce the commitment of members of this sect by emphasizing to them their exalted position as part of an exclusive cognitive and moral elite. Worthy of note also is the fact that many Internationalists add to their Chinese-style English certain usages based on the linguistic practices of the sect leader who is of Punjabi background.

The high degree of identification with the person of their leader exhibited by Internationalists is of interest, for Simmel's assertion that 'insofar as a number of people are equally subject to one individual, they are themselves equal'[28] appears to be relevant to the discussion of these sectarians' uniformity of thought and action.

Reinforcement of commitment to the sect on the basis of the abandonment of individuality appears to be the most important aspect of the frequent national, 'mass' gatherings organized by the sect. These occasions appear to have little importance in terms of decision-making and are probably best understood as ritual activities. In an atmosphere of speech-making, banner-waving, rhythmic Chinese-style applause, and group singing and slogan-chanting, individual Internationalists have their commitment to the sect 're-charged'.[29] After one such conference, a number of Internationalists spoke of the uplifting experience and of the renewed dedication they felt towards their sect and its cause. A female member declared : 'The conference was marvellous, especially the last night when we all chanted the slogans together and sang the Internationale—that was terrific!'

SATISFACTIONS OF SECT MEMBERSHIP

The Internationalists claim to be successfully building a mass movement and to be proselytizing intensively in order to increase their numbers. Although the point cannot be argued at any length or in detail here, close scrutiny of the sect casts doubt upon this claim.

Assertions by Internationalists that they are part of a large, growing 'new democratic' movement of 'broad masses of the Canadian people' are belied by close observation of the sect. Despite their avowals that expansion of the group is desirable, necessary and occurring, Internationalists leave an impression that they are only concerned with expansion and progress 'on paper' and in their grandiose pronouncements. Members of the sect, indeed, seem to be more concerned with purity than proselytization; with exclusivism rather than expansion; and appear content with a situation of minimal growth in membership. Investigation of Internationalist proselytization activities suggests that it would be superficial to view these as simply genuine attempts to gain support and recruits. Rather, these activities might be better interpreted as occasions on which sect members are able to assert with pride their status as members of an elite, in the face of representatives of the wider society, and as situations in which they may experience the honour of persecution at the hands of the 'Anticonscious' and unrighteous.[30]

Certainly, to most outsiders, the Internationalists appear as an arrogant, intolerant, exclusivist group whose frequent appeals for 'discussion' and 'co-operation' do not disguise their real nature as a small, self-satisfied, self-proclaimed elite, whose official humility masks a deep pride. Even a sympathetic observer notes:

> . . . I reacted against the aggressive attitudes of members of the group—to individuals, myself being one, not directly associated with it . . . the tone of approach of the Internationalists served to alienate more than endear . . . they seemed to equate rejection of their criticisms as the mark of ignorance or satisfaction with the system outside the group; they did not seem to accept anyone to be in a transient stage, they seemed to make no allowances for people without the necessary intellect to evaluate their attitude to their immediate context. . . . In a word, they seemed intolerant, a closed circle.[31]

Observation of Internationalist proselytization activities including literature selling, pamphlet distribution, and public meetings confirms the assertion that the approach of sect members seems calculated 'to alienate more than endear'. Again, at times the Internationalists act quite overtly as a small exclusivist 'closed circle' by turning away from the world, identifying their own group as 'the masses', and engaging only in unpublicized meetings designated 'strictly by invitation only'.

In such circumstances, it seems mistaken to view the commitment of Internationalists as maintained on the basis of their satisfaction in involvement with a growing social movement. Rather, those who remain within the sect might better be considered as gaining satisfaction from th*e sectarian experience itself*, an experience actually very different from that portrayed in Internationalist descriptions of a grand 'new democratic' alliance of oppressed and progressive people.[32]

A clue to the real rewards experienced by members of this sect may be found in the writings of the sect founder himself, for referring to the fact that some Internationalists derive a 'kind of security' from their 'new society', he notes :

> For many people, the Internationalists have become a new historical crib, a new perspective through which they can rationalize their position in nearly all circumstances, they can say that 'I am an Internationalist, therefore I am a developing person by definition' . . . the malaise of the Internationalists can be thought of in this way : they reinforce their own personalities within the group, and derive satisfaction from being called rebels outside of it.[33]

The outside observer should accept and extend this perception, viewing the sect as an 'expressive' rather than 'instrumental' movement,[34] which provides its members with an *alternative* to the world rather than the *means* of changing it. Members of this sect appear to derive satisfaction from being part of a small, totally politically isolated, cognitive and moral elite, a 'closed circle' with a certain notoriety in the outside world. Sharing a distinct sense of reality derived from 'facts' in which 'relevant things [are] relevant and irrelevant things irrelevant',[35] the Internationalists accord themselves elevated status further enhanced by its exclusive nature and its rarity.

This sect may be interpreted as offering a closed environment in which members, and the significance of their acts, are totally transformed. Within it, certain young intellectuals attain cognitive certainty, a sense of status and moral worth,[36] a feeling of comradeship[37] and 'belonging', and an awareness of 'meaning' in life.[38] Rather than viewing this sect as a means to an end, it is worthwhile attempting to understand it as an end-in-itself.

The Socialist Labour Party

Though founded over thirty years ago, the Toronto branch of the Socialist Labour Party is a relatively recent addition to what has been called the 'Grand Old Party'. The SLP can claim the distinction of being the oldest Marxist organization in North America, with a history of over eighty years' continuous activity.

The SLP is a living fossil, a small sect surviving as a relic of a once larger and more powerful organization, in the manner of such similar organizations as the modern IWW and the Socialist Party of Great Britain.[39] Although it essentially ceased to be an effective North American political force by 1914, this sect survives in the 1970s in the form of tiny groups scattered throughout major cities. In contrast to the Internationalists, the SLP is composed of working men from middle to old age. Politically ineffectual and largely unknown, the Socialist Labour Party proclaims itself the only 'genuine' Marxist organization in the world, founded as it is on the distinctive doctrine of 'Marxism-De Leonism'.[40] Thus, the SLP in Canada proclaims proudly: 'The Socialist Labour Party of Canada is the only bona fide party of socialism in Canada. It has no connection whatever with other parties calling themselves Socialist or Communist.'[41]

MEMBERS' COMMITMENT TO THE SECT : WHEN PROPHECY FAILS[42]

Neither De Leon nor any other major SLP figure has ever, to our knowledge, made a *specific* prediction regarding the date of the proletarian revolution and SLP accession to power. However, De Leon's followers at the turn of the century were led to expect these events sooner rather than later. De Leon's addresses strike a note of urgency, and the message that 'there is no time to lose' is nowhere more apparent than in his jibes at the 'gradualists' and 'reformers' who oppose the 'revolutionary' stance of the SLP :

> Give us a truce with your 'reforms'! There is a sickening air of
> moral mediocrity in all such petty movements of petty childish
> aspirations at times like these when gigantic man-issues [sic] are
> thundering at every man's door for admission and solution.[43]

Declaring the capitalist class to be 'on its last legs,'[44] he stated in
1902 that 'the condition precedent for proletarian emancipation
[had] been reached.'[45]

Contemporary SLP members thus belong to an organization
which pronounced capitalism to be in its 'death-agony' over half-
a-century ago. Far from concealing this fact, however, SLP members
draw attention to this diagnosis, maintaining its 'scientific' accuracy.
Arguing that De Leon gave no precise schedule for capitalism's
imminent collapse, that a death-agony may be prolonged, and that
capitalism has, indeed, been 'on its last legs' for the whole of the
present century, they assert its essential validity. Members of the
sect, therefore, unashamedly make declarations which are virtual
echoes of De Leon's pronouncements :

> . . . Capitalism is today . . . mired in its own decomposition.[46]

> It is too late for reform! Giant industrialism has written FINISH
> to any social betterment within the framework of class rule. . . .
> At this late date reforms can only serve as concealed measures of
> reaction. . . . The hour of revolution has struck.[47]

The SLP may be viewed as being in a protracted 'state of emergency' in which a sense of urgency combines with one of extreme
patience, and in which shrill proclamations of the imminence of the
doom of the present order are accompanied by an apparently
lethargic waiting upon events :

> Revolutions are not *made*, they *come*. Before there can be a
> revolution there must be a revolutionary situation. A revolution-
> ary situation can no more be created by socialist agitators than
> a hurricane can be created by meteorologists. It is a consequence
> rather of the coming to a head of contradictions that are inher-
> ent in the old society. These contradictions . . . are already gnaw-
> ing at the vitals of capitalism. Sooner or later they will create
> the conditions of capitalist crisis and breakdowns which, in turn,
> will jolt the workers out of their apathy and compel them to face
> the task history has assigned them.[48]

Thus, SLP members stoutly deny the disconfirmation of De Leon's assertions and maintain his eschatology intact as the creation of a scientific genius. They link a belief that members must be prepared for an almost immediate collapse of capitalism with a caution that nobody should be impatient, disappointed or disillusioned if the possibility of this event seems to recede. All that is certain is that De Leon's forecast will prove accurate 'sooner or later' (and sooner rather than later), and that the 'socialist reconstruction of society' will begin.

THE DEFENCE OF THE SECT—IS THE SLP 'GETTING ANYWHERE'?

SLP members' attitude to their eventual triumph must be considered in the context of the nature of their organization. Whatever the possibilities of a collapse of capitalism, its culmination in the triumph of the SLP appears, to the outsider, most unlikely. SLP members are aware that their grandiose claims of destiny are rejected by non-members and that they are stigmatized as 'dogmatists', 'dreamers', 'armchair philosophers' and 'crackpots'[49] belonging to an obscure, tiny, impotent group, a pathetic relic of better days, with no 'destiny' other than eventual demise. So self-conscious of this image are SLP members that a section of the sect's political catechism is devoted to the question: 'Why hasn't the SLP Gotten Anywhere?'[50] The suggestion that SLP activity in the past half-century has proven fruitless and that its present members are engaged in a futile enterprise is viewed by the sect with official scorn. The sect condescendingly presents the outsider with the argument that a correct perception of 'reality' cannot fail to demonstrate the health, vigour, success and destiny of the sect. Starting from the premise that 'Revolutions cannot be made to order, nor can their realization be fixed at such and such a time,'[51] the SLP asserts that all is going according to plan, that it is in good shape for the battles to come, and that some of the hardest work of revolutionary preparation has already been completed. With long-practised skill it presents a picture of itself as a thriving group whose members are earnestly and systematically engaged in a full schedule of tasks. Proclaiming that its work over the years has been 'great and fruitful' and that it is 'stronger and more determined than ever',[52] it rejects suggestions that it is merely a small, unsuccessful, isolated and impotent group fighting for survival. This official position is enthusiastically upheld by sect members.

In defending the vitality and destiny of their organization, SLP members adopt a strategy entirely different from that of the Internationalists. Whereas the latter respond to assertions that they are a tiny, insignificant, isolated group by maintaining a grandiose image which exaggerates their support and effectiveness, SLP members acknowledge, and even emphasize, the fact that their group is small and isolated. Denying that smallness and isolation imply insignificance, they regard these characteristics as marks of honour rather than of failure. Arguing that 'quality rather than quantity' is the only measure of the worth of a revolutionary group, members of the sect see the smallness and isolation of the SLP as confirming rather than contradicting their conception of its historic role. Smallness is identified with total dedication and with the preservation of doctrinal purity. Thus, the instructor of the weekly 'study class' held by the Toronto SLP has stated :

> You know, people sometimes come to these study classes for a while and then get disillusioned and stop coming because they don't see numbers! What they don't realize is that in an organization like this, numbers aren't really important. We say 'quality is more important than quantity'. Not that we wouldn't like a few more members than we've got, but we're not going to sacrifice our principles for members! There's another advantage to a small movement : it's easier to *keep clean*! to keep your members loyal and dedicated.

These sentiments have been echoed by the National Secretary of the SLP of Canada :

> A lot of people play us down and attack us because we're a *small* group but what they don't realize is that there's nothing great about size. The smallness of the SLP is a good thing! It's much better to have a small group of people who are dedicated—who are willing to die for their cause—rather than lots of people who can't be relied on. The SLP is small but it's a dedicated group.

Thus, SLP members point to their lack of numbers with pride, attributing it primarily to their concern with upholding rigorous standards of membership. Arguing that though many are called, few are chosen, sect members emphasize their status as an elite. In their view, the SLP is small in size but great in knowledge, dedication and potential. It is a unique organization composed of individuals carefully selected from the best elements in society.

The SLP views its political isolation in the same way as its size : as a matter for pride rather than shame. Isolation, like smallness, is proclaimed as desirable, especially for the defence of doctrinal purity. Maintaining that 'only the Socialist Labour Party has achieved and retained Marxist integrity',[53] the sect conspicuously declares its isolation from all 'other parties calling themselves Socialist or Communist'.[54] Declaring itself the *only* genuine revolutionary Marxist movement, the SLP vilifies other 'radicals' as 'reformists' and 'fakers':[55] 'The SLP stands alone in the clarity of its idea of how socialism must be constituted, and equally important, how the workers . . . must organize to get it.'[56]

Thus, SLP members have little knowledge of, or interest in, the activities of other radical political organizations, and take pride in this.

SLP PROSELYTIZATION : SPREADING THE WORD?

Although it declares its satisfaction with a condition of smallness and isolation, the SLP also claims to 'spread the message of Socialism by conducting a ceaseless, vigorous programme of Socialist education among the workers'.[57] It states : 'This educational programme is carried on by every legitimate means available to the Socialist Labour Party—public lectures; study classes; widespread distribution of leaflets; street sales of pamphlets and its official organ, the *Weekly People*; as well as the use of radio and television whenever and wherever possible.'[58] Underlining this professed emphasis on proselytization, the sect announces : 'We do not seek to develop mere bookworms or barren philosophers. Men of *action* are the need of the hour.'[59] The SLP is at pains to document its missionary activities in precise detail, and such entries as the following typically appear in its regular Canadian publication :

> One of the highlights . . . was a trip made to Oshawa, Ontario . . . under the direction of National Office. 3,235 leaflets and 54 back copies of the *Socialist Press Bulletin* and *Weekly People* were distributed on this occasion.[60]

> A Daniel De Leon Commemoration public meeting was held on December 14th. In honour of the occasion Comrade ————— delivered a thought-provoking address entitled 'The Issue is Survival' to a small but attentive audience.[61]

However, the close observer is aware that rational book-keeping methods are never applied to the *results* of proselytization, and that 'a small but attentive audience' denotes a handful of individuals, mostly sect members. He learns also that when 'literature distribution continues to result in a good number of write-in enquiries, personal visits and 'phone calls to Section Headquarters in search of further information,'[62] a maximum of one or two responses is involved. Thus, SLP members appear to be meeting disappointment and 'keeping their spirits up' by transforming their failure into mild success.

Certainly, the sect disguises the failure of its proselytizing activities by emphasizing the energy and diligence with which they are carried out rather than their results; and by stressing the 'potential' effect of such endeavours. Yet, a simple conception of SLP proselytization as a sincere attempt to spread the De Leonist word and to seek recruits to the sect seems ill-founded. Plausible though it is, a view of SLP members engaging in earnest proselytization and coming to terms with failure and disappointment by the construction of a rationalization which demonstrates their 'success', is not supported by close analysis of the sect. Far from engaging in the energetic activity of which they boast, SLP members appear to be merely 'going through the motions' of educational and propaganda activities, and, indeed, seem to aim many such activities at targets which virtually guarantee their failure. The members of the sect may be interpreted as maintaining what Robin Williams terms a 'cultural fiction' :

> A cultural fiction exists whenever there is a cultural description, explanation, or normative prescription that is both *generally accepted as a norm and is typically followed* in conduct but is at the same time markedly at variance with the subjective conceptions or inclinations of participants in the pattern, or with certain objective scientific knowledge.[63]

It may be suggested that participants in the sect's proselytization activity are not really disappointed by its failure, firstly because they are aware that 'objectively' it has little chance of success, and secondly because it goes against their 'subjective inclinations'. This point may be illustrated in the context of the main form of SLP proselytization : the anonymous distribution of leaflets which present the basic ideas of the sect. Compared to the sophisticated canvassing and propaganda techniques used by many modern political groups, SLP leafletting seems traditionalistic, uneconomical, unproductive, and rather 'shame-faced'. Unpromising as it might seem to leave bundles of such literature in the lobbies of apartment buildings, or behind the windscreen wipers of cars parked at shopping centres,[64] the activity appears to be assured of failure by a calculated avoidance of its most strategic targets. Thus, leaflets are never distributed in factories or outside factory gates, a situation which parallels the refusal of sect members to present their ideas in a trade-union setting. So entrenched is leafletting as the traditional way of spreading the De Leonist word, that sect members use this method in order to advertise special events, such as infrequent SLP public meetings, in preference to more effective devices.

Analysis of leafletting provides support for the view that SLP members are engaged in the creation of a 'cultural fiction' when they assert their commitment to vigorous missionary work. The 'token' nature of this activity as pursued by sect members leads the outside observer to infer that such conduct is 'at variance with the subjective conceptions or inclinations of participants'. In this context, SLP members appear to be paying lip-service to the goal of proselytization and their insistence that they 'do the best they can', given their numbers and resources, is unconvincing. The challenge of snatching recruits from the enemy's lair by directing a leafletting campaign towards factory workers, for example, seems to impress SLP members less than the possible hostility towards their ideas which they might encounter. The nature of SLP leafletting appears to be symbolized by an incident in which the present writer asked a leading member of the sect which leaflets had been chosen for distribution on a recent leafletting campaign, and the reasons for this choice. Rather than replying in political terms by stating that, for example, a particular issue was important or timely and that a certain leaflet dealt with it, he merely stated: 'We decided we'd better get rid of this pile as they were beginning to yellow. They've been around for some time and we decided we'd better move them.'[65]

The lack of enthusiasm of SLP members for whole-hearted proselytization seems apparent also in their attitude to 'firebrands'. Although the sect claims to seek 'men of action', its members express great hostility towards those who can be labelled with this well-established SLP epithet. One sect member expressed his sentiments thus:

> The sort of people we don't want in the movement are 'firebrands'. *They're* going to shape-up the movement, they're going to put it into action, and so on! A friend of mine was just like that but he burned himself out, they always do—burn themselves out—and then drop out of politics because they get disillusioned. We generally tell these guys—'look, *calm down*, that's not the way we work in the SLP!' For us, building a revolution is

slow, painstaking work—there's no big drama. Unless someone is willing to submit to the discipline of the party and drop all these ideas . . . we tell him to get out. The party can do without him!

The fate of such 'men of action' is disillusionment, and expulsion for 'disruption'.

Consideration of SLP leafletting activity and attitude to zealous activism leads the informed observer to view with scepticism the sect's claims to energetic involvement in 'spreading the word'. Rather than the frantic, widespread, urgent activity portrayed by sect members, an outsider is likely to perceive seemingly 'half-hearted' ritualistic, and by now traditional attempts at proselytization. SLP members appear to be 'play-acting' a role as revolutionary evangelists and their activities seem to constitute a 'pseudo-proselytization' aimed, at best, at maintaining the sect at its present strength. Despite their avowed aim of carrying 'the life-giving principles and programmes of Marxism-De Leonism, the one hope of humanity, the beacon light'[66] to the working class, the activities of members of the sect seem less than heroic.

SATISFACTIONS OF SLP MEMBERSHIP : ELITISM

The attitude of members of the sect towards proselytization suggests a resistance to changing the smallness and isolation of the *status quo*. Thus, it is worth considering the satisfactions of membership in the SLP in its present form. Like the Internationalists, SLP members appear to derive satisfaction from membership in a small, exclusive, cognitive and moral elite.

Just as the Internationalists see themselves as in exclusive possession of 'Consciousness', so SLP members view themselves as exclusive guardians of an absolute 'scientific' truth. They are 'cognitively deviant' and 'cognitively defiant'[67] in maintaining a distinct and exclusive sense of reality. Like religious sectarians who claim to possess the grace which eludes the practitioners of more powerful established religions, SLP members declare themselves in possession of the truth which 'official' science is incapable of recognizing, and which 'intellectuals' with years of formal education are unable to grasp. With the anti-intellectualism which has long characterized the sect,[68] members express their satisfaction at attaining knowledge denied to those hampered by formal learning.[69] As one has expressed it : 'We don't get many intellectuals. We find that most of them are "too clever" in the sense that they think important ideas must be complicated when, in fact, all the most important and true ideas in science are very simple. . . . So we draw most of our support from workingmen who may not be so intellectually sophisticated, but can recognize truth when they see it!'

SLP members are not reluctant to describe how the possession of truth affects them. One member has stated : 'I'll tell you this from my own experience. I'm a great sleeper! I always sleep soundly. That's because I'm *at ease*. *Peace of mind*! That's what the SLP can give you—nobody can shake that from me. So, whatever happens in the world, and even though the SLP is only a small party, the fact that I know the truth gives me confidence and peace of mind.' Another has observed : 'Knowing you have the truth no matter how people ignore it or suppress it gives you great strength. . . .'

Thus, SLP members derive satisfaction from being a *cognoscenti*. As guardians of truth, they are an exclusive 'band of the chosen'[70] with status very different from that which they enjoy outside the sect. The possession of truth gives them fortitude and 'peace of mind', while exclusive possession provides them with the satisfaction of sharing secret knowledge.[71]

SLP members belong to a moral elite as well as a cognitive one. To the satisfaction of exclusive possession of truth they add that of an exclusive hold on morality. As a small, unique group, charged with the historic moral task of showing mankind the way of redemption they constitute a 'select group of sacred souls'[72] and '[regard] the outsider as not participating in grace, as not belonging to the select, as not yet having the fortitude or capacity to adhere to revolutionary principles [and] as an exponent of a lower morality.'[73]

The moral satisfaction of SLP activity is underlined by an official SLP publication :

It were a pity that the knowledge of scientific Socialism be acquired and not put to use in the service of our class. Much is lost then. But it is not the movement alone which is the loser; the individual who deprives the movement of enlightened devotion loses also. As Daniel De Leon who gave of his energies and genius without stint, put it : 'We count him happy whose lot is to contribute his efforts to help forward the banner of the proletariat to final victory. . . .'[74]

Like the Internationalists, SLP members deny that they regard themselves as an elite, and adopt an attitude of humility, portraying themselves as mere servants of mankind. However, the sect's own phrase 'enlightened devotion' aptly sums up the SLP stance as a cognitive and moral elite. Membership in this elite appears to be a source of satisfaction.

The emphasis given by the SLP to the 'fellowship' to be found within its ranks is striking. Certainly, *esprit de corps* can be important in maintaining members' commitment to sect beliefs, as a leading SLP member has suggested : 'I've been in the party for twenty years, and I've held on to the party ideas—and God knows, it's been a hard job at times to hang on to them with the pressures of work and life—and I've been tempted just to let it all go. . . . But I'd come here [to SLP Headquarters] and talk to the other SLP fellows, and do you know, that was a real help in meeting all the problems. . . .'

Although this statement illustrates the effect of group reinforcement on individual commitment, it is more interesting for its demonstration of a sect member's awareness that his relationship to SLP 'comrades' helped him to meet 'all the problems' which he identifies with 'the pressures of work and life'. This individual credits the congenial companionship he has found within the sect with enabling him to overcome the difficulties of life outside it. Other SLP members confirm that the sect provides a warm, supportive environment in which private troubles may be shared with sympathetic listeners : '. . . no matter what pressures get you down in work and life—and they get us all at times—you'll find that belonging to the SLP will make you able to live with those pressures better and to get over them.'

The emphasis given to 'fellowship' by the SLP is shown in published reports of the sect's activities, for accounts of public meetings and leaflet distribution are accompanied by items which appear odd as progress reports of an avowedly revolutionary organization :

> The section held its annual picnic on Sunday, August 2 . . . the weather was excellent and forty comrades and friends from Toronto, Hamilton and as far away as Buffalo, Detroit and Ohio enjoyed a fine day of SLP fellowship. Games were held for the women and children and plenty of corn on the cob was available.[75]

One of the highlights of the first quarter of 1969 was a house social held on February 15, in honour of Comrade —— (retiring SLP National Secretary). Members and friends of the SLP enjoyed a social evening and . . . contributed $90 to further Party work.[76]

The attempt to infuse a 'serious purpose' into such activities by an appeal for funds appears to emphasize rather than deny their essentially 'social' nature. The best attended sect activities are similar to those of such non-revolutionary voluntary associations as veteran and church groups. Such events provide a congenial, familial[77] atmosphere in which individuals may experience a sense of 'belonging'.

SLP emphasis on 'fellowship' is perhaps the cornerstone of the sect's existence, in terms of which, members' lack of concern with changing the sectarian *status quo* may be most fully understood. SLP members gain satisfaction from belonging to a cognitive and moral elite, but this is sustained by their satisfaction with the sect as an oasis, a place of refuge from the pressures of the outside world. The SLP, like the Internationalists, appears to be best understood as providing an alternative to the world rather than a means of changing it; as an 'expressive' rather than an 'instrumental' movement. It might be suggested that, for its members, 'the movement is everything, the final goal nothing'.[78]

Conclusion

The above discussion raises a number of points relevant to the sociology of sectarianism but three in particular seem worthy of further comment.

Stress has been laid on these sects' primary concern with maintenance of the *status quo*, despite claims that they strive for growth. Their efforts to remain small, exclusive and isolated, reflect an unwillingness to compromise with the wider society, and indeed, a lack of enthusiasm for expansion or change *per se*. Such a situation lends support, in a political context, to a critique of the Niebuhr 'denominationalization thesis'.[79] It indicates that this classic formulation of the process by which the sect 'compromises' with the world and becomes the more tolerant 'denomination' may be atypical.[80] The more typical case may be that exemplified by the SLP, in which the sect *remains* a sect.

The designation of Internationalist and SLP missionary endeavours as 'pseudo-proselytization' appears to be of interest. It suggests the necessity for close analysis of the precise nature of proselytizing activity in different sectarian situations, and cautions against the acceptance of proselytization at face-value.

Finally, emphasis on the 'expressive' aspects of Internationalist and SLP activity is relevant to consideration of the relationship between religious and political sectarianism. A stereotype of religious activity as purely expressive has long been rejected, and attention given to such issues as the 'pre-political' nature of certain religious behaviour and the role of religious sects in social revolutions.[81] But, this rejection of a stereotype of *religious* activity has been accompanied by perpetuation of a stereotype of *political* activity, for criticism of the 'irrationalist' perspective on religion has implicitly regarded political activity as its model of 'rational' action.[82] Analysis of the Internationalists and the SLP indicates that this assumption is unwarranted, and that political sects may be expressive rather than instrumental organizations, just as religious sects may be instrumental rather than expressive. Thus, the student of sectarianism must avoid an 'over-rationalized conception of politics,'[83] and, whether his concern is with political or religious phenomena, it is important that he be alert to the complexity of the religious-political distinction.[84]

Twenty years ago, Peter Berger observed : 'On the modern scene we find the dynamics of sectarianism at work in places far removed from religion proper—in politics, art, literature, and even within the sacred precincts of science itself.'[85] Sociologists have been slow to investigate sectarianism in such 'far removed' places, but the above analysis of sectarianism in politics may suggest the worth of such investigations.

NOTES AND REFERENCES

1 See for example D. G. Macrae, 'The Bolshevik Ideology' in *Ideology and Society: Papers in Sociology and Politics*, Heinemann, London, 1961; E. Heimann, 'Atheist Theocracy', *Social Research*, Vol. 20, No. 3, Autumn 1953; David E. Apter, 'Political Religion in the New Nations' in C. Geertz (ed.), *Old Societies and New States*, The Free Press, Glencoe, 1963; E. B. Koenker, *Secular Salvations: The Rites and Symbols of Political Religions*, Fortress Press, Philadelphia, 1965.

2 They have tended to concentrate on the role of 'political religion' in nation-building etc., rather than, for example, on statistically less important

secular sects and cults in modern urban centres. Some of the kinds of phenomena discussed, for example, in Orrin E. Klapp, *Collective Search for Identity*, Holt Rinehart and Winston, New York, 1969, have not generally been explored in terms of 'secular religion'. In recent years, however, the study of 'quasi-religious' movements has become a fast-growing field. See for example, B. R. Wilson's discussion of 'Sects with the imprint of secularity' in Chapter 8 of his *Religious Sects: A Sociological Study*, McGraw-Hill, New York, 1970; Susan Budd, 'The Humanist Societies: The Consequences of a Diffuse Belief System' in B. R. Wilson (ed.), *Patterns of Sectarianism*, Heinemann, London, 1967; Colin D. Campbell, *Toward a Sociology of Irreligion*, Macmillan, London, 1971; and Christopher Evans, *Cults of Unreason*, Harrap, London, 1973.

3 These investigations are reported fully in the author's unpublished doctoral thesis, 'The Sociology of Political Sects: Four Sects in Toronto in 1968–69' (University of Toronto, 1972) available on microfilm from The National Library of Canada, Ottawa. The author wishes to acknowledge the intellectual support of Professor Lewis S. Feuer and the financial support of the Canada Council for this work.

The use of the term 'sect' in a non-religious sense may strike many sociologists as unusual. Such usage has a number of precedents in sociological literature some of which are discussed in the present author's 'A Consideration of "sect" as an Exclusively Religious Concept: Notes on the "Underground" Use of the Concept', presented to the 1971 Annual Meeting of the S.S.S.R., Chicago, Illinois. For examples of such usage the following works should be consulted: Wellman J. Warner, 'Sect' in Julius Gould and William L. Kolb (eds.), *A Dictionary of the Social Sciences*, The Free Press, New York, 1964; Thomas F. O'Dea, 'Sects and Cults' in *International Encyclopedia of the Social Sciences* (ed. David L. Sills), Macmillan and the Free Press, New York, 1968, Vol. 14; Peter L. Berger, 'The Sociological Study of Sectarianism', *Social Research*, Vol. 21, No. 4, Winter 1954; Lewis A. Coser, 'Sects and Sectarians', *Dissent*, Vol. 1, No. 1, 1954; Robert E. Park, 'Characteristics of the Sect' (1932) in *On Social Control and Collective Behaviour*, Ralph H. Turner (ed.), University of Chicago Press, Chicago 1967. In referring to 'political' sects the author is following a general usage, rather than (as will be clear below) making judgements regarding the instrumentality or rational goals of these groups. Eichler's critique of Murvar (*Journal for the Scientific Study of Religion*, Vol. 11, No. 2, June 1972, pp. 187–191) is well-taken, but there is much to be said for following general usage and labelling organizations in terms of their own conceptions of themselves. Thus, a sect is 'political' or 'religious' etc. depending on whether its members perceive it as a 'political', 'religious' or other organization. The political sects discussed below might be regarded as 'secular' sects.

4 The sect was founded in Vancouver, B. C., in 1963. When its leader settled briefly in Eire it effectively 'emigrated', to return in 1968 and be refounded in Montreal. Although we have used the title 'The Internationalists' this sect uses many names, and many observers become puzzled by these and by the plethora of 'fraternal organizations' with which it claims to be involved. During the period under discussion the sect called itself 'The Internationalists' but also acted under the name 'Canadian Student Movement'. In early 1969 it styled itself 'Canadian Communist Movement (Marxist-Leninist)', while later in that year it changed its title to 'Communist Party of

Canada (Marxist-Leninist)', the title by which it is now generally known.

5 *Mass Line*, Vol. 2, No. 26, 7 June, 1970, p. 2. This was the organ of the 'Canadian Communist Movement (Marxist-Leninist)' and is now the official organ of the 'Communist Party of Canada (Marxist-Leninist)'.

6 Hardial Bains is a Punjabi microbiologist who taught at the University of British Columbia and at Trinity College, Dublin in the mid-1960s.

7 The basic-writings are his pamphlet *Necessity for Change!*, The Internationalists, Dublin, 1967; and the 'Resolution' passed at the 'First Historic Conference of the Internationalists' whose text is available in *Mass Line*, Vol. 1, No. 10, 17 September, 1969. The student of Bains's thought should also consult his pamphlet *One Struggle, Two Enemies, Three Guidelines, Four Levels of Analysis*, The Internationalists, Montreal, 1968, and his 'Public Statement Delivered by the Chairman of the Internationalists' reprinted in *Mass Line*, Vol. 1, No. 10, 17 September, 1969.

8 *Mass Line*, Vol. 1, No. 10, 17 September, 1969, p. 29.

9 On the Oxford Movement see for example Alan Eister, *Drawing Room Conversion*, Duke University Press, Durham, N.C., 1950, especially pp. 161–162, or Hadley Cantril, *The Psychology of Social Movements*, John Wiley and Sons, New York, 1941, pp. 144–168. On Scientology see for example George Malko, *Scientology: The Now Religion*, Dell Publishing Co., New York, 1970; Robert Kaufman, *Inside Scientology*, The Olympia Press, New York, 1972; and Roy Wallis, 'The Sectarianism of Scientology' in M. Hill (ed.) *A Sociological Yearbook of Religion in Britain*, No. 6, S.C.M. Press, London, 1973.

10 *Necessity for Change*, pp. 15–16.

11 An obvious parallel with M.R.A. is worth noting here. See Werner Stark, *The Sociology of Religion* (Vol. 2), Routledge & Kegan Paul, London, 1967, pp. 316–318.

12 As the Internationalists have termed him. See *Mass Line*, Vol. 1, No. 10, 17 September, 1969, p. 29.

13 We borrow the term 're-make' from M.R.A. usage. Peter Howard, for example, entitled a book *Re-Making Men*. The term 'historical crib' is Bains's: 'The particular prejudices of the society, transmitted through the parents and the social institutions constitutes a *historical crib* into which we are born which, like the womb of the mother, provides us with everything we need. . . . This perspective is an active blindfold of *anti-conscious-ness*. . . .' (*Necessity for Change*, pp. 4–5.).

14 The process of 'conversion' is discussed in, for example, William James, *The Varieties of Religious Experience*, The Fontana Library, London, 1960, pp. 194–257 (First published 1902); William Sargant, *Battle for the Mind: A Physiology of Conversion and Brain-Washing*, Pan Books, London, 1957, pp. 79–107; Hans Toch, *The Social Psychology of Social Movements*, The Bobbs-Merrill Co., Indianapolis, 1965, pp. 111–129; John Lofland and Rodney Stark, 'Becoming a World-Saver: A Theory of Conversion to a Deviant Perspective', *American Sociological Review*, Vol. 30, 1965, pp. 862–875.

15 Herbert Blumer, in A. M. Lee (ed.), *Principles of Sociology*, Barnes and Noble, New York, 1951, p. 216.

16 The Internationalists' main slogan is 'Seek Truth—Serve People'. Bains states: 'To seek truth is to serve people. . . .' (*Necessity for Change*, p. 13) and 'for the revolutionary, service to others *is* seeking the truth', (Ibid., p. 8).

17 Compare them with M.R.A. endorsements of 'soul surgery' in Eister, op. cit., pp. 180–182, and also the testimonials of members of Alcoholics Anonymous. See I. P. Gellman, *The Sober Alcoholic: An Organizational Analysis of Alcoholics Anonymous*, College and University Press, New Haven, Connecticut, 1964.

18 *Canadian Student*, Vol. 2, No. 1, 1, January, 1969, p. 3 (An Internationalist organ).

19 J. M. Yinger, *Religion in the Struggle for Power*, Duke University Press, Durham, N.C., 1946, pp. 22–23. See also Lewis A. Coser, op. cit., p. 361.

20 This phrase of Lenin's was made famous (or infamous) by Gitlow; see V. I. Lenin, 'The Urgent Tasks of Our Movement' in *Selected Works* (3 Vol. Edition), Progress Publishers, Moscow, 1970; and Benjamin Gitlow, *The Whole of Their Lives*, Western Islands Publishers, Belmont, Massachusetts, 1965 (First published 1948).

21 'Resolution' of the 1967 Necessity for Change Conference, reprinted in *Mass Line*, Vol. 1, No. 10, 17 September, 1969, p. 9.

22 Ibid., p. 9.

23 The Internationalists try to ensure that the family is at least neutralized as a rival claimant on an individual's loyalty, and if possible attempt to involve it in the sect. The family may be said to present the greatest challenge to the sect in this regard. On this point see Coser, op. cit., p. 362; Edwin Lemert, *Social Pathology*, McGraw-Hill, New York, 1951, pp. 220–221; Egon Bittner, 'Radicalism and the Organization of Radical Movements', *American Sociological Review*, Vol. 28, 1963, pp. 928–940; and G. Simmel, *Conflict and the Web of Group-Affiliations*, The Free Press, New York, 1955, pp. 132–157.

24 Coser, op. cit., p. 363.

25 *Mass Line*, Vol. 1, No. 1, 16 July, 1969, p. 21.

26 Ibid., p. 7.

27 See for example, *Mass Line*, Vol. 2, No. 26, 7 June, 1970, p. 1.

28 Quoted in Coser, op. cit., p. 367. The Internationalists lend support to Coser's assertion that 'sects . . . tend to be strongly authoritarian and subject to the powerful control of charismatic leaders'. (Ibid., p. 367).

29 For the classic discussion of this process, see Emile Durkheim, *The Elementary Forms of the Religious Life*, Collier Books, New York, 1961. See also some of the descriptions in William Sargant, op. cit.

30 Internationalists quote with approval Chairman Mao's maxim: 'To be attacked by the enemy is a good thing.'

31 Letter to *Words International*, Vol. 1, No. 2, 1967, p. 3. (An Internationalist magazine.)

32 See Mao Tse-tung, *On New Democracy*, Foreign Languages Publishing House, Peking, 1964.

33 *Necessity for Change*, p. 5.

34 These terms have a long history in the subdiscipline of Collective

Behaviour and Social Movements. The origins of the distinction may be seen in Sighele, and in the work of Park and Blumer on 'expressive' and 'acting' crowds. See R. E. Park and E. W. Burgess, *Introduction to the Science of Sociology*, University of Chicago Press, Chicago, 1924, pp. 870–874; H. Blumer in A. M. Lee, op. cit., pp. 214–216. See the critical discussions of the distinction in K. and G. Lang, *Collective Dynamics*, Crowell, New York, 1961, pp. 500–511; and in J. R. Gusfield, *Symbolic Crusade*, University of Illinois Press, Urbana, Illinois, 1963, p. 179. See also the similar distinction in R. Turner and L. Killian, *Collective Behaviour*, Prentice-Hall, New Jersey, 1957.

35 *Necessity for Change*, pp. 7 and 22.

36 The sect provides 'status' to 'up-and-outers' as well as 'down-and-outers'. See the discusison of M.R.A. in C. S. Braden, *These Also Believe*, Macmillan, New York, 1949, p. 409. See also on this topic: B. R. Wilson, *Religious Sects*, McGraw-Hill, New York, 1970, pp. 31–32; H. Cantril, *The Psychology of Social Movements*, John Wiley, New York, 1941, pp. 41–45; and W. Stark, op. cit., pp. 37–46 and 48–51.

37 See the discussion of *esprit de corps* in H. Blumer, op. cit., pp. 214–215; and Eric Hoffer, *The True Believer*, The New American Library, New York, 1958, pp. 44–45.

38 On the problem of 'meaning' see Talcott Parsons's introduction to Max Weber, *The Sociology of Religion* (trans. Fischoff), Beacon Press, Boston, 1963, pp. lvii–xlix. See also H. Cantril, op. cit., pp. 53–77.

39 On the modern IWW see S. Holbrook, 'Last of the Wobblies', *The American Mercury*, Vol. 62, April 1946, pp. 462–468. On the SPGB, see G. Thayer, *The British Political Fringe: A Profile*, Anthony Blond, London, 1965, pp. 148–150; and R. J. Alexander, 'Splinter Groups in American Politics', *Social Research*, Vol. 20, 1953, pp. 288–289.

40 SLP doctrine has remained essentially unchanged since it was expounded at the turn of the century by the movement's towering figure, Daniel De Leon. The SLP boasts that De Leon is the *only* person to have made important additions to Marxism, and has published a number of eulogies to him. See, for example, *Daniel De Leon: The Man and His Work, A Symposium* (1934); A. Petersen, *Daniel De Leon: Social Architect* (1941); and I. M. Johnson, *Daniel De Leon: American Socialist Pathfinder*. But see also Don K. McKee, 'Daniel De Leon: A Reappraisal', *Labour History*, Vol. 1, No. 1, Winter 1960, pp. 264–297. The SLP publishes all of De Leon's writings.

41 This statement appears prominently on all Canadian SLP publications.

42 An allusion to L. Festinger, H. W. Riecken and S. Schachter, *When Prophecy Fails*, Harper & Row, New York, 1964, (first published 1956).

43 Daniel De Leon, *Two Pages of Roman History: Plebs Leaders and Labour Leaders, and the Warning of the Gracchi*, New York Labour News Co., New York, 1962. (Inset quotation at beginning of pamphlet.)

44 Ibid., p. 69.

45 Ibid., p. 61.

46 'Resolution of Re-Affirmation of Adherence to Principles', adopted by 36th National Convention of SLP of Canada. Reprinted in *Socialist Press Bulletin* (organ of SLP of Canada), June 1969, p. 3.

47 Ibid., p. 3.

48 Eric Hass, *The Science of Socialism: A Home Study Course*, New York Labour News Co., New York, 1967, pp. 41–42.

49 SLP members claim that outsiders so characterize them.

50 This refers to the pamphlet *Socialism: Questions Most Frequently Asked and Their Answers*, New York Labour News Co., New York, 1967. This document is catechistic in intent and in its question-and-answer format. See p. 59.

51 Ibid., p. 59.

52 Ibid., p. 60.

53 *The Science of Socialism*, p. 5.

54 This is declared in all the sect's publications.

55 SLP 'conspiracy theory' assigns a major role to all other radical groups. The present writer has explored the SLP view of them in two papers: 'Aspects of Conspiracy Theory in Social Movements: The Case of the Political Sect' in R. R. Evans (ed.) *Social Movements*, Rand McNally, New York (forthcoming) and 'Perceptions of Social Control by Political Sectarians', unpublished paper presented to the A.S.A. Annual Meeting, Denver, Colorado, 1971.

56 *Socialist Labour Party: Position and Programme* (Leaflet).

57 *Socialism: Questions Most Frequently Asked and Their Answers*, p. 60.

58 Ibid., pp. 59–60.

59 Arnold Petersen, National Secretary of the SLP of America 1914–1969, in a document presented to all new members. Quoted in *The Science of Socialism*, p. 59.

60 *Socialist Press Bulletin*, August 1969, p. 5. (This paper is the official organ of the SLP of Canada. Canadian SLP members also read and sell the *Weekly People* published by the SLP of America and regard this as the major SLP publication.)

61 *Socialist Press Bulletin*, January 1970, p. 6.

62 *Socialist Press Bulletin*, April 1969, p. 6.

63 Robin M. Williams Jr., *American Society*, Knopf, New York, 1961, p. 391.

64 In terms of classic social science knowledge such activity would appear likely to prove unproductive. See Paul Lazarsfeld, Bernard Berelson and Hazel Gaudet, *The People's Choice*, Columbia University Press, New York, 1948, in which the famous statement is made: 'In the last analysis, more than anything else people can move other people.' (p. 158).

65 'Urgent' propaganda yellowing at the edges might almost be taken as symbolic of the SLP. George Thayer noted that the literature of the Socialist Party of Great Britain was similarly yellowing with age. See Thayer, op. cit., p. 150.

66 *Socialist Press Bulletin*, June 1970, p. 5.

67 These terms have been coined by Peter Berger. See *A Rumour of Angels*, Doubleday, Garden City, N.Y., 1970, pp. 17–19.

68 Hostility to intellectuals (with the notable exception of De Leon) is long-

G

established in the SLP. Indeed De Leon himself set the tone for this in 1905 when he presented what Lewis Feuer has called 'probably the ugliest portraiture of the "Intellectuals" that an intellectual ever wrote'. (See L. S. Feuer, 'The Political Linguistics of "Intellectual": 1898–1918', *Survey*, No. 1 (78) Winter 1971, p. 165.) Anti-intellectualism established itself in the SLP between 1905 and 1914 when intellectuals left its ranks to join the new 'Socialist Party'.

69 Just as Eduard Bernstein noted of the communistic sects of seventeenth-century England that they exhibited '. . . a contempt for academic learning combined with a great interest in education'. (*Cromwell and Communism*, Schocken Books, New York, 1963, p. 235. First published in German in 1895.)

70 This phrase has been coined by Michael Waltzer, see his *The Revolution of the Saints*, Atheneum Publishers, New York, 1968, pp. 317–319.

71 See G. Simmel, 'The Secret and the Secret Society', in Kurt H. Wolff (ed.), *The Sociology of Georg Simmel*, The Free Press, New York, 1950, pp. 307–316.

72 H. Blumer, op. cit., p. 216.

73 L. Coser, op. cit., p. 361. Compare also L. Trotsky *et al*, *Their Morals and Ours: Marxist Versus Liberal Views on Morality*, Merit Publishers, New York, 1966.

74 *The Science of Socialism*, p. 59.

75 *Socialist Press Bulletin*, September 1970, p. 6.

76 *Socialist Press Bulletin*, April 1969, p. 6.

77 'Familial' in both a metaphorical and literal sense. The sect seeks to involve members' families in its social gatherings. See footnote 23.

78 This is, of course, Bernstein's famous phrase. It is used here in a different sense from that which he intended. See Eduard Bernstein, *Evolutionary Socialism*, Schocken Books, New York, 1961, p. 202 and p. xxix for a discussion of his 'proposition'. (This work was first published in 1899.)

79 See H. Richard Niebuhr, *The Social Sources of Denominationalism*, World Publishing Co., Cleveland, 1957. (First published 1929.)

80 This has been argued in David Martin, 'The Denomination', *British Journal of Sociology*, Vol. 13, 1962, pp. 1–14.

81 See for example, P. Worsley, *The Trumpet Shall Sound*, MacGibbon & Kee, London, 1957; E. J. Hobsbawm, *Primitive Rebels*, The Norton Library, New York, 1965 (first published 1959); M. Waltzer, op. cit.; N. Cohn, *The Pursuit of the Millennium*, Mercury Books, London, 1961; and V. Murvar, 'Messianism in Russia: Religious and Revolutionary', *Journal for the Scientific Study of Religion*, Vol. 10, No. 4, Winter 1971.

82 See Gusfield's discussion of the terms 'rational' and 'irrational' as applied to social movements in op. cit., p. 179.

83 This phrase plays on Dennis Wrong's 'Oversocialised Conception of Man'. See D. H. Wrong, 'The Oversocialised Conception of Man in Modern Sociology', *American Sociological Review*, Vol. 26, No. 2, 1961.

84 On the 'religious-political' and 'religious-secular' distinctions as related to sects and social movements, see J. L. Gillin, 'A Contribution to the Sociology of Sects', *American Journal of Sociology*, Vol. 16, 1910–11, p.

246; N. J. Smelser, *Theory of Collective Behaviour*, The Free Press, New York, 1962; P. Wilkinson, *Social Movement*, Pall Mall Press, London, 1971; K. Westhues, *Society's Shadow*, McGraw-Hill Ryerson Ltd., Toronto, 1972, pp. 33–34; W. Stark, op. cit., pp. 51–59; and Lang and Lang, op. cit., p. 182.

85 P. Berger, 'The Sociological Study of Sectarianism', (cited above), p. 467.

R. K. Jones

10 Some Sectarian Characteristics of Therapeutic Groups
with Special Reference to Recovery, Inc.
and Neurotics Nomine

Transcendental groups have often displayed an organization and structure either very similar to secular groups or in many ways difficult to separate. Alcoholics Anonymous, for example, exhibits quite clearly patterns of ideology and organization which are transcendental or sect-like.[1] Various studies of Humanist societies have again suggested that these groups are very reminiscent of religious sects.[2] Studies of overtly secular groups such as the Socialist Party of Great Britain, the Internationalists and other fringe political movements highlight them as possessing many of the characteristics of transcendental groups.

Others have indicated a similar pattern to be found in therapeutic and revolutionary groups. For example, Schwartz sees convincing 'parallels between the development of chiliastic and apocalyptic religious visions in earlier phases of Western history and contemporary revolutionary doctrines of both the right and the left'.[3] This observation is not limited simply to political ideologies. Rieff's work on the schismatic followers of Freud,[4] and Slater's analysis of analytic groups, further suggests that the notion of *sect* is not to be confined to the transcendental realm.[5] Some time ago Berger suggested that 'the dynamics of sectarianism' is to be found 'at work in places far removed from religion proper—in politics, art, literature, and even within the sacred precincts of science itself'.[6]

Recovery, Inc. and Neurotics Nomine are both movements which reveal similarities to religious sectarianism both in their belief-structure and organization. An examination of some of the resemblances will, it is hoped, throw some light both on the groups themselves and also confirm or modify our perception of the way in which sects are structured. The two movements are commonly referred to as 'ex-patient' organizations, that is, groups specifically formed for members to share common problems and experiences arising out of their life-situations as former mental patients.[7]

Growth and Development

Wechsler attributed the growth of ex-patient organizations to the 'other-directed' and 'organization-oriented' drift in modern society in which the mentally ill are becoming joiners as much as any other section in the population.[8] There are naturally important differences in the *style* of participation. In the community as a whole, and especially in the United States, voluntary association membership can be as high as 65 to 80 per cent. But as others point out,[9] often as many as 65 per cent drop out, suggesting that an individual's membership profile varies considerably even in a short period of time. Many have multiple memberships. Affiliation is most common in the middle years and is linked to family status and life-cycle. After the age of seventy there is a decline in affiliation. Generally speaking voluntary associations fall into two main categories[10] which have been termed *social influence* and *expressive* groups, the former endeavouring to achieve a condition of change in some aspect of society and the latter formed to express or satisfy the interest of their members. Employing these categories, Gordon and Babchuck framed a typology incorporating what they regarded as the main factors involved in voluntary affiliation, that is, (i.) degree of accessibility, (ii.) status conferring capacity, (iii.) function.

In contrast to these voluntary associations belonging to the general community the particular problems and status of ex-mental patients makes it difficult for them to affiliate easily with most voluntary organizations and enhances the need for affiliative groupings of a more suitable order. Ex-patients find it particularly difficult to sustain social relationships and to encounter new ones. The whole problem of the stigma[11] attached to mental illness forces ex-mental patients to create their own stress-free situations operating on the principle of 'like to like'. This is the major motivating factor given for the emergence and perpetuation of these therapeutic groups.[12]

Studies of Types of Ex-Patient Organizations

Wechsler ranged ex-patient organizations on a continuum based on the way they relate to the 'supportive milieu',[13] and categorized 20 per cent as being patient-led as compared with 80 per cent which

are professionally led : 'Professionally-run groups are usually sponsored by state agencies, hospitals or mental health associations, while
patient-run groups must obtain their own funds and facilities.'
Examples of the former include Fountain House, San Francisco
Fellowship Club, and Center Club, and of the latter, Recovery,
Inc., Search, and Club 103. Some of these are in fact halfway
houses, that is, 'a residential institution designed with the ostensible
goal of affecting the transition of the ex-patient from the mental
hospital to the community.'[14] Wechsler sees the choice as a reflection
of the particular ideology which is held. The professional-based
group views the patient as not yet ready to assume the reponsibilities
inherent in running such an organization. The patient-based group,
on the other hand, is often seen as promoting initiative and independence. In practice, of course, the two extremes often come
together. A further differentiation of type noted by Wechsler is
between groups which base themselves on a 'sociability' function and
those which employ other methods of treatment.[15]

Membership of ex-patient organizations throughout the world is
not more than some twenty thousand. Most organizations 'are
relatively small in size, with two thirds having twenty or fewer
regularly attending members'.[16] Groups themselves differ over membership policy. 'Alumni' organizations are open only to ex-patients
from specific hospitals, while 'total' or 'inclusive' organizations
permit anyone who has been treated for illness to become a member.
Some, like Recovery, Inc., have some members who have never been
hospitalized. Professionally run groups operate a screening procedure, and aspirants who are alcoholics, psychopaths or sexual
deviants are dissuaded from joining, generally on the grounds that
they will disrupt other members.

Activities of groups vary enormously. Some are essentially social
rehabilitation centres while others place an emphasis on a 're-
education' of members.[17] Visits, indoor games, talks, and so on, are
all part of the recreational pattern that these clubs attempt to
convey. In theory it is felt that such activities offer a rehearsal procedure that will facilitate entry into the community.

Lay-run groups have a shorter life-span[18] than professionally run
groups, due not only to the difficulty in obtaining members but also
to conflict in self-governing policies. Recruitment difficulties mainly
reside in the individual having to assume the 'ex-patient role', which
makes 'passing' in the community more difficult. Many patients wish
to avoid the 'labelling' which would accompany affiliation to these
clubs.[19] In addition, lay-run groups are far less formally and effi-

ciently organized than professional ones. For example, Goertzel, Beard and Pilnick's study of the Fountain House Foundation, one professionally organized group, reveals a highly formalized organization with a thirty-eight-member Board of Directors and thirteen Standing Committees.[20] In 1960 it had an annual budget of over $200,000, and a total active membership of five hundred and fifty. The referral pattern was as follows:

Referrals to Fountain House Foundation

Source of Referral	No.
Psychiatric hospitals	24
After-care clinics	19
Other agencies	15
Friends of members	16
Publicity, family members, professional not employed by agencies	26
	100%

and the members were a mixture of schizophrenics, psychotics and non-psychotics.

Men outnumbered women three to two. Only five per cent are twenty years or younger and only eight per cent are over fifty years of age. Two thirds of the members are in their twenties and thirties. Only one out of twenty is currently married.[21]

Looked after by a full-time staff of thirteen, this organization sponsors a transitional employment programme and a social recreation programme. The former includes placement at various occupations, as 'trys', and the latter an evening and weekend series of organized activities. This kind of formal organization stands in marked contrast to many of the lay-run bodies, and indeed to some other professional ones.

Landy and Singer were concerned primarily with the way that clubs for former mental patients were socially organized, and with their general culture. Basing their observations mainly on Club 103 they make the interesting point that a club movement may in time become a kind of cult involving highly ritualized and formalized behaviour with a 'charismatic' leader who expounds the 'Word'.[22] Such cults have their dogma and exegesis. They instance Recovery, Inc., as a movement in which the 'Book', *Mental Health Through*

Will Training, has become a 'bible', a point to which we will later return. In discussing organizational development, Club 103 had no formalized rituals of admission. There was a hard core of daily attenders (fifteen frequent and twelve regular) who met for about six hours a day. The 'older' (longest and most frequent) became *de facto* representatives on the club-hospital steering committee. There was the emergence of an informal leader, but this did not last for long. Basing their analysis on Redfield's 'Folk-culture' theme,[23] they showed that the club offered both positive and negative benefits. For example, not only did members share a common culture to 'feel out' their hospital experiences but they saw in the club a community which offered freedom from the demands of the outside world, for example, 'dating' and social ranking. The social organization of the club consisted of a small inner core and a larger peripheral membership. There was a loose structuring of social relationships and an apparent need for leadership and fellowship. Social relations were 'equal' but separate, with a general levelling of social status. The basis of relationships was socio-emotional, and in the sense that it was a self-perpetuating group for the perennially sick it resembled an informally organized deviant sub-group.

Rapoport[24] describes how the community meetings of one group, the '8–30', resemble group-therapy sessions, with the exception that there are some one hundred and twenty-five members rather than a dozen. The group has an intimate self-confessional aspect that he likens to that found in the congregations of religious sects, such as Buchmanites and Quakers, that stress leaderless public confessionals. It is not viewed as primarily a treatment group although treatment does undoubtedly occur, and there are powerful forces at the disposal of the treatment aims of such a group, principally social control. The devices used are varied and include the 'defaulters'' meeting at which the culprit's misdemeanour would be highlighted by the group, and steps taken to bring him into line. The groups are further organized into ward meetings, departure groups, family groups, socials, doctors' groups, and leisure groups.

Sugarman[25] has described in detail the activities of Daytop, a community therapy institution for ex-criminals and addicts. Daytop displays a strong hierarchy of leadership. On admission senior residents tell the addict that he is *responsible* for his condition and no one else (a form of 'reality therapy'). In effect the addict is receiving a ritualized 'dressing down' after which, gradually, by a seemingly harsh programme, he begins to *relate* to his fellows. The morning meeting is highly ritualized and includes a time devoted to formal 'pull-ups'. After the 'pull-ups' there is a series of announcements. Groups in Daytop are *static* (the same people meet each time) or *encounter* (based on grievances residents might entertain against each other). He sees them as providing two functions—(a) offering controlled release of hostility and verbal aggression; (b) forming a setting for 'reality therapy'. In his description of the Phoenix Unit,[26] Sugarman stressed the importance placed on the patient's relationships with other inmates and non-medical staff. The Phoenix Unit is a heterogeneous therapeutic community serving sixty-five 'in' and twenty-five 'out' patients, with an ideology which views illness as intimately bound up with interpersonal relationships and an inability to cope with deep-seated emotional feelings. Consequently, an expression of such feelings becomes an important aspect of the Phoenix treatment.

A community similar to Daytop, Synanon, is described by Volkman and Cressey.[27] Basically it is run on the same lines. It does not claim to 'cure' drug addicts but merely to help them stay away from drugs. There is a hierarchical movement up through the 'stages' from new entrants to 'graduates' which reflects the success of the passage through the movement, and represents 'stages of graded competence'.[28]

Recovery, Inc.: The Association of Nervous and Former Mental Patients

Recovery, Inc. is the largest and probably the oldest existing self-help group for former mental patients with over six thousand regular members and seven hundred and twenty-five groups in forty-one states in America. Little has been written about it and consequently most of the information is to be gleaned from the 'Book' of the movement, *Mental Health Through Will Training.*[29]

The movement was founded on 7 November, 1937, by thirty patients, or rather ex-patients, who had previously been treated at the Psychiatric Institute of the University of Illinois. Between 1937 and 1940 the organization was limited to patients admitted to wards of the Psychiatric Institute, but in 1940 it extended its work to outpatients in that establishment. In September 1941 the group broke away from the University and established its own headquarters in 116 South Michigan Avenue. In the years after 1942 the bulk of the membership was recruited from the private practice of the chief founder and writer of the Recovery Book, Dr Abraham Low.[30]

Recovery, Inc. offers group psychotherapy classes prior to patients leaving hospital in order that they might better face the problem of community living. The organization also offers a complete programme of recovery during both the 'phasing-out' period and also for those who have left the psychiatric institution. Members are protracted chronics, that is their range of suffering is from two to twenty years. Panel members' groups or listeners' groups take place some three times a week during which time, generally speaking, members discuss a chapter or an article from one of Low's books, or from *Recovery Journal* or *Recovery News* (the *News* having succeeded the *Journal*). Group psychotherapy classes are conducted by a physician. The Public Meeting is 'open', and consists of a panel discussion and the physician's address. Panel meetings are led by a panel leader. Throughout, the appearance of 'setbacks' is catered for by veteran Recovery members being at hand to be contacted in distress. If the veteran fails to accomplish anything the panel leader is called, and if that fails the chairman of the organization is called. As a last resort the physician is called, although this rarely occurs.[31]

RECOVERY LANGUAGE

The symptomatic idiom has to be learned by members, including facial expression and gestures.[32] The 'Recovery language'[33] includes conceptually important phrases such as 'sabotage' and 'authority'. The authority of the physician is 'sabotaged' if the member presumes to make a diagnostic, therapeutic or prognostic statement. Once a physician has diagnosed a member's condition the latter is dissuaded from 'self-diagnostic revelry'. The 'spotting technique'[34] encourages the member to 'spot' inconsistencies and fallacies in his own language in order to check his sabotaging propensities. 'Spotting' brings home to the member the fact that there is no danger involved in a situation. One of the functions of the Recovery language is that it enables the member to bring a situation within his control.

DEVELOPMENT

In the early days [35] social events and activities were quite common but Low later tended to play these down. In the beginning they consisted of what were tantamount to personal chats on an informal basis with refreshments, or *Kaffeeklatsch* as Low called them. In

1950[36] membership was $3 per year, and since then the movement has been open to any psycho-neurotic or former mental patient. In January 1950 the membership was three hundred and seventy-six, 75 per cent of whom were procured from Low's private practice. The movement largely finances itself by private donations, fees, sale of Recovery literature and collections at meetings, although in the early days Low met the yearly deficit. The affairs of the organization[37] are now conducted by a Board of three directors, all ex-patients. There is also a vice-president, a secretary, and treasurer and six counsellors, although Low himself never held office.

LITERATURE

The editor of *Recovery News*,[38] which after the eleventh issue replaced *Recovery Journal* (which ran from June 1946 to June 1947 and collapsed owing to publishing costs), is a former mental patient and the publication itself appears eight times a year. Recovery literature between 1938 and 1941 consisted of a bi-monthly magazine *Lost and Found*, edited by Low, who also contributed most of the articles. In 1943 this material was issued in book-form in three volumes under the title *The Techniques of Self-Help in Psychiatric After-Care* which has now sold several thousand copies. The first edition of *Mental Health Through Will Training* appeared in 1950 and the sixteenth edition in 1968. The book is essentially a series of case studies designed to illustrate examples of post-neurotic symptoms and a proposed aid to recovery.

Recovery, Inc., controls the publications of the movement, a pattern shared by such sects as the Swedenborgians, the Catholic Apostolics or Irvingites, the Exclusive Brethren and the Witnesses, as well as many others.[39] To some extent, of course, control of the published information means in effect control of the *ideology* of the movement. With the Christadelphians the editor of the official journal became, effectively, leader of the sect, and in 1917 the directors of Christian Science took action in the courts to gain control of the publishing enterprise in order to consolidate their leadership. Such an analysis is not to be confined purely to religious groups. Alcoholics Anonymous and the Socialist Party of Great Britain have a similar value placed on their publications. Such publications not only determine to a large degree the external image of the movement but they become in turn a source of social control in groups lacking formal leadership roles. For example, in Recovery, Inc. a literalistic adherence to the Book is both encouraged and in turn utilized as the official yardstick for the group's ideology.

LATER DEVELOPMENTS

After the original publication of the Book, Low made several changes. However, it was not until after his death in 1954 that the organization assumed a different and independent character. Now Recovery meetings are open to the public; social activities are no longer part of the Recovery method—in fact Low, just before his death, asked that these aspects be played down. There is now a maximum training in self-help activities.

During its formative years Recovery, Inc. was a professionally supervised organization. The initial aims were, gradually : to help reduce the incidence of relapse in mental illness and prevent a chronic state developing; to save time for the physician and expense for the patient; and to create an independent self-help lay group without professional supervision. In 1952 Low established the 'panel example' method (three or four experienced members discuss a chapter from Low's three volumes on self-directed after-care) which became a model throughout the entire organization. Panel leaders (a) have received authorization by Recovery's Board of Directors; and (b) have received a thorough training (at least one week!) in the method. Each group contains some thirty members, and a trained leader is responsible for procedure. Referral is through doctors, psychiatrists, mental hospitals and clinics. After Low's death in 1954 the organization withstood the death of the founder and emerged as an independent self-help, lay organization. Because of its lay character it does not replace the physician whose authority remains constantly paramount, and neither does it purport to offer diagnosis, medical treatment or counselling. It is non-denominational, non-political, and has no affiliation with any other organization or individual. It is non-profit making, and ultilizes psychotherapeutic methods to deal mainly with post-psychotic and psychoneurotic persons.

WECHSLER'S CASE STUDY

The results of a questionnaire survey, undertaken by Wechsler, indicated that the model Recovery member was middle-class, middle-aged, married and female.

She has had at least some high school education, and may have attended college. Her husband is employed in a non-manual occupation and the yearly income is approximately $6,000.[40]

He goes on to describe the profile as having one or more independent children.

She is active in community and church affairs, belongs to one or more voluntary community associations and attends church services weekly. She takes part in various leisure time activities. . . . Thus she is an individual who appears to be integrated into her community and who, at least on the basis of certain socio-economic criteria, appears to hold an average or perhaps better-than-average status.[41]

One hundred and twelve of the returned questionnaires were from leaders of Recovery groups, who approximated to the general profile with the exception that they were of a higher socio-economic status and displayed more voluntary activity. Wechsler cites three reasons for joining Recovery. First, the patient suffered from psychological symptoms such as fears, delusions and 'nerves'. Second, the patient suffered from psychosomatic symptoms, such as tremors and heart palpitations. Third, there was a genuine curiosity as to whether the organization could help.[42]

The Recovery method seeks to alleviate the fears of the patient that psycho-neurotic or post-psychotic symptoms are dangerous, and part of the method's success lies in the patient accepting the diagnosis of the doctor and subsequently applying his 'will' to alleviate threatening symptoms. The Recovery principles include 'spotting', the Recovery language, and so on, but furthermore the patient is taught to distinguish between the external environment, which cannot be changed, and his own internal environment, which is subjective. The patient is to refrain where possible from a commitment to judgements of 'right' and 'wrong', and to consider himself at all times as average rather than exceptional.

Wechsler's account of Recovery meetings illuminates the organization and structure of these groups. The meetings are strictly routinized or liturgical and are attended by between eleven and thirty members. According to him such meetings are divided into four parts. The first part is devoted to readings from the Book, which has the dual effect of therapeutically engaging the participant more actively and also familiarizing him with the contents of Low's method. The second part is concerned with the presentation of the examples for which there exist procedures which are strictly adhered to. Various 'models' are incorporated in Low's book which exemplify the procedures. The examples can be characterized by: (a) familiarity—the context is always that of the familiar; (b) concreteness—specificity of illustration; (c) somatization of symptoms—a general symptomization expressed most frequently as air hunger, heart palpitations, perspiration and tremors; (d) uniformity of symptoms—the same symptoms are referred to; (e) exclusive use of Recovery concepts—extraneous terms are excluded and the Recovery terminology adhered to; and (f) the testimonial—the success of the method is demonstrated by its use. The third part comprises group participation during which the principles and techniques of the Recovery method are utilized. The fourth and last part is a question-and-answer period which is usually no longer than fifteen minutes. After all this refreshments are served during 'mutual aid' periods.[43]

Wechsler particularly draws out the cathartic value of the Recovery confessional[44] which, he suggests, may well 'aid the individual in removing some of the anxiety associated with his symptoms'. The act of public admission reinforces in the patient the knowledge of the similarity his symptom has to others. In most respects this is similar to the confessional period of Alcoholics Anonymous and many religious sects. Wechsler also stresses the religious or semi-religious nature of Recovery as a total programme.

> The Recovery method and its practice at panel meetings is clearly reminiscent of various elementary characteristics of certain organized religions. The method involves faith and acceptance of regulations handed down by a higher authority. The method stresses self-discipline and the volitional aspects of human nature. This type of approach is more amenable to certain religious beliefs than is the Freudian and Darwinian notions of man as an instinct-driven animal. The emphasis on the the power of positive thinking and on inspiration is also clearly analogous to some religious tenets.

He goes on to add that

> the analogy between Recovery and religion may be extended further. Recovery has a bible, the textbook of Dr Low. Hero worship of Low sometimes assumes the proportions of making him almost appear a god-figure. The leaders assume the role of disciples. In certain Recovery groups the desire for expansion and for national recognition is analogous to the missionary zeal in

religious groups. In addition, the repetitive ritual-like panel meetings resemble certain forms of religious ceremonies.[45]

The group leader in Recovery, Inc. 'assumes the role of a nervous patient'. He must appear expert in the nuances of this specific methodology. He can also, however, curtail a critical discussion of the method by passing the group onto something else. In this way the exercise of the role is also the exercise of a powerful means of social control which ensures that members retain their fervour and adherence to the aims of the movement.

Neurotics Nomine

Neurotics Nomine is a voluntary organization under the presidency of Dr Joshua Bierer. It was established some fourteen years ago to meet the increasing anxiety felt by some at the rise of the number of people with nervous or mental illness. It was thought that such illness prevented a successful adjustment to normal activity within the community, and that such an organization as Neurotics Nomine could provide a supportive role in bridging the gulf that existed. A precedent had already been established by the formation of several other self-help groups such as Alcoholics Anonymous, societies for the blind, the hard of hearing, the crippled, and so on. In other words, there have been several secular responses to what Glock and Stark call 'organismic' deprivation.[46] 'Helping groups' were formed by ex-mental patients and others interested in nervous and mental illness.

Neurotics Nomine benefits from the advice of the psychiatrist but is lay-run and controlled, essentially by ex-patients and patients who are still in the process of receiving treatment although community-integrated to some extent. Like Alcoholics Anonymous, Neurotics Nomine stresses anonymity, although outside the organization this is left to individual choice. It is now a registered charity with a membership of some five hundred.

The aims of the organization are as follows : (a) to help ex-mental and mental patients to meet each other and people outside the organization; (b) to assist the patient in taking the first steps towards social adjustment; (c) to support each other by meetings at home or talking over the telephone in an emergency; (d) to provide a panel available to discuss or answer questions to an audience of GPs or members of the Social Services; (e) to help remove the stigma and fear that still surrounds mental illness; and (f) to help the members by providing, through these activities, opportunities for useful work, social contacts and self-expression.

THE ORGANIZATION AND ITS ENVIRONMENT

The aims listed above involve us in a complex problem which has constantly confronted sociologists of organizations. It is not at all clear, for example, that the goals of formal organizations are as self-evident as some writers have implied.[47] Can we, in fact, make logical sense when we attribute goals to educational organizations? Or are we in fact simply falling into the trap of reification?[48] These sorts of problems involved in the study of organizations require separate treatment. Suffice it to say here that the stated goals or aims of Neurotics Nomine may, as the organization develops, become displaced, original goals may make way for current goals, and observers of such organizations may infer quite different goals from those inferred by members.[49]

'Helping groups' such as Neurotics Nomine may have a certain ambiguity in relation to their environment simply because membership is not at variance with that environment but is undertaken in order to function adequately within it. The stigmatization which mental illness brings to those who function in the normal environment creates a gulf between the individual and that environment. Neurotics Nomine attempts to bridge that gulf by a series of inter-personal activities. Members may visit exhibitions and concerts, speakers from 'outside' may be brought in, and so on.

DIVISION OF LABOUR AND COMMUNICATION

Neurotics Nomine (Neurotics by Name) is a lay-run ex-patient organization with some official backing, i.e. some psychiatrists take a strong interest and sit on committees, as do some full-time Council of Social Service employees. In areas where official backing is weak or non-existent then groups tend to oscillate. Between fifteen and twenty persons attend group meetings on average. Activities in these groups generally consist of informal activities such as bingo-playing, table tennis, and the occasional dance. This set of rudimentary activities is designed to draw the members into a form of social interaction. Illness is rarely, if ever, discussed. The principal organizer of such group meetings is usually an ex-patient who calls everyone by their first names, and to my knowledge there is no professional attendance at these meetings.

The main means of both formal and informal communication is through the infrequent issue of *Contact*, the Neurotics Nomine magazine, which is usually cyclostyled. The contents consists of reminiscences of travel abroad, poetry composed by members, and 'confessional' accounts of personal illness, often accompanied by religious overtones. Other matters contained in *Contact* are concerned with the debate as to whether the name of the organization is a suitable one, and whether more personal help could be given by the lay members, for instance, someone to telephone when in distress, or to write to. Some branches have their own newsletter and news of branches is reported in the national magazine.

SYSTEMS OF ENGAGEMENT AND REWARD[50]

In the case of ex-mental patients the need for a gradual re-entry process into the normal activities of the environment is important, and this is particularly so in view of the process of overt and covert depersonalization which exists in many of our mental hospitals. The stigmatization of the mentally ill is still a reality in contemporary society, and these social clubs assist to some extent in breaking down this stigma. Further, such ex-patient organizations form a kind of *rite de passage* for the patient to gain entry into the community and re-establish satisfactory relationships, which become vitally important for the perpetuation of the recovery process. These groups present a gradual induction for the re-establishment process, and they are self-supporting in the sense that most members have been stigmatized in roughly the same manner and consequently can be assumed to understand each other's problems. There is no compulsion to join in the activities of the groups, and individuals may enter into an engagement whenever this suits them. The environment provided by the group is, perhaps, a sheltered and artificial one, but to some extent this is necessary when dealing with so susceptible a membership. The ultimate goal is complete resocialization into the community.

The demarcation suggested by Wechsler of lay and professional therapeutic groups is not really as clear as he suggests. Neurotics Nomine, for example, has professionals on its committees and many professionally run organizations have ex-patients on their committees. Another difference is that some of these groups, as we have suggested, are purely social while others have a psychotherapeutic function. Some groups are open only to ex-patients while others admit people who are still hospitalized on 'release evenings'. Some are completely closed and admit no outsiders while others welcome the community 'normals' who profess sympathy with the aims of the organization. Neurotics Nomine no longer confines itself to neurotics or people with a history of psychiatric illness but extends its membership to the lonely, the depressed and the obese.

We have already suggested that some ex-patients may not wish to identify themselves formally with an ex-patient role, seeking rather to 'pass' in the normal community. Consequently some would argue that there are disadvantages associated with belonging to an ex-patient group which may well outweigh the advantages. For example, affiliation may well serve as a means of differentiation from the wider community—members may regard themselves as ex-patients rather than as husbands, teachers, business executives or clerks who have been ill—and such clubs may operate manifest or latent mechanisms of reinforcement to this end. Some have been attending groups for over six years and have neither attempted nor wished to allow their membership to lapse.

Organizational Structure of the Two Groups

Neurotics Nomine lacks rigid control and centralized authority. Recovery, Inc., on the other hand, has a more obvious structure and local groups must adhere to a formalized procedure. Neurotics Nomine is organized on the basis of autonomous groups[51] run by a voluntary secretary and a committee composed of a relatively flexible membership. The Executive Committee of Neurotics Nomine is composed of ex-patients. Usually two people are assigned to each task in order to ensure that continuity is maintained. The most successful Neurotics Nomine groups are to be found in areas where there is 'good' official backing, i.e. London, Liverpool and Norwich. On 18 January, 1970, Neurotics Nomine held its Annual General Meeting. All paid-up members of the organization who had given their ten shillings subscription to the Central Office were invited to attend. The main concern of this meeting was the establishment of the organization as a registered charity. Officers were elected and the main aims and objectives of the association were drafted. Nevertheless, in practice, the autonomy of the regional groups remains. Explicit leadership is absent in the groups although the local secretary is the prime agent in cajoling the members to participate in the recreational activities. Commitment to the organization some-how lacks the intensity of a movement such as Alcoholics Anony-mous, partly due to a lack of clearly established procedure and to the diversity of 'ailments' possessed by Neurotics Nomine members. Clearly established procedures for social control are absent. There is no pivotal focus and meetings are mostly of a recreational kind.

In contrast, Recovery, Inc., a very similar sort of organization, exhibits a far more rigid and formalized structure. Procedures are strictly adhered to and the groups follow those established in the Book. Meetings are liturgical in character, and the panel leaders are guardians of the method. Undoubtedly, Low had some of the elements of *charisma* which were subsequently transferred to his Book. Both have a formalized ritual of admission, namely coming to terms with the members' condition, and in this they share Alcoholics Anonymous' stress on the acceptance of that condition.

Cultural and Religious Aspects of Therapeutic Groups

It is apparent that what we normally designate as sectarian characteristics are not confined simply to religious sects but are to be found in many of the areas that Berger suggested. Wechsler, for example, has demonstrated the religious nature of Recovery, Inc. in its use of a confessional technique, and both Recovery, Inc. and Neurotics Nomine frequently display conversion and resocialization procedures. Low's group makes persistent references to 'the Founder'. Both these associations display a totality of concern which distinguishes groups of this nature, whether transcendental or secular. Members exhibit some of the characteristics of Goffman's 'colonization' where the group lays down interpretations of the outside world (although these interpretations are to be distinguished from those made by the inmates of total institutions) and the mem-bers build upon that sample. The outside world of the normal com-munity is used as a reference point to accentuate the desirability of the group's procedures. The two elements compliment each other and otherwise unavoidable tension between the group and the 'normal' world is considerably reduced.[52]

Both the groups we have discussed exhibit sectarian characteristics of organization and structure.[53] They are small, value-oriented groups possessing a voluntary membership which is conditional upon some mark of merit[54] (i.e. the overt admission of mental illness, alcoholism, and so on). Membership is nearly always voluntary[55] with the exception of some day therapeutic clubs at which attendance is part of the professional treatment. Although ostensibly the main goal of these groups is to enable the individual to obtain integration into the community, nevertheless one of the criticisms levelled against organizations such as these is that they inevitably display separatist tendencies to society in general, and withdrawal from the world and its institutions and values. There is a substantive element of self-perpetuation latent in organizations which meet specifically in order that individuals with similar problems may discuss their common ailments. Wechsler maintains that when no formal mechanism exists for the termination of ex-patienthood, individuals may be limited in growing out of it. Here, then, these organizations display a characteristic of sectarianism, that of withdrawal and separation.

Recovery, Inc. exhibits some aspects of conversion activity common to value-oriented movements. The individual must display faith in the Recovery Programme and acceptance of the general regulatory pattern to be found in the organization. Confessional characteristics are shown not only in the group meetings but also in the overall acceptance of the movement's tenets and the pragmatic aspect of the Testimonial.

Both transcendental and secular movements of this kind exhibit a 'totalitarian ideology'[56] which manages the individual in his dealings with the 'normal' community. It is in the meetings that the member is taught, either formally or informally, a set of techniques for coping with the day-to-day exigencies of living. These techniques can consist of either a set of instructions such as those Recovery, Inc. offers or the possession of a certain singlemindedness and fervour which will provide combatant stances with which to cope with his problems. The formal structure of Recovery, Inc. is certainly much tighter than that of Neurotics Nomine, although both offer a structured system of goals, methods and taboos. The former is organizationally geared to the achievement of its goals in a way that Neurotics Nomine is not, although the latter is geared in an *informal* way to such achievement.

Recovery, Inc. places significant reliance on the writings of Low, which are regarded almost as 'new' knowledge received from outside the everyday world. The movement, by use of panel leaders, sustains its concern for the purity of these writings. The ideology of the movement is consequently based on Low's work and any deviation is used to crystallize the orthodox stance by being utilized as an example of 'straying' or 'back-sliding', which serves to consolidate the main position. Members of both groups exhibit a totality of concern in which accommodation to the 'normal' society is the primary goal.

It has been argued that similar patterns of organization and structure are to be found in both secular and transcendental movements. The therapeutic groups under discussion are overtly secular organizations which only inadvertently display 'religious trappings'. Nevertheless, although the identification is not necessarily complete, secular movements do resemble religious groups. Some of the points of similarity have been suggested. Others could include the suggestion that both types of groups are concerned with the management or resocialization of the identity of their members in some way. In other words, to do the job required, whether it be the legitimation of an ideology or a form of resocialization, these groups offer a locus for solving both personal and social dilemmas which confront us. They are not functional alternatives to one another nor to religious sects but rather fulfil the same 'competences', to quote Nadel, which are located in society to legitimate both private and public cosmologies.

NOTES AND REFERENCES

1 Robert K. Jones, 'Sectarian Characteristics of Alcoholics Anonymous', *Sociology*, Vol. 4, No. 2, May 1970, pp. 181–195.

2 Susan Budd, 'The Humanist Societies: the consequences of a diffuse belief system', in Bryan R. Wilson (ed.), *Patterns of Sectarianism*, Heinemann, London, 1967, pp. 377–406. See also Colin Campbell, *Towards a Sociology of Irreligion*, Macmillan, London, 1971.

3 Gary Schwartz, *Sect Ideologies and Social Status*, University of Chicago Press, Chicago, 1970, p. 10.

4 Philip Rieff, *The Triumph of the Therapeutic*, Harper Torchbooks, New York, 1966.

5 Philip Slater, *Microcosm*, Wiley, New York, 1966, *en passant*.

6 Peter Berger, 'The sociological study of sectarianism', *Social Research*, Vol. 21, No. 4, Winter 1954.

7 Henry Wechsler, 'The ex-patient organisation: a survey', *Journal of Social Issues*, Vol. 16, No. 2, pp. 47–53.

8 Henry Wechsler, op. cit., p. 47.

9 Nicholas Babchuck and Alan Booth, 'Voluntary association membership: a longitudinal analysis', *American Sociological Review*, Vol. 34, No. 1, 1969, pp. 31–45.

10 C. W. Gordon and Nicholas Babchuck, 'A typology of voluntary associations', *American Sociological Review*, Vol. 24, No. 1, 1959, pp. 22–29.

11 Erving Goffman, *Stigma: Notes on the Management of Spoiled Identity*, Pelican, London, 1968.

12 Wechsler, op. cit., p. 48.

13 Ibid., pp. 48–9.

14 Harold L. Raush with Charlotte L. Raush, *The Halfway House Movement: a Search for Sanity*, Appleton-Century-Crofts, New York, 1968, p. 189.

15 Wechsler, op. cit., p. 50.

16 Ibid.

17 Ibid.

18 Ibid., p. 52.

19 Ibid., p. 53.

20 Victor Goertzel, John N. Beard and Saul Pilnick, 'Fountain House Foundation: a case study of an ex-patient's club', *Journal of Social Issues*, Vol. 6, No. 2, pp. 54–61.

21 Ibid., p. 57.

22 David Landy and S. Singer, 'The social organisation and culture of a club for former mental patients', *Human Relations*, 16, 1961.

23 Robert Redfield, *The Folk Culture of Yucatan*, University of Chicago Press, Chicago, 1941.

24 Robert Rapoport, *The Community as Doctor*, Tavistock, London, 1962.

25 Barry N. Sugarman, 'Daytop Village' (unpublished manuscript) 1968. Also 'Daytop Village: a Drug-Cure Co-operative', *New Society*, 13 April, 1967, pp. 526–529.

26 Barry N. Sugarman, 'The Phoenix Unit: alliance against illness', *New Society*, 6 June, 1968, pp. 830–833.

27 Rita Volkman and Donald R. Cressey, 'Differential Association and the Rehabilitation of Drug Addicts', *American Journal of Sociology*, Vol. 60, No. 2, pp. 129–142. See also Lewis Yablonsky, 'The anti-criminal society: Synanon', *Federal Probation*, 26, 1962, pp. 50–57; and also *Synanon: the Tunnel Back*, Penguin Books, Baltimore, 1965.

28 Other relevant literature on therapeutic communities and ex-patient organizations include: M. B. Palmer, 'Social rehabilitation for mental patients', *Mental Hygiene*, 42, 1958, pp. 24–28; D. A. S. Blair, 'The social therapeutic club: an important measure of social rehabilitation in the treatment of psychiatric cases', *Mental Hygiene*, 39, 1955, pp. 54-62; Joseph A. Shelly and Alexander Bassin, 'Daytop Lodge—A new treatment approach for drug addicts', *Corrective Psychiatry*, 11, July 1965, pp. 186–195.

29 Abraham A. Low, *Mental Health Through Will Training*, Christopher Publishing House, Boston, 1968.

30 Ibid., p. 16.

31 Ibid., pp. 18–21.

32 Ibid., p. 21.

33 Ibid., p. 24.

34 Ibid., p. 25. A Recovery meeting may begin with an 'endorsement'

(giving oneself credit for one's efforts) followed by recitations by members of incidents that have an emotional upheaval, an enumeration of the symptoms displayed, how the individual coped with the situations, and how Recovery helped. Part of the technique involved is in spotting each symptom as it arises, and especially 'sabotaging', which takes the following forms: 1 literalness (blocking the physician's efforts by means of a literal interpretation); 2 ignoring or discrediting the initial improvement; 3 disparaging the physician; 4 challenging the physician's diagnosis. 'Spotting' is also used to spot enthusiasm, sentimentalism and lack of muscle control. Examples of sentimentalism might be expressed in the following words: 'I like to think of myself as a lost soul. I feel I am irretrievable'. Emotionalism is demonstrated by a patient as follows: 'I am disgusted with myself. I can't control my temper. The other day it was so bad that I cried out, "I am sick and tired of living". Of course, they were alarmed. I knew they would be.'

35 Ibid., p. 25.

36 Ibid., p. 27.

37 Ibid., p. 28.

38 Ibid., p. 28.

39 See Robert Kenneth Jones, 'The Catholic Apostolic Church: a study in diffused commitment', in Michael Hill (ed.), *A Sociological Yearbook of Religion in Britain*, No. 5, S.C.M. Press, London, 1972, pp. 137–160, especially p. 143; R. K. Jones, op. cit., 1970, pp. 184–5; Robert Kenneth Jones, 'The Swedenborgians a case of new wine in old bottles: an interactionist analysis', in Michael Hill (ed.), *A Sociological Yearbook of Religion in Britain*, No. 7, S.C.M. Press, London, 1974.

40 Henry Wechsler, 'The self-help organisation in the mental health field: Recovery, Inc., a case study', *Journal of Nervous and Mental Disease*, 130, No. 4, 1960, pp. 297–314

41 Ibid.

42 Ibid., p. 302.

43 Ibid., p. 301.

44 Ibid., p. 307.

45 Ibid., p. 307.

46 Charles Y. Glock and Rodney Stark, *Religion and Society in Tension*, Rand McNally, Chicago, 1965, pp. 242–59.

47 David Silverman, *The Theory of Organisations*, Heinemann, London, 1970, pp. 8–14.

48 Ibid., p. 9.

49 Ibid., p. 10.

50 Tom Burns, 'The comparative study of organisations', in Victor Vroom (ed.), *Methods of Organisational Research*, University of Pittsburg Press, Pittsburg, 1967, pp. 130–1.

51 Although affiliated to the central organization many branches of Neurotics Nomine prefer to call themselves by another name such as New Horizons Club, The Endeavour Club, and so on. Other organizations with a common interest are the Henry VI Society (with the aim of studying the life of the king and praying for the re-opening of his cause in Rome: entry not

restricted to Roman Catholics) and the Open Door (principally for the estimated one hundred thousand agrophobia sufferers in Britain) and the Red Badge of Friendship (in Australia). On a national scale there exists a correspondence club in which members can write to each other about their problems.

52 Erving Goffman, *Asylums*, Doubleday, New York, 1961, pp. 62–63.

53 Recovery, Inc. has developed differently from Neurotics Nomine in a number of ways: more explicit leadership, intense commitment; more homogeneous recruits; more procedures for instituting social control; more rigid and formal structure; liturgical character of meetings; charismatic element in the founder; structure tighter and more strictly defined; structured system of goals, methods and taboos; more bureaucratic structure; more distinct leadership and so on. No doubt some of these differences are to be accounted for in terms of social and historical circumstances in development. Because of these characteristics the suggestion appears to be that Recovery, Inc. approximates more than Neurotics Nomine to the social structure and organization of transcendental groups. If this is the case then we may be led to the implication that the social structure and organization of groups, whether secular or transcendental, if the resemblance is sufficient, will be the over-riding factors in drawing out similarities, irrespective of the extent of the dissimilarities of the ideologies, goals and so on.

54 For an account of the therapeutics of fellowship, which these two groups share with Alcoholics Anonymous, see R. K. Jones, op. cit., 1970, pp. 185–186.

55 B. R. Wilson, *Sects and Society*, Heinemann, London, 1961. See also Bryan Wilson, *Religious Sects*, Weidenfeld and Nicolson, London, 1970, pp. 23–35, for an up-to-date analysis regarding the problem of definition. The main characteristics of sectarianism appear to be voluntariness, exclusivity, merit, self-identification, expulsion, conscience and legitimation. I am following here the yard-stick which I adopted in an earlier study (R. K. Jones, op. cit., 1970) as follows: 'There is now quite general agreement concerning the characteristics of religious sects. Wilson (1961) defines sect as "that small religious group in which membership is voluntary and conditional upon some mark of merit—understanding the group's teachings, or experience of some personal religious ecstasy—upon the basis of which association can arise." The sect is small and exclusive, and its voluntary membership is generally adult . . . ( ) separation from society . . . ( ) exclusiveness both in attitude and in social structure (are characteristics).' Other features include symbolism, voluntary joining, spirit of regeneration, singlemindedness and fervour of adherents, members kept under scrutiny and the pattern of their lives regulated in particular ways, equal to total commitments and subjective fellowship and community.

56 Partly because of the high level of commitment but also because such ideologies approximate to a *total* explanation, usually by applying an over-riding idea to 'the various realms of reality'. For example, Recovery, Inc. bases its ideology on the principle that mental health can be both attained and sustained in day-to-day social interaction in the normal world by the systematic application of techniques relating to the mastery of the 'will'.

Notes on Contributors

JAMES A. BECKFORD, Ph.D. is Lecturer in Sociology at the University of Durham. He has conducted research on the Jehovah's Witnesses and the Unified Family. He is author of *Jehovah's Witnesses in Britain*, Blackwell, Oxford (forthcoming), and 'Religious Organizations', *Current Sociology*, 1974.

FRANCINE J. DANER, Ph.D. has taught in the Department of Anthropology of the University of Illinois. She has conducted research in the fields of archaeology and anthropology.

ROBERT K. JONES is Staff Tutor in Sociology for the Open University. He is currently engaged upon research into a number of ideological collectivities. He is the author of *Sociology in Medicine*, University of London Press, London (forthcoming) and many articles in *Human Relations, Sociology, Philosophy*, and the *Sociological Yearbook of Religion in Britain*.

ROGER O'TOOLE, Ph.D. is an Assistant Professor of Sociology at the University of Toronto. He has conducted research in the field of political sectarianism, and is the author of 'Aspects of conspiracy theory in social movements : the case of the political sect', in R. R. Evans (ed.), *Social Movements*, Rand McNally & Co, New York (forthcoming).

BARRY SUGARMAN, Ph.D. is Director of Research at Marathon House, Inc. He has conducted research and written widely on education and the therapeutic community. His latest work is *The School and Moral Development*, Croom Helm, London (Barnes Noble, New York).

ROY WALLIS, D.Phil. is Lecturer in Sociology at the University of Stirling. He has engaged in research on marginal religious movements and moral crusades. He is the author of various articles for *The Sociological Review*, *Social Research*, and the *Sociological Yearbook of Religion in Britain*, and a monograph, *The Road to Total Freedom: A Sociological Analysis of Scientology*.

JOHN MCKELVIE WHITWORTH, D.Phil. is an Assistant Professor of Sociology at Simon Fraser University, British Columbia. He has engaged in research on communitarian sects, and on the sociology of West Africa. His book *God's Blueprints*, is published by Routledge, London, 1975.